SOCIAL WORK
DAY TO DAY

Third Edition

SOCIAL WORK DAY TO DAY

The Experience of Generalist
Social Work Practice

Carolyn Cressy Wells
Marquette University

*With a Chapter on Macro-Level Practice at a
Central City Middle School by*

Janice M. Staral
Marquette University

Book and Section Introductions by the late

Ronald Federico
Updated for the third edition by Carolyn Cressy Wells

An imprint of Addison Wesley Longman, Inc.

New York • Reading, Massachusetts • Menlo Park, California • Harlow, England
Don Mills, Ontario • Sydney • Mexico City • Madrid • Amsterdam

Editor-in-Chief: Priscilla McGeehon
Acquisitions Editor: Janice E. Wiggins
Senior Marketing Manager: Wendy Albert
Project Manager: Bob Ginsberg
Design Manager: Rubina Yeh
Text and Cover Designer: Rubina Yeh
Prepress Services Supervisor: Valerie A. Vargas
Electronic Production Manager: Heather A. Peres
Print Buyer: Denise Sandler
Electronic Page Makeup: Heather A. Peres
Printer and Binder: Maple-Vail
Cover Printer: Coral Graphic Services, Inc.

Although events related in the following chapters are narrated exactly as the author experienced them in her year of rural social work practice, the names of all places, clients, schools, school boards, colleagues, supervisors, and agencies have been changed to protect clients' privacy.

Library of Congress Cataloging-in-Publication Data

Wells, Carolyn Cressy.
    Social work day to day : the experience of generalist social work practice / Carolyn Cressy Wells; with book and section introductions by the late Ronald Federico, updated for the third edition by Carolyn Cressy Wells. — 3rd ed.
        p.   cm.
    Includes index.
    ISBN 0-8013-1800-9
    1. Social work education. 2. Social case work—United States
—Case studies.   I. Federico, Ronald C.   II. Title.
    HV11.W44 1998
    361.382—dc21   97-53257
                                                                           CIP

Please visit our website at http://longman.awl.com
ISBN 0-8013-1800-9

2345678910—MA—010099

In memoriam Ronald C. Federico, outstanding social work educator, who encouraged me to begin as a writer and then opened the way; and to James Herriott, whose wonderful stories served as inspiration and example

CONTENTS

CHAPTER 16

PART FOUR

Policy Issues   147

CHAPTER 17

CHAPTER 18

CHAPTER 19

CHAPTER 20

CHAPTER 21

PART FIVE

Values, Social Justice Issues, and Populations at Risk   197

CHAPTER 22

CHAPTER 23

CHAPTER 24

CHAPTER 25

PART SIX

Epilogue   233

CHAPTER 26

Preface

Developing the third edition of this book has been an honor for me. When I began the original, I wondered if anyone would be interested in such simply written yet heart-felt stories about the work of an ordinary social worker. To my delight, the answer was affirmative. The book has found a niche as a supplemental text helping students understand the intricate interweaving of personal and professional lives, policy and practice issues, individual and environmental perspectives, and social work values and social justice concerns.

The events described in the original edition cannot be revised, of course, since they happened in a certain place at a certain time. The third edition, therefore, like the second, leaves the original text largely intact. However, a new chapter, Chapter 10, has been added to the Practice Skills section, illustrating macro-skills in the organization and community settings as demonstrated by the current social worker in "Orangetown" today. The Human Behavior in the Social Environment section has been expanded and retitled Human Diversity and Human Behavior in the Social Environment, reflecting a new curriculum area for social work education, human diversity, mandated by the revised Curriculum Policy Statement of the Council on Social Work Education (CSWE). A new chapter in this section, Chapter 16, examines sexual orientation concerns.

In addition, an entire new section has been added: Values, Social Justice Issues, and Populations at Risk. These topics comprise the three other new curriculum areas in social work education mandated by the CSWE's revised Curriculum Policy Statement. This section of the book explores social work values and examines how they affect social workers' perceptions of social justice in America today. It also examines the interactions between values and social workers' perceptions of populations at risk, among whom are unfortunately the children and the women who usually care for them. Chapter 25 describes various specific effects of welfare reform.

Finally, the Epilogue section has been updated with information about current organizational and political changes that have impacted special education programs in the towns herein described as "Kingston" and "Orangetown."

This book is a teaching tool that can be useful in engaging prospective majors in introductory courses in social work. It may also be used as a supplementary text in more advanced courses, helping illustrate practice skills in the complex context of changing social policy. Its organizational framework includes sections on practice skills, human diversity, human behavior in the social environment, social welfare policy, social work values, social justice issues, and populations at risk, seven of the nine required curriculum areas of the Council on Social Work Education, so that the text may be used to tie together an entire curriculum in a course such as a senior integrating seminar. An eighth major CSWE curriculum area is field instruction; the book may also serve as an excellent teaching tool for a field instruction seminar.

ACKNOWLEDGMENTS

This acknowledgment section is heartfelt but belated; I did not include acknowledgments in the first two editions of this book. The reason was that I was worried about getting my deeply respected colleagues in "Kingston" and "Orangetown" in trouble because of some of the things they told me that I put into print.

However, many years have passed since the original edition of this book was written, and administrations of both the schools and the special education programs have changed. Many of the changes are described in this edition, but I do not believe anything I have included will be problematic for the people kind enough to consult with me. Hence I now feel free to thank those who made this book possible.

First and foremost, I want to thank the committed social workers, psychologists, and educators whose continuing hard work and willingness to describe their experiences made the third edition of this book a reality: Roger Goppelt, Richard Helmick, Joseph Kuzak, Michael Lisowski, Kathleen Masch, John Rawinski, and Jody Searl Wnorowski.

Next, I want to thank the late Ronald Federico, who was an inspirational social work educator during his all too brief life. It was Ron who initially suggested I write this book. He followed up on his suggestion with consistent encouragement and patient editing, not only for this book but for two others that followed. I also want to thank Irving Rockwood, who worked closely as editor and publisher with Ron and the authors Ron recruited. Working with such a supportive team was a real privilege for me.

I would also like to thank the reviewers who provided thoughtful feedback for the third edition: Terry Tirrito, University of South Carolina; Harper Dean, University of Maine, Orono; Martha K. Wilson, Boise State University; Kathleen Perkins, Louisiana State University; and Carol Boyd, Delta State University.

Finally, I want to thank the acquisitions editor of the third edition of this book, Janice E. Wiggins, for her excellent suggestions as to additional content, and for her encouragement, hard work, patience, and good humor. I also want to thank Janice's editorial assistant, Katya McElfresh, and production manager Bob Ginsberg.

Carolyn Cressy Wells

SOCIAL WORK DAY TO DAY

Introduction

THE PARTNERSHIP OF PRACTICE AND KNOWLEDGE

The purposes of social work require that professional social workers understand situations holistically and know how to organize interventions that link people with the resources they need. To accomplish these purposes, social work is built on skills derived from knowledge and values. The values are codified in the National Association of Social Worker's Code of Ethics, but the knowledge is somewhat elusive. Nevertheless, a consensus has emerged around several areas of knowledge that undergird professional social work practice. These areas include the following: the institutional structure of social welfare and social work's place within it, human behavior in its social environment, human diversity, social welfare policy as a codified set of programs and a decision-making process, social justice issues, populations at risk, and research. These knowledge areas enable practitioners to understand practice situations, to make carefully considered decisions about when and how to intervene, and to assess their practice efforts. Throughout these activities, knowledge is joined with values so that the practice that results is both effective and ethical.

In the course of practice, social workers apply and test knowledge as well as generate new practice knowledge. In their efforts to understand and use social welfare policies, for example, practitioners identify the knowledge that led to the development of these policies. Then they have to learn which specific programs have resulted from the policies so that they can be used effectively as resources in practice. Specifically, social workers have to know what programs exist, basic eligibility requirements, potential barriers to their use, effective methods of linking people with needed services, gaps in service, and so forth. As they become involved in policy, social workers realize how important it is for their practice to include helping to change existing but insufficient policies and programs or helping to create new ones.

Much valuable knowledge in many areas of biological, psychological, and social functioning has come from such attempts to apply knowledge in practice. As an illustration, consider behavior theory. The theory postulates that the nature and the timing of reinforcements are powerful factors in behavior change. However, a clearer understanding of how reinforcements are specifically related to the life situations of diverse groups (such as the elderly, ethnic groups, and so on) has come from practice. For example, positive reinforcers that will be effective in motivating behavior change with one group may be neutral or negative stimuli for another. These factors can only be learned through a combination of careful study and applied practice experience. There is also a distinctive body of knowledge about practice itself that has come from practitioners. Knowing how feelings affect behaviors in helping situations and how contracting provides a structure for both goal setting and mutuality in helping are two examples.

Although it is clear that practice is closely linked with knowledge and values, it has been difficult to keep these linkages intact throughout the educational process. The need for sequential learning that progresses in complexity from knowledge mastery through integration to application has tended to create somewhat linear educational processes. The curriculum begins with knowledge mastery courses (such as basic foundation courses in the social, behavioral, and biological sciences). It then moves to what are heavily knowledge integrating courses in social work. Social policy and human behavior in the social environment courses illustrate this level. Application is generally the major task of the field learning and practice courses (although they have knowledge mastery and integration components as well). Here, knowing in order to act provides the focus of the integration of the total learning process.

Unfortunately, it is sometimes difficult for students to maintain a holistic perspective in such a linear learning process. As a result, they may have difficulty seeing how policy or research or human behavior in the social environment relates to their developing practice skills. They may find it easier to relate values to practice than to see the way knowledge also underlies practice. The purposes of social work, however, demand practitioners who are skillful users of both knowledge and values. Improving the transactions between people and their environments and improving the functioning of people and the systems in which they live require highly knowledgeable, as well as thoroughly ethical, practitioners. Although the task of holistic learning may be difficult, it is also critical for attaining professional competence.

ISSUES IN TEACHING SOCIAL WORK PRACTICE MORE EFFECTIVELY

It is unlikely that the structure of professional education in social work will change substantially from its current linear model in the near future. While the new CSWE Curriculum Policy Statement allows for more flexibility than in the past, the organization of most colleges and universities militates against rapid change. Nevertheless, many programs are grappling with the issue in a number of ways. There is an increasing clustering of courses so that students see how courses interrelate and how concepts in one are relevant to concepts in the others. Team teaching is also a mechanism to provide for wholeness in a basically linear system. The use of media, role plays, and community involvement are additional ways to work toward integrated learning. Another strategy used by many social work educators is to organize and evaluate class and field learning around a set of objectives that provide a unitary focus for the various curriculum elements. Individual faculties will no doubt continue to exercise their creativity to find still other strategies.

This book builds on an integrating technique with a long history in social work education—the case study. However, it extends and enriches this technique in a number of ways, which are enumerated as follows:

1. Most cases illustrated are from one social worker's professional practice over a given period of time. The overall approach of this social worker to her practice and to the way she goes about her work is the focus of the book. Having this focus accomplishes two important objectives. First, it illustrates generalist social work practice in action. Second, readers are presented with social work practice as a totality. Many different situations are illustrated that require social work practice skills, only some of which involve client systems. Agency systems, community systems, and professional systems are very important additional parts of practice as portrayed here. Seeing how a social worker tries to use knowledge and values to act skillfully in this range of situations provides a wholeness to the knowledge-value-skill components of practice.
2. Specific practice situations that emphasize the knowledge-value-skill triad are illustrated. The feelings experienced by both social workers and clients are described. Interaction between societal beliefs and attitudes about social problems and the social welfare policy and programs that result are also illustrated. Other interactions between people and their environments, including the major social institutions of society, are explored from the perspective of social work practice. This approach reinforces for readers the continual interplay between the knowledge and the values that they have learned (and are learning) and the practice skills that they are gradually mastering.
3. The structural unity of the curriculum is reinforced by using practice as the focus around which the other curriculum areas are organized. It becomes clear in this book that the competent practitioner is one who has mastered knowledge and clarified values in order to develop specific practice skills.

THE PLAN OF THIS BOOK

This book has the following conceptual and chapter plan. It contains a "story" in that it spans one social worker's experience in one job. It begins with her decision to apply for the job and follows her through the interview process. This part of the book focuses on issues of professional career decision making and the values involved in that process. It also focuses on beginning the new job, including relating to co-workers, learning organizational structures and procedures, and clarifying professional goals and purposes. Then follows a section examining specific practice skills used in a range of practice situations with diverse client systems. Understanding human diversity, the multiple sources of human behavior and the systems within which it occurs, provides the major focus of the next section. Situations in which policy and research issues have to be understood and confronted are used to organize the following section. Last, a section is included providing case studies that illustrate social work values, social justice issues, and populations at risk. The problem situations and social work intervention efforts described in the various sections are presented according to their pertinence to each section, rather than in chronological order. The original edition of the book ends with the social worker's decision to move to a different job, returning to the opening themes of professional decision making and personal growth as a professional. The third edition concludes with an epilogue describing contemporary work in Kingston and Orangetown today.

Seen as a whole, the book provides the reader with a clear, realistic, and lively view of professional social work practice. It captures well the excitement, rewards, frustrations, and problems of social work. It also provides an excellent introduction to the range of knowledge, values, and skills the professional social worker must have to function competently in the variety of situations that are encountered when working to achieve the purpose of social work: helping people function more effectively by intervening in people-environment transactions and systems. Above all, the book is a real, human account of a profession that responds to human life in all its complexity and diversity.

SUGGESTIONS FOR INSTRUCTIONAL USES

There are many points in the curriculum where this book can be used. Indeed, given its holistic approach, it will serve to provide an integrating function wherever it is used. In beginning courses, it introduces readers to the work of the profession in a way that emphasizes the importance of knowledge, values, and skills in achieving the purposes of the profession. It will be especially appreciated and enjoyed at this level for its humor, warmth, and "realness." The book can be a valuable supplementary resource in institutions, human behavior in the social environment, and policy courses because it clearly shows how each of these areas is basic to the development of practice competence. It also clearly illustrates many social justice issues.

Most importantly, this book fills a long-recognized gap in field seminars and practice courses. It is an excellent vehicle for helping students integrate their field practice with the conceptual learning they have had in the other major curriculum areas (policy, research, and so on). The practice situations in the book can be used to focus on issues every social worker confronts in practice. The field experiences students are having can then be organized around these issues, and strategies used in the book and by students can be compared and evaluated. The breadth of the practice situations discussed and the consistent attention to the purposes of the profession should help developing professionals maintain some balance and perspective in their own practice efforts. These same features are useful in practice courses, especially in conjunction with a more standard, theory-oriented practice text.

Throughout the curriculum, this book's value as something that readers will enjoy and be able to relate to in a very personal way must not be ignored. It is a rare blending of what is sometimes called the "art and science" of social work. There is much feeling; yet it is always linked to knowledge. Skills are demonstrated yet always closely linked to values. The professional in this book makes mistakes but is able to assess them professionally and grow in her competence as a result. The book leaves no doubt that social work is a profession with well-developed knowledge, value, and skill resources. At the same time, social work professionals are portrayed as caring, skillful, persistent, but ultimately very human. It is a view of professional life to which we can all relate and be proud.

RONALD FEDERICO
Westchester Social Work Education Consortium

Informal Authority Structure

*(who generally exercised the most personal influence
in decision making among the special education staff;
of course, these are my own perceptions)*

Orangetown (Elementary School and Junior High)

David Chase — (*ED Teacher*)

→ Mrs. Glass — (*LD Teacher, Elementary Grades*)
Hope Shasta — (*LD Teacher, Junior High Level*)

→ Carolyn Wells — (*Half-time Social Worker*)
Polly Hinkle — (*Title I Teacher*)
Isaac Jacobs — (*Guidance Counselor*)
Remedial Reading Teacher
Speech Therapist

→ Mr. Lou Bachus — (*Director, Pupil Services*)

→ Mr. Martin Murdock — (*County Supervisor*)

If you check the model for the *formal* authority
structure, you will see that the informal pattern is
quite different and includes non-special education
personnel.

Kingston

Dan Dwyer (*County Supervisor*)

→ Norman Werner — (*Director, Pupil Services*)
Gertrude Baker — (*Social Worker*)

→ Carolyn Wells — (*Half-time Social Worker*)
Jim Atkins — (*Psychologist*)

→ Grace Conway — (*Nurse*)

→ *ED Teachers*
LD Teachers

Speech Therapists

If you check the model for the *formal* authority
structure, you will see that the informal pattern closely
parallels the formal model.

Formal Authority Structure
Regular Education
Orangetown

Superintendent
Mr. Brent Norseman
▼
School Principals
Elementary and Junior High, Mr. Burr
High School
Kindergarten
▼

Regular Education Professional Staff

Guidance Counselor
Isaac Jacobs

"Nurse-Social Worker"
Polly Hinkle (by function, not title)

Disciplinary Classroom Teacher
Robert Marein

Other Regular Education Teachers
▼
Remedial Reading Teacher

Regular Office Staff
Secretaries, etc.

Formal Authority Structure
Emmett County Special Education Program

County Director — Dr. Myrtle Knight
Assistant Director — Mr. Martin Murdock
Administrative Assistant — Ms. Jean Fillmore

ORANGETOWN SPECIAL EDUCATION PROGRAM	KINGSTON SPECIAL EDUCATION PROGRAM
County Supervisor — Martin Murdock	*County Supervisor* — Dan Dwyer
▼	▼
Director of Pupil Services — Lou Bachus (Psychologist)	*Director of Pupil Services* — Norman Werner (Psychologist)
▼	▼
Special Education Professional Staff	*Special Education Professional Staff*
Half-time Social Worker — Carolyn Wells	*Psychologist* — Jim Atkins
LD Teachers — Hope Shasta, Mrs. Glass, Constance Chase	*Social Worker* — Gertrude Baker
	Half-time Social Worker — Carolyn Wells
ED Teachers — David Chase, Constance Chase	*Nurse* — Grace Conway
Speech Therapist	*LD Teachers*
	ED Teachers
Physical Therapist (part-time)	*Speech Therapists*
	Physical Therapist (part-time)
Secretarial Staff — Mrs. Julia Green, Assistant	*Secretarial Staff*

Formal Authority Structure
Regular Education
Kingston

Superintendent
Mr. Sorensen
▼
School Principals
Country School, Mrs. Gilmore
Elementary Schools
▼

Regular Education Professional Staff

Guidance Counselors

Regular Education Teachers

Regular Office Staff
Secretaries, etc.

Note: All special education staff were hired through interviews with both special and regular education administrators. They were paid by each town, but each town was reimbursed by the county. Hence both special and regular education administrators expected obedience from special education staff.

PART ONE

Professional Choices and Development

INTRODUCTION

The day-to-day practice of social work is a tapestry of many interwoven strands. This book will try to separate many of these strands so that each can be more easily examined. However, there will inevitably be a certain amount of overlap and repetition because practice in reality occurs this way. Indeed, as you become familiar with the various people and work environments with which the author deals, you will feel more and more as if you are actually a part of them each time they are encountered.

In this part, the focus is social work as a job. The professional decisions that are part of the job search, the interviewing process itself, and the issues involved in getting started as a social worker in a new job are examined. As will become apparent, the decision to seek a job involves a careful analysis of one's career objectives, one's personal values, and one's immediate financial needs. Social work is a richly diversified profession, and most social workers aspire to work in particular areas of the profession—with children, perhaps, or with troubled families or the needy elderly. Many jobs offer a combination of opportunities. Later in the book, for example, it will become clear how the author worked with both children and their families, among others.

The clearer one's focus on preferred work, the more directed one's job search can be. In addition to working with children, the author preferred to work in a particular geographical area. She also rejected a potential job because she felt it would not allow her to work toward the purposes of the profession of social work as she saw them. On the other hand, she accepted a position about which she had some reservations because she needed employment and the income it provided. Her experience is a very realistic example of how the job search is a careful balancing of our own professional career objectives, our own professional values, and our own particular life situations. This balance will vary somewhat for each of us and at different points in our lives.

Once a job is obtained, its dimensions and procedures have to be understood. The tasks that are absolutely required and those that are optional must be differentiated.

The organizational procedures, both formal and informal, must be understood. People with whom one can or must work have to be assessed in order to understand how to best relate to each. A new job is far more than a job description. It is a complex network of people and activities, some of which are enjoyable and helpful and others of which may be experienced as tedious obstacles. A social worker is part of many systems, and all must be understood and used effectively if the social worker is to be successful.

The author's experiences show that settling into a job can sometimes be difficult. Her responsibilities were not altogether clear, nor were the procedures she was expected to use. The formal network of professional relationships was often not very helpful and had to be supplemented—very carefully—with informal networks. As the only social worker in her work setting, the author often missed the counsel and support of other social workers. This is not an unusual situation for many social workers, by the way, especially those in rural areas. This part of the book, as well as some chapters in the next part, focuses on the issues the author faced as she attempted to settle into her new job. However, throughout the book, you will see her continue her struggle to clarify her role as a social worker and to better understand her work environment.

The Kind Man at Ash Arbor and How It All Began

or: Looking for a Job

Concepts Covered in This Chapter

1. The process of seeking a social work job
   a. Strategies for locating job openings
   b. Strategies for performing effectively in job interviews
2. What to look for in a job
   a. Professional factors
   b. Personal factors

Learning Objectives After reading this chapter you should be able to

1. Identify at least four strategies usable to locate social work job openings
2. Describe the potential effects of gender, ethnicity, and racial variables in job interviews
3. Discuss how power is a variable that affects job interviews
4. List at least three types of information that can be obtained before a job interview that can facilitate a successful outcome
5. Identify at least three professional values that are important to you and that would affect whether you accept a particular job
6. Identify at least three working conditions that would affect whether you accept a particular job
7. Identify at least three personal needs that would affect whether you accept a particular job
8. Discuss your own strengths and limitations in an interview situation

It was hard for me to believe that I was heading east in my car toward my job interview. I had done all the things about job hunting that I had advised my students to do: opened a placement file with my alma mater, scanned their job notices religiously, kept my eyes scrupulously alert to the want ads in the newspapers and professional journals, and asked around.

To my own surprise, the strategy worked. I wasn't even seriously looking yet when I heard about this job through both a friend and my friendly placement office. I scheduled an interview and shot off a postcard to have my placement file forwarded. It all seemed much too easy, and this really was the kind of job I thought I might want to do: social work with the special education program of the public schools in Ash Arbor.

I had been teaching undergraduate social work and sociology courses at a university for nearly five years; it had been that long since I had been job hunting. Contrary to what I had advised my students to do, I was becoming very nervous. You're being ridiculous, I reminded myself. You probably don't even want this job. It's too far away. And that part was true. The Ash Arbor school district was located over an hour's drive from my home.

I was in luck. The interviewer turned out to be one of those rare, fine persons who really is interested in fitting the right person to the job. After the first few minutes, my hands stopped shaking. I never have been able to create a calm and assured presence, although I have practiced and preached such skills.

In fact, I just get nervous at job interviews, and depending on the interviewer, I make it through well or I don't. This is probably unpardonable in a field where I am supposed to grasp interviewing skills and actually do quite a bit of interviewing myself. I'm usually very good at calming down the *other* person, of course.

After I decided that this interviewer was sincere, I relaxed and began asking the right questions. Soon, I was pretty sure both that I could have the job and that I didn't want it. I learned that special education was a game at this school, a matter of checking out referrals in such a way that most of the children wouldn't qualify.

The interviewer made it clear that this was primarily a paperwork position. My job would be to "process" as many special education referrals as I could in the shortest possible time and to justify in carefully worded reports that would stand up in court why the children being evaluated were unacceptable for special services.

The interviewer wasn't a callous person. He was an ordinary man in the middle of a difficult situation, one in which new special education laws required services for children with disabilities but did not provide funds to hire adequate staff. So with limited money at hand, the school system in Ash Arbor was choosing to resolve its legal dilemma by hiring, not treatment staff, but a team of testers and evaluators to keep the papers flowing that would satisfy the judicial machinery in case irate parents brought suit.

"Well," the interviewer said at the end of this candid interview, "I'm sorry you aren't interested. But I wanted you to know how things really are here. It's a zoo, to tell the truth, and sometimes I wonder why I stay myself. It's a job, I guess, and it's close to home for me."

"But you say you are from out near Branbury?" he continued. "That would be quite a trip for you to make every day, anyway. Did you know that the new special education law will be implemented this year throughout the state? Since Branbury needs some new staff too, I can give them a call and recommend you."

The interviewer made a couple of telephone calls but couldn't reach the people he was seeking. He apologized and gave me the names of some people I could call myself, with permission to use his name as an introduction.

I left, wondering whether special education would be a paper game everywhere.

I went home and began dialing the names and numbers I had been given by the kind man in Ash Arbor. The particular job he had in mind was already filled, but I called several other schools in the area to check for special education openings. The result was a series of interviews for a social work position with the Emmett County special education program. Working in Emmett County would entail dividing my time between Kingston and Orangetown. Interviews went well with a cheerful assistant administrator at the Emmett County special education program office and with the well-spoken superintendent of the Kingston public schools. The interview with Mr. Brent Norseman, the superintendent of the Orangetown public schools, went less well. A furtive little man, his pale, tea-colored eyes shifted constantly throughout our interview between my left shoulder and my toes, and his questions were muttered in a monotone. I doubt I would have hired the superintendent for much of anything on the basis of that interview, but apparently he had other ideas about me.

The next step in the interview process was an interview with the Orangetown School Board, chaired by the school superintendent, Brent Norseman. At the meeting, I found that the school board was comprised entirely of men. The little superintendent slid up to me, and eyes fastened this time at approximately my middle, he greeted me as "doctor." Would the doctor like to sit down? The word seemed absurdly out of place among the farmers' overalls and the red and blue flannel shirts. To be sure, there were a few three-piece suits in evidence, most notably the smooth tan one worn by the superintendent. I had come clad in my only dress, complete with purse and nylon stockings, figuring that rural America wouldn't appreciate too liberated a woman. Hence my inner cringe at the use of that most unfamiliar and distancing term, which seemed to echo and reverberate about the place.

I tried to look demure and hometownish as I sat down at the long conference table, but it seemed that now all the men were staring rather coldly at me. Maybe the superintendent really *didn't* want to hire me, and this was his safest way not to do it. I moved my left hand up onto the table, where my wedding ring would show. Of course, I felt a little guilty; the game was too obvious. But I wanted to look like a normal, well-behaved married lady. That felt like the safest way to land this job. And I knew I needed a job by now. I had formally taken a leave of absence from my university teaching position and I was the only wage earner at this time while my husband was busy building our new home. Because I had been impressed with my interviewer at the county special education office and with my interviewer in Kingston, I felt the position with Emmett County was one I would accept, if it were offered to me.

The town dignitaries puffed on pipes and cigarettes. Smoke rapidly began to obscure the atmosphere, and my eyes began to water. I wished I hadn't come. Four interviews for one job really were too much, anyway. If only the job at Branbury hadn't been filled before I called and I hadn't so diligently called all the other schools in the area.

And then everything broke loose. Questions came out of everywhere. Nobody paid the least attention to Mr. Norseman, now seated in the far corner, and it didn't seem as if anybody else was supposed to direct this interview, either. Questions came from anyone about anything and flew across the room, one after the other. Yes, I was married. Yes, my husband was employed—er—self-employed. Construction, yes, house building. Our house. No, we didn't have any children. Yes, I hoped to have some someday. No, I didn't think I'd have any in the coming year. Yes, I was new to the area. Yes, we planned to live here a long time. No, I wasn't related to so-and-so of the same maiden name.

Was this interview exploring my professional qualifications for the job? I could have legally refused to answer almost all the questions, and probably would have been upheld in court, but then I also wouldn't have gotten the job without a long, drawn-out fight. Court litigation would have cost too much in terms of energy, time, money, and emotion.

Then came a new train of questions. What did I think of working mothers? Weren't they the cause of all Orangetown's troubles today? Unsupervised children broke the windows in the homes of local authorities and called the authorities nasty names and wrote wicked things on the walls of the schools. What did I think about that? And what was I going to do about it? What was I going to do about the kids who drank beer at the age of fourteen and bashed up the family car? Just how was I going to stop delinquency in Orangetown? And what would I do if I needed to speak to the mother of a rowdy kid if she was always holed up in a bar?

The school board members came across as dreadfully overwhelmed by the problems they perceived in Orangetown. I began to mirror their desperation. What overwhelmed me most was what seemed to be the limited nature of their perceptions. The men talked angrily about the high degree of delinquent behavior in the town's children and about the mothers' alcoholism. They then squarely blamed the children and their mothers for behaving irresponsibly. They directly asked me what I planned to do to make things right. I surely didn't know, not offhand. I did know that I had a very different framework for perceiving and defining problem behavior. In accordance with my social science background, I believed the behaviors described would be shaped by social and environmental conditions in Orangetown. But it was clearly not the time to introduce social science concepts to the eloquent and angry men on the school board.

Suddenly, in walked a most refreshing addition to the meeting, a woman whose face expressed warm serenity and a lively intelligence. She smiled into the staggering silence and said here she was, the assistant superintendent. She smiled at me, and I smiled back with relief, waiting to be introduced. The superintendent seemed deferential as he explained to this mysterious assistant who I was. He didn't tell me who she was. But there was a steady encouragement in her quiet eyes as she looked at me and a welcoming acceptance in her smile. Her presence was somehow commanding; even the men seemed to step back a pace. I was impressed. Here I had been playing such a demure role, partly a game calculated to win me a job, but partly just my habitual way of coping with a stressful situation; and this woman strode into the meeting like a queen and was clearly respected. I lifted my shoulders into what I fantasized to be a stately posture.

The little superintendent raised again the last question I had been directed: Just what *would* I do if I couldn't reach a troublesome mother because she was always at the bar? As had so frequently occurred during this interview, I guessed I would be foolish to reply with complete honesty to a question that seemed intentionally provocative. But I was feeling a little reckless by now, and I didn't care. I was emboldened by this potent new female presence. Besides, an old social work practice guideline popped into my mind, and it seemed humorously appropriate to these circumstances. The social work profession guides its practitioners to "start where the client is." The advice isn't necessarily to be taken literally, but—

So I jauntily replied that I'd find out what bar the mother preferred and go talk to her there. That got to them. They didn't know what to say. After a few gasps, frowns, and tentatively cleared throats, the questions that came next were relatively lifeless compared to what had gone before. The assistant superintendent didn't ask me any questions, but she smiled broadly throughout the remainder of the interview. And I got the job.

DISCUSSION AND STUDY QUESTIONS

In a nation where one of the first questions asked of a stranger is, "And what do you do?" we are all aware of the importance of a career. Career provides not only income; it provides a good part of our identity once we enter the working world. Our sense of an appropriate career for ourselves comes from many sources. Parental guidance, aptitude tests, personal experiences, and education all play a part. However, social structure factors also shape our career choice—the financial rewards and prestige attached to different careers or the accessibility of careers to various categories of persons. For example, social work has traditionally been considered a good career for women, whereas a career in engineering has been most accessible to men. Minorities of color have traditionally been underrepresented in all the most financially rewarding and prestigious careers.

Yet another important variable in a choice of a career is a sense of life goals. Managing a career for most people must be accomplished in and around managing a primary relationship, a marriage, and/or a family. Social work has often been found attractive by women because it is a career that allows women to withdraw for several years to raise families. Similarly, nursing is an attractive career for women in part because its flexible hours allow for part-time work. For those who see their career and financial success as their primary life goals, different sorts of careers might be more appropriate and more rewarding.

With these ideas in mind, consider the following questions:

1. What are your life goals, and how do you see whatever career you select for yourself fitting into them?
2. What factors in your life have influenced (or are now influencing) your formation of life goals and your choice of career? Be sure to consider the

influence of your parents, your siblings, other relatives, your peers, teachers you have had, the mass media, and your own life experiences.

3. Analyze social work as a career, using the following criteria: the level of income it provides, the prestige it confers, the appeal of the people with whom one associates, the amount of free time, the flexibility in jobs available, the amount of power one has, the amount of responsibility one has, the opportunity to be creative, the opportunity to express oneself, and the opportunity to create a better world. (Note that a very useful way to get information to answer this question is by interviewing social workers in your community.)

*4. How does your choice of social work relate to your planned life goals? Specifically, how do you see it relating to your plans for marriage, child rearing, financial security, self-expression, and personal happiness?

Every career starts with a first job and a first job interview, and even the best-prepared person may find job hunting a stressful experience. The literal interpretation of the word *interview* is given in *Webster's New Collegiate Dictionary* as "to see another, meet." This historical perspective of the term is a little different from the first modern definition listed in *Webster's:* "a formal consultation usually to evaluate the aptitude, training and progress of a student or prospective employee." The literal meaning of the word seems best to illustrate a very important part of any job interview: the fact that the "seeing" between prospective employee and prospective employer is mutual.

It is clear in this chapter that the person being interviewed, the author, is "seeing," in fact, examining, her prospective new employers as critically as they are "seeing" or examining her. It goes without saying that the applicant's own powers of observation and their conscious exercise are crucial in job selection if the applicant cares about what kind of job he or she will be able to perform when hired. With these ideas in mind, consider the following:

1. Think back to a situation in which you were interviewed for something (admission to college or for a summer job, for example). What kinds of things did you "see"? Looking back, would you say your "sight" was accurate and complete?

2. When you were an applicant (as in question 1), did you feel that there was a power element in the interview? Did you feel you had any power? Are there ways you could have increased your power? If you had had more power, would you have felt differently about the interview?

3. When the author describes one of her job interviews, she says she attempted to look as "normal" as possible. Have you ever felt the pressure to

---

*Questions notated with an asterisk are intended for advanced students who have had or are currently having some social work practice experience and who have made at least a tentative commitment to the profession.

look or act "normal" to get something you wanted? How did you feel about being pressured in this way?

*4. The author states that many of the questions asked of her during one of the interviews were illegal. Which questions were these? Why are they illegal? Why did she answer the questions even though she believed they were illegal? Would you have done so?

*5. If the author were male, do you think the process of the interview and the way it was experienced would have been the same? Would it have mattered if the author were a male minority of color?

CHAPTER 2

Getting Started

or: Learning How to Be Effective on the Job

Concepts Covered in This Chapter

1. Strategies to move into a new position quickly and effectively
   a. Managing one's own feelings
   b. Learning organizational procedures
   c. Identifying key people
   d. Locating needed resources
2. Establishing effective working relationships with professional colleagues
3. Establishing effective working relationships with support staff
4. Establishing productive work patterns
5. Assessing resources and developing plans to ensure the availability of needed resources
6. Managing work-related stress

Learning Objectives   After reading this chapter you should be able to

1. Draw an organizational chart that demonstrates your knowledge of organizational structure
2. Describe the formal procedures that govern relationships between two levels of your organizational chart
3. Compare and contrast the formal and informal relationships that exist in an organization with which you are familiar
4. Describe your role in an organization to which you belong
5. Describe an experience you had in an organization, focusing on your feelings and how you managed them
6. List at least three factors that are likely to influence your relationships with professional colleagues
7. List at least three factors that are likely to influence your relationships with support staff

8. List at least four factors that will influence the productivity of your personal work patterns
9. Identify at least five resources that social workers need to practice effectively
10. Discuss the relationship between organizational structure and obtaining needed professional resources
11. Identify at least three strategies for managing work-related stress

---

Because of the memorable experiences I had in my four separate interviews for the job with Emmett County, I began my position with the special education program genuinely convinced that things were going to go better for me in Kingston than in Orangetown. So when the end of August rolled around and it was time for me to go to work, I set up my week so that I would begin it and end it in Kingston. This was truly an inspired arrangement, and I came to bless it increasingly as the year progressed. Monday was a day I could contemplate cheerfully, and so I could enjoy my weekends.

My first Monday in Kingston was an awesome experience. First, I met my social work colleague, Gertrude Baker, who seemed to have enough energy and enthusiasm for 10 people. In fact, she scared me to death with her aura of brisk competence. Surely Gertrude would be able to solve every problem that came to her, whereas I would get stuck at times. She took me on a tour through the three schools that would be my primary responsibility in Kingston and filled me in on a great deal of local folklore surrounding the various school administrators and the respective special education staff. I probably took in less than 10 percent of what she told me.

I also met many of the other members of the special education team in Kingston: two psychologists, two speech therapists, a physical therapist, and even a full-time nurse. One after another, the staff in Kingston provided me with pep talks and friendly advice about how to get started. I couldn't have been more delighted. It even pleased me that all our desks were located in the same room. What a welcome change from the relative isolation of my university office. Besides, working together spatially provided for natural communication channels among the various members of the special education team. There were also plenty of private rooms available to use for confidential interviewing with children and families when needed, both in the general office building and in the individual schools.

Then along came Tuesday, and it was time for Orangetown. Really, I told myself, there was no reason to start the first Tuesday with such a sense of dread. After all, the school building was located next to the little green house with the welcoming porch, and the school itself looked like a friendly enough place from the outside. I counseled myself to be rational as I headed toward Orangetown the first day. To have an upset stomach before I even got there was totally unreasonable, especially as I'm just not the kind who gets upset stomachs very often. They really had rattled me, all those guys on the school board, I guessed—they and their odd superintendent. Maybe the assistant superintendent could help turn my innards around, somehow.

I hoped the school would disappear before I got there, but stubbornly, it didn't. Once inside, I wandered for some time down long hallways and dreamed of roller skates. Kids were running everywhere, and their energy and enthusiasm propped up my spirits. It was before 8:00, of course. Promptly at 8:00, an incredible bell nearly blasted me off my feet, and all the littler ones disappeared into doorways along the hall. I found myself alone in an eerie quiet.

Eventually I found the main office. A kindly secretary, who introduced herself as Mrs. Green, gave me the number of the room where I was supposed to have an office. She explained how to get there. Several long corridors and mysterious turns later I arrived at the room and figured immediately there must be some mistake. The room was an ordinary classroom filled with tiny children's desks and one big teacher's desk of the regular variety. The teacher's desk was obviously fully occupied. Seated there with an important demeanor was a fine-looking, dark-haired gentleman sporting an impeccable charcoal gray suit. Energetic in appearance, smoothly groomed, regular and handsome of feature, he gave every appearance of having stepped directly out of the Ivy League. There was something efficient and brisk, rather than welcoming, about his greeting. He had been expecting me.

"David Chase," he introduced himself.

"There must be some mistake," I stammered after introducing myself. "I was told this room was my office, but obviously it can't be."

"Well, I certainly wish it weren't," David articulated brusquely. "I spent all of yesterday trying to get you moved out of my room. No offense, but we certainly can't share my classroom. But it looks as though we're going to have to. Believe me, I've looked everywhere, and this school hasn't an extra square inch to spare. Neither has the high school or the kindergarten. I checked them all."

I looked around for something to sit on, at least for this temporary conversation. Nothing particularly suitable revealed itself, so I pulled up one of the tiny desks and sat on top of it. This perch raised my eye level no higher than the young man's belt buckle, and I immediately began to feel some empathy for the tiny superintendent next door. If this were how he always felt, no wonder he came across so shifty-eyed. I felt somewhat shifty too. I leaned my head back and shouted, "Have you asked around about another desk?"

"Yes, and there isn't another one available. I felt a little guilty about taking this one, but I'm sure you'll understand." With finality. Well, he was pretty smooth, and besides, he was also bigger than me. Possession is nine-tenths of the law, anyway. It looked as if this were going to be a marvelous place to work.

At about this point, a middle-aged man with a cheerful air of authority breezed into the room. I recognized him from the county orientation meeting prior to the beginning of school. I had taken special note of his name because I knew I would be working with him: Martin Murdock. Mr. Murdock had been introduced at the county orientation meeting as the new supervisor for the Orangetown special education staff from the county office.

Mr. Murdock was a moist sort of person—moist handshake, moist clothing, moist blue eyes, a moist way of speaking, so that you liked to stand back a bit when he started talking to you. And he really liked to talk. It seemed that the fewer things he had to say, the more words he liked to use. It was apparently a sort of sport with him, a real challenge. He had been given an opportunity to introduce himself at the county orientation meeting, and a half hour or so later somebody politely managed to get him stopped. So it was with some trepidation that I asked Mr. Murdock about the peculiar office arrangement I had found in Orangetown, without a place to sit.

"Well, well, well!" he shouted. "Really now, you're right! There doesn't seem to be a place to sit. You're right, there doesn't! There doesn't! Oh, oh! Well, well!" This approach went on for some time, but finally I managed to insert a question: Did he know whether there might be some chance for me to obtain a desk somewhere? That was really a tactical mistake on my part because the "yes-yesses," "well-wells," "no-noes," and "maybes" went on almost indefinitely.

I became too weak to interrupt, and David gallantly took over for me. David said that he had heard of some county funds to help new programs get equipment. Could these funds be tapped for supplies like a desk or room dividers to provide us with some privacy? Or a telephone? Or file drawers? But David had made a mistake too. Now the strings of phrases contained words like "complicated," "doubtful," "forms," "approval processes," "time-consuming," and the world began to look bleak indeed. But the fellow was still very cheerful about it all, and I surely felt grateful for that. A joyful noise generally improves the quality of an austere environment.

When eventually he stopped, he looked hopefully at David and me for more questions. But we outfoxed him and just smiled. He looked around for a place to sit. Since Mr. Murdock was rather too large to be safe on one of the tiny desks that served as my precarious perch, he eventually drifted away, with many promises to return to our assistance.

I spent the rest of my day repeating David's rounds of the day before, including even a visit to the principals' offices of both the Orangetown elementary school (where my shared classroom was located) and the high school next door. I walked a mile down to the kindergarten building. I felt like an explorer, and I enjoyed the sense of adventure and of discovering new places. I even rather liked the principals and felt my meetings with them were pleasant, if unproductive in terms of my immediate need. For I was unable to locate so much as an empty closet. Not only was there no place for me to have an office of my own, but there was not even a private room available for occasional use for special conferences with parents or children.

The schools had simply been constructed with only classroom space in mind, and all that space had been fully allocated to regular instruction. The special education program had been introduced to the town by an outside entity, the county, and no one in the local school system had made any space allowance for it. Worse yet, the county had made little or no effort to secure physical space for us, either. David and I were lucky—the only reason we got the classroom we had was that, in the name of efficiency, classes for children with cognitive disabilities in elementary grades in Kingston and Orangetown had been combined, and these classes were being held in Kingston this year for the first time. The decision to move the combined classes to Kingston had been made by the county late in the summer, and the local school system hadn't yet gotten around to reassigning the space. So when David and I arrived on the scene, that's where we were put.

David and I, while still circling each other, trying to lay claim to the limited booty we had in our room, made a mean team, although we didn't trust each other. He worried about me because he liked to counsel children, and he wondered whether I, as a social worker, might try to claim some of his potential clientele. Besides, he told me later with an open grin, he had always had a terrible opinion of social workers, and he expected me to be a real nuisance. I worried about David because, after all, he had colonized the only place to sit in the room and it was supposed to be my room too. But we were both resourceful. We were able to agree that we did not need all the present classroom furniture; we would rather have the space to develop an inviting environment for the special education kids we expected would be referred to us sometime or other.

David was, it turned out, the newly and duly appointed teacher for children with emotional disturbance of elementary school level. That sounded straightforward enough. I didn't know yet exactly what I'd be doing with special education children, but I did hope to become involved in counseling in one way or another, and children with emotional disturbance seemed a likely group to need counseling services. I think I was less concerned than David about losing some of my potential clientele to him, perhaps because I am congenitally lazy.

David was able to hustle up a couch from a speech therapist, and I was able to hustle up a rug from a reading teacher. And then I hit the jackpot. I ran into the assistant superintendent—quite literally. In my characteristic way, I was racing up the hallway, dreaming of roller skates and not particularly watching where I was going, when I came to a dead halt up against an enormous bucket. I got only slightly sprinkled by the dirty water I jostled onto my clothing. Leaning on a mop next to the bucket and surveying me with an amused yet serene expression was a woman with a very familiar face. I couldn't quite believe it, but there was no mistake. The woman I had dared hope to be the real assistant superintendent of schools was, in fact, a custodian. I had forgotten that when women break into men's job territory, they generally do it at a low level. "Hi," she greeted me. "You're the one that talks to mothers in bars."

Custodian or not, her voice as she spoke to me conveyed the same self-assured, slightly amused presence that her eyes and smile had transmitted at the school board meeting. She looked regal despite her dripping mop.

Once I got my dignity and my breath, I sang for her my song of sorrows. It surely was hard getting a place to work around here, I complained. Maybe I'd have to set up shop in a bar. No this, no that, too many little desks in our classroom, and no place to get rid of them.

I had met providence. My friend had keys to the basement. That meant storage space and a veritable treasure trove. By the end of the day, David and I had a bare, gleaming classroom. Now we could lay the rug, install the couch, and set up some low but useful room dividers enclosing the few desks that David felt he would need when children began to come to him for special instruction. Most exciting of all, for me anyway, I had a desk—not a real desk, but a serviceable alternative. My assistant superintendent friend had found an ancient table for me behind a pile of junk in the basement, and she also came up with, not one, but two sets of file cabinets, one for David and one for me. She also gave us several bookshelves, which we set up partly for books and assorted toys but also for additional room dividers.

Now we had almost everything we needed—except, of course, any real privacy for confidential interviews and a telephone. Already in Kingston, part of my job involved contacting families of children referred for special services. I figured if I needed to do that in Kingston, I would probably need to do it in Orangetown too.

That was a must, and that was going to take money. For that reason alone, I broached the topic the next time Martin Murdock paid us a visit. "Yes, yes! No, no!" he cried as usual. "Certainly you need a telephone. Certainly you do. Certainly. Social workers do use telephones, don't they? Now just what would you need a telephone for?" he asked. I explained about calling parents. "Oh," he said. "So you do that in Kingston. Well, I don't know anything about that. You know I'm new here too. Well, we shall have to do something, we shall have to do something. What shall we have to do? Why, why, why—I know there isn't anything to be done. There isn't any money to do anything. At least not now, no, not that I know of—"

A few days later I talked to the elementary school principal, Mr. Burr, about a telephone. To my relief, he immediately recognized my request as reasonable. The closest telephone to my room was located in Mrs. Glass's room, about half a mile of corridor away. But then he began to talk about the possibility of transferring the telephone out of Mrs. Glass's room.

That terrified me. I had met Mrs. Glass. Mrs. Glass was not the kind of person from whom you steal a telephone. A few years before, apparently when the county special education program was just getting started in Orangetown, Mrs. Glass had been hired to teach students with learning disabilities. She was a good teacher; excellent, in fact. And because she had been the first teacher in special education to be placed in Orangetown, when she arrived there had even been space available for her program. She had constructed a homey environment in two tiny adjoining offices; with meticulous care she had created a bright and friendly little miniworld for herself and her students. Mrs. Glass took meticulous care with her own appearance as well. Everything in its place, and all's right with the world. You could feel a marshaled order the minute you entered Mrs. Glass's world, and you absolutely had to behave yourself there.

And proudly perched on a shapely little table in the middle of that world was the telephone. Mrs. Glass had told me of the number of parents she regularly contacted with that telephone. She was obviously diligent about communicating with parents and was proud of her efforts. Take Mrs. Glass's telephone?—good grief, not Mrs. Glass's telephone!

I begged the principal, Mr. Burr, not to consider giving me that phone. I explained why Mrs. Glass needed it. I offered to pay for another telephone out of my own salary, if it came to that. Mr. Burr said he would think things over. But two days later, when I returned to Orangetown, the first thing I heard from David was that Mrs. Glass had complained bitterly to him. She said she had been told that the new social worker was going to get her telephone. I went back to see Mr. Burr, and it was true. Mr. Burr said he had discussed the situation with Mr. Norseman; Mr. Norseman had insisted that I must have Mrs. Glass's telephone or none at all.

So I stopped to see Mrs. Glass. Her eyes virtually annihilated me as I walked into her tiny universe. Coldly, but cordially, she greeted me much too correctly. "Mrs. Glass," I exclaimed, falling all over myself. "I've been told that the superintendent plans to transfer your telephone to my office. Have you heard the same thing?" "Yes," she hissed. "Look," I said. "I do need a telephone. But I don't want yours. You've been here longer than I have, and you need it. Do you know how to fight this?"

"Around here," she said, "you don't fight anything."

"Look," I said. "I'm willing to pay for a telephone myself. But I think our case would be stronger if we went together to the superintendent and asked for a second phone. You could explain how and why you use yours to contact parents. If we said we would split the cost of a second phone, maybe we could get him to change his mind from social pressure, if nothing else." I waxed positively eloquent about the potential power of a serious coalition between the two of us.

There's no question that Mrs. Glass lowered the intensity of the glare in her gaze a bit as I continued in this vein. She definitely got the message that I was willing to do what I could to keep her telephone where it belonged, on her table. But she wouldn't do anything with me to alter the situation. This puzzled me. She did not come across as a pushover. What had her experiences been here? I tried a few more approaches, but eventually I had to give up. Mrs. Glass didn't want to get involved, even when something dear to her heart was at stake. It bothered me.

In a pensive and definitely cautious frame of mind, I walked across the schoolyard, back again inside the comforting porch that served as the superintendent's office. Today the breeze was blowing a little cold. I asked the secretary whether it would be possible to make an appointment with the superintendent. "Brent," she threw back nasally over her shoulder, "that doctor lady is here to see you again."

The office door opened immediately, and Brent Norseman himself stood back and motioned me to enter. I tried to catch his eye, to communicate something that might reach him, but to no avail. The little head that literally came only to my chin remained inclined at a 45 degree angle downward. It wagged back and forth a few times as I began to speak. I got the impression of a naughty boy who had put one over on his mother. His eyes took one fleeting peek at mine toward the beginning of our conversation, and there seemed to be a smirk in them.

The next half-hour of reasoning, and then finally pleading, got nowhere. And not a week later, Mrs. Glass's little telephone was sitting awkwardly on my table.

DISCUSSION AND STUDY QUESTIONS

Nonverbal messages do not necessarily come only from people themselves. They may also come from inanimate objects in the physical environment. This is why the place in which social work practice occurs is so important. It is difficult to establish trust and an atmosphere of interpersonal caring in a highly impersonal environment. It is equally difficult when there is a great deal of noise and movement and when there is little privacy. The way clients are treated by receptionists or other support persons also affects their frame of mind when they finally encounter their social worker.

Social workers may have rather little control over where they work. Their offices are usually in buildings and locations that are selected by others. When they make visits to clients in their homes or their places of work, they have to make the best of whatever circumstances they find. Whereas social workers may be subject to decisions about the working environment made by others, this chapter illustrates some of the ways they can be creative *if* they recognize the importance of the physical environment. We do tend to live in a wasteful society in which many usable things are pushed aside. In many cases one can find needed items stored in basements or in back rooms of agencies. It is also possible to use a few of one's own personal things to create a warm environment. Here, as in so many aspects of social work, creativity and initiative are critical components of successful practice. But as the author suggests, it isn't necessarily easy!

1. How sensitive are you to your physical environment? For example, have you spent a lot of time fixing up your room at home or at school? Are there some classrooms you like to have classes in and others you hope to avoid? What do you think your particular reaction to your environment tells you about yourself?

2. What examples of nonverbal messages do you recognize in this chapter that come not from actual persons but rather from the inanimate environment that people have created? For example, what nonverbal messages does the Orangetown school system convey to its new special education staff? How does it convey these messages?

*3. What effects on staff relations can be byproducts of administrative decisions concerning allocation of scarce resources (such as the telephone in this chapter)? What efforts can staff exert among themselves to help avoid some of the undesirable effects?

*4. Compare and contrast how the same environment in which you worked as a social worker affected different clients. You might think, for example, about clients who had different types of problems or who were different ages or had different cultural characteristics. What, if anything, did you try to adapt to their different responses?

---

*Questions notated with an asterisk are intended for advanced students who have had or are currently having some social work practice experience and who have made at least a tentative commitment to the profession.

CHAPTER 3

Sherlock Wells Gathers and Assesses Information

or: Increasing One's Knowledge About the Job

Concepts Covered in This Chapter

1. Defining professional purpose and establishing one's professional role
2. Relating social work roles to those of colleagues in other professions
3. Establishing productive relationships with colleagues
4. Developing professional support networks
5. Understanding supervision and using it effectively

Learning Objectives   After reading this chapter you should be able to

1. Define the purpose of social work, using material from the National Association of Social Workers as needed
2. Define the role of a social worker in a school setting
3. Define the role of social workers, generalizing from what you know about the role of a social worker in a school setting
4. Identify at least two differences between the role of a social worker and that of a psychologist
5. Define a professional support network and list at least three strategies for developing one
6. List at least three purposes of supervision
7. Define the difference between friendship with a colleague and a professional relationship with a colleague
8. Discuss how the formal and informal aspects of an organization interact

T here I sat at a battered little table in a battered old classroom in Orangetown, and I didn't have a thing to do. David sat at his official big desk, and he didn't have a thing to do either. We spent some time looking at each other, trying to size up whether each was friend or foe. At least, that's how things felt to me.

During the days when I was off working in Kingston, David would rearrange the precious items in our room; once he even gave away a little table I had planned to use for play therapy with the youngest children. David's handsome features always seemed to be particularly evenly composed on those days when I came to work in Orangetown to find things changed around in the room, and I sensed a challenge. I was mad and I knew it, but I didn't know yet how to approach him constructively with angry feelings.

Orangetown itself felt like a relatively hostile environment, and somebody's quotation from the American Revolution kept popping into my mind: We had better hang together or assuredly we shall all hang separately! We had too little to fight over, and besides, I rationalized, David had to be in this school every day. No wonder he was trying to throw his weight around.

We started to talk. Just what were we supposed to be doing here? David's job title looked self-explanatory on paper: teacher for children with emotional disturbance. The school hadn't had a teacher for children such as these before, however, and just how did we identify emotional disturbance? Moreover, I had a job title that didn't prescribe any specific job function: social worker. Social worker was too broad a title to mean anything definite right offhand. The social work job description in a school setting could cover everything from the role of truant officer, which I definitely didn't want, to group worker to psychotherapist to family liaison.

And David considered counseling to be part of his own job, so perhaps the job title "teacher" wasn't all that self-explanatory, after all. How would we share that role; supposing we both wanted to counsel the same children? We edged nervously around the borders of a professional territorial dispute. This particular sense of territoriality turned out to be ridiculous because later on we were to be desperate for more people and places to refer our overflow of children and families who needed counseling.

We both knew from our job interviews and county inservice sessions prior to the beginning of school that we were supposed to work with children referred for special education services only. But how did we get these referrals? And once we had them, how could we determine whether the children who were referred to us were indeed qualified for special education services? I remembered how my interviewer at Ash Arbor had warned me that most of the children referred in that town were intentionally disqualified during the evaluation process.

I was in Orangetown the morning that David asked Martin Murdock how the county determined eligibility for services to the emotionally disturbed. David had been getting to know the second-grade teacher down the hall, and that teacher had mentioned to him that one of his students seemed to have emotional disturbance. The teacher had asked David whether he should refer the student for formal evaluation by special education or whether David just wanted to work with the boy a little. David saw a chance to get started, but he first wanted to learn and use the appropriate organizational procedures.

Mr. Murdock was our supervisor from the Emmett County special education office rather than the woman with whom I had originally interviewed and whom I had expected to find in that position. I was disappointed by the change, as I had looked forward to working with my lively interviewer. But Mr. Murdock it was, and Mr. Murdock would have to do. He was brand new to his job, as both David and I were to ours.

Martin Murdock didn't know how the county determined a child to have emotional disturbance, and he had no guidance to offer. But inspired by the sheer practicality of David's technical questions, even though they were not answered, I asked Mr. Murdock whether he knew what the social work job description was supposed to include. "Oh, oh, why, why!" he began somewhat to my astonishment. "Of course I know what a social worker does. Everyone knows what a social worker does, correct? Now of course I'm correct. Of course. Now, what would a social worker do *here*—that is the question. That is the question indeed. Indeed!"

At this point I expected Mr. Murdock to stop and to move on to another topic where he could be of more assistance. But he didn't. He went on with his "indeeds" and "why-why's" for quite some time, forming his words carefully and distinctly and seeming to derive enormous satisfaction from his pronunciation. He toyed with my question for quite a while, in fact, but he didn't come up with any answers. Finally, Mr. Murdock promised to get some written materials for both David and me from the county office. And he really did get us written materials after we reminded him sometime later on, but they didn't relate to what we wanted to know.

I suggested to David that we talk to the Orangetown school psychologist to gain some direction on what to do with a potential referral. In Kingston, where I spent half the week, teachers and other staff members referred children to a school psychologist for special education evaluation. The psychologist coordinated all the special education referrals and contacted the children's parents for permission to evaluate. No special education evaluation could be initiated by law without a written permission from the parents, I had been told by the psychologist in Kingston.

I had already participated in a meeting with a child's parents in Kingston. The meeting was called an "initial staffing," and the reason for the child's referral for special education evaluation was discussed with the special education staff and the parents by the referring teacher. The purpose of the initial staffing was to decide whether there was enough evidence of a problem to go through a complete evaluation. There was in this case, and the psychologist decided to conduct psychological tests. The teacher for children with emotional disturbance was commissioned to observe the child in the regular classroom, and I was asked to develop a "social history," or a history of the child's emotional and physical development in the family setting.

It all seemed very logical and orderly in Kingston. The staff there told me that students with problems could only receive help from the special education team if they were found to fit one of the five categories of special need: cognitive disability, learning disability, speech pathology, physical disability, (which could include pregnancy), or emotional disturbance. I was told by my colleague, Mrs. Baker, the full-time social worker in Kingston, that generally the social worker was asked to develop social histories only for the children referred as potentially emotionally disturbed.*

---

*Today, the categories of need have been refined and expanded to include hearing and visual disabilities, traumatic brain injury, orthopedic impairment, autism, occupational therapy, physical therapy, and other health impairment in adddition to the original categories.

I had already talked with the school psychologist in Orangetown, Lou Bachus, on several occasions since I joined the Orangetown staff. Lou was a big, slow-moving man with a ready grin. Almost totally bald but sporting a brave mustache, he looked a good deal older than his thirty-odd years. He had a comfortably pudgy body build, teddy-bear-like, the kind you could hug on the least excuse. But everything about him rather sagged—his body, his clothing, his facial features, his spirit. He carried the tired air of a person who has decided he is past his prime before ever feeling he has attained it.

But Lou tried to comport himself with a mild sort of flair, and the verbal signals promised a relaxed, debonair sort of relationship. He used a lot of phrases like "hey, man," and "boy, oh boy." I really did expect, in the beginning, that we would become friends. And in fact, Lou never said a cross word to me during the entire year I worked with him. He liked to joke and to banter, but somehow it felt forced. Lou seemed all bound up inside.

And he didn't have what it took to coordinate a pupil services team. Lou's official position in Orangetown, director of pupil services, was virtually overlooked by that good gentleman himself, although it took me quite awhile to figure this out. I had originally expected that Lou, like the psychologist in Kingston, would have work he wanted me to do. When I first met Lou, I hopefully introduced myself as the new school social worker for special education, and I almost expected this large pleasant man to sit me down and swamp me with work. After all, the Orangetown school board had impressed me that the town was overwhelmed with incredible problems that I was supposed to solve singlehandedly. Certainly the psychologist would welcome at least some assistance in this monumental task.

I had explained to Lou that I didn't know precisely what I should be doing in Orangetown but that I was available for counseling, social histories, and various other family contacts, and did he have any other ideas? Lou's reaction had been warm, kindly, and just obviously disinterested. Well, he had said, he and the school guidance counselor took care of counseling at the school, but the families in the town hated the school and didn't like to be contacted, so he didn't really expect there would be any work in that area.

Following this first conversation, the quality of my contacts with Lou Bachus neither improved nor deteriorated. Whenever I asked him about possible work assignments or ideas, his response was invariably warm, kindly, and disinterested. When I came up with some ideas of my own to sound out with him, he would just say, "Hey, man, that's an interesting idea. Why don't we just think about that for a while?"

The elementary school guidance counselor, Isaac Jacobs, had provided a similar experience. Although sympathetic to my attempts to get started, he had nonetheless confided that he doubted whether I'd ever work out a job description. He said he had developed one every year for his own job position, which the local school administration turned down as a matter of course. That had been going on for some seven years! The problem, he said, was power. I remember he used that specific word. He just didn't have any power in the school, Isaac Jacobs lamented.

Mr. Jacobs went on to explain that informal group work just wasn't safe with the older students. They wanted to talk about sex and drugs. Once when conducting a discussion group with students from the junior high wing, he had permitted these topics to be introduced. Irate parents had nearly run him out of town. The school administration had formally censured him. Although Mr. Jacobs sometimes did individual counseling, he thought the families were often the problem, and he hadn't had any luck with the ones that really needed to change. Now he spent most of his time arranging academic schedules for students and feeling frustrated.

I got the clear message from both Lou Bachus and Isaac Jacobs that whereas school personnel were wary of both the parents and the school administration, the parents were wary of anything to do with the school.

Wearying of the effort to obtain work assignments, ideas, or referrals from the obvious places, I sought out the two teachers of students with learning disabilities at the elementary school. They had been working in Orangetown for a few years. Maybe they would have some ideas. And good heavens, they did. Mrs. Glass, the elementary school teacher for children with learning disabilities, suggested the names of two young boys whom I might be able to counsel. Hope Shasta, who worked with learning-disabled students in the junior high wing, had several suggestions to make regarding children she thought might benefit from counseling.

Next, I went to visit the guidance counselor at the high school. He seemed interested when I discussed with him the possibility of working with pregnant girls, but he had no particular ideas of his own about how I might be useful to the school.

And then I met Constance Chase, David's wife. Constance was the first and only teacher of children with learning disabilities (LD) and those with emotional disturbance (ED) in Orangetown High School. What a job title! Constance had glorious and incredibly natural blond hair that glowed straight down to her waist, and her sensitive, intelligent face was highlighted by lovely, deep blue eyes. She could have stepped directly out of a movie magazine. I must confess that I had sized her up as altogether too beautiful when I first saw her and imagined that she would be aloof, probably even supercilious toward ordinary mortals such as myself. Besides, she was David's wife, and as I didn't feel very comfortable with David, I expected it would be worse with this gorgeous young lady. I went to see her last of all the members of the pupil services team.

I couldn't have been more wrong. Constance became my first real working partner in Orangetown and, more than that, my friend. She became a friend almost immediately, and I rarely make immediate friends. I almost never do in work situations. Although I try to develop working relationships that are constructive and cooperative, my friends are the persons I am completely myself with, and the two categories rarely overlap.

In Constance's case, I met an exception. What I was most aware of in my first conversation with her was her open nature and my own sense of relief to find an open person at last in Orangetown. We were going through the same growing pains of getting started in a new school system, and we could talk about it with each other. We could discuss both the frustrations and the various strategies we had been using to try to create our respective jobs. We became a virtually instantaneous minisupport system.

Constance told me she had met several students who had asked her to be their teacher. For some reason, she said, they just kept coming into her room and hanging around, and almost all these students were boys! I didn't have a whole lot of trouble figuring out what that was all about, but I felt it was a hopeful beginning. Certainly emotionally disturbed students, however defined, would work better if they actually wanted Constance to be their teacher.

But it was time to figure out how special education evaluations were to be conducted. Constance could not handle all the students who wanted to be in her room. Her room was only half the size of a regular classroom, and she needed somehow to coordinate schedules for two types of students, those with learning disabilities and those with emotional disturbance.

Constance also had several ideas regarding students she thought might need counseling. But again, how did we determine eligibility? Providing this information was, of course, the job of Martin Murdock or Lou Bachus, but neither of these men was doing it.

So by the time David and I went to talk to Lou Bachus about David's potential new referral from the second-grade teacher down the hall, I was already beginning to have some ideas about how I could develop a role for myself within the school system. But through David's potential referral, we finally learned from Lou how special education was actually organized and administered in Orangetown, at least in the elementary school. Lou told David to wait until the weekly special education staff meeting to do anything with his potential referral. That came as quite a shock; nobody had mentioned to us before that there was such a meeting! So there was a system after all!

The meeting was held on Thursday, fortunately a day I was in Orangetown. To my amazement, the meeting was conducted by a person I had never met, a woman named Polly Hinkle. She was not on the special education staff, I learned later, but she was an informal force among the special education team. She was officially hired by the Title I program as a teacher for culturally deprived or low-income students, but she didn't like to teach. So she had appointed herself as an ex officio member of the special education evaluation team. She functioned on a day-to-day basis as a combination school nurse and ever-ready surrogate mother.

She could do that because there was no active Title I supervisor at the county level, and nobody in the local school administration cared one whit about Title I. Mrs. Hinkle's office, in which she was officially supposed to tutor Title I students, was, in fact, the school nursing office, where children came to spend time healing wounds, both physical and spiritual. There was a real county nurse who spent some time there one day a week, but she was a grouchy lady and everybody avoided her. Mrs. Hinkle, on the other hand, was wonderfully nurturant, and people liked to spend time with her—including, later on, myself. She was to alert me to many students with special needs. She had a telephone in her office, which she used to call the parents of ill or truant children. She functioned in many ways as a social worker as well as a nurse, unofficially meeting the emotional and physical needs of many children and parents.

Mrs. Hinkle brought to the pupil services meeting a handful of forms, which were referral forms for children whose teachers had requested special education evaluations for them. She had been given these forms by Julia Green, the secretary for the special education staff.

I now began to learn that Mrs. Green, the secretary, was the de facto coordinator of the Orangetown pupil services team. It was to her that teachers brought their referral forms for special education services; it was she who delegated the task of running weekly pupil services meetings to the various staff members. She made up a rotating schedule so that no one would have to perform the leadership function very often.

Now I was learning about the vital informal network of shared responsibilities in Orangetown. The formal locus of direction, Lou, was simply nonfunctional in that respect. The rest of the staff and some people not on the staff but in related areas (such as Title I staff like Mrs. Hinkle and the school remedial reading teacher, Sara Brown, from whom I previously had begged an ancient rug to use in my shared classroom) filled in the breach of leadership.

But certainly, important information was getting lost along the way. For example, Mrs. Green collected referral forms and was a conscientious and efficient secretary, but she did not know exactly what happened to referrals after they left her desk until she received the final evaluation reports to type. There was no one to fill in the gap of educating new staff to their potential roles and responsibilities. And there was no one to make sure that the special education evaluations were actually completed and followed through.

My first special education staff meeting in Orangetown was a stimulating and disturbing experience for me. There were several referrals from regular classroom teachers of children who seemed to exhibit symptoms of emotional disturbance, at least as described on the referral form. David offered his services to observe and evaluate the classroom behavior of these children. His offer was accepted. But nobody wanted me to get involved in visiting families and developing social histories.

The staff was, in fact, horrified at the idea of routine home visits and interviews with parents of disturbed children. What? Are you crazy? the staff members gasped in various ways. Home visits to families of emotionally disturbed children? The families around here wouldn't let a social worker come up the front walk, much less in the front door. They have guns in their closets around here, you know. No, no, we don't want you to do social histories. Lou, in particular, was emphatic on that point.

David left the staff meeting looking taller, more important, and purposeful. He had a caseload of a half-dozen children to observe, a real job at last. I was still without official function, and I didn't feel so hot.

But now I knew that I was going to have to get input from outside Orangetown to become involved in social histories, and I certainly thought social histories were important in evaluating children referred with suspected emotional disturbance. Some children who act up at school might be fine at home, and the problem at school could relate to treatment at school, not to some kind of internal "disturbance." Perhaps contact with and information from the home could help regular teachers cope with the child's behavior in the normal classroom without requiring separation from peers. Moreover, I felt that that sort of perspective could be a valid contribution from the profession of social work to the Orangetown special education team.

I thought that I would begin developing my strategy toward incorporating social histories routinely in special education evaluations by consulting in earnest with my Kingston colleague, Mrs. Baker. She would probably have useful perspectives and experiences to share with me. Then I thought I might go talk to some people at the county level. Surely there, however, I would have to consult with someone other than Martin Murdock.

DISCUSSION AND STUDY QUESTIONS

Getting started in a job entails getting to know people and learning procedures. The procedures describe the formal organizational structure, but as one gets to know people, an informal structure also emerges. Sometimes these two structures are quite different, as is the case in the work environment described in this chapter. In such cases, a careful analysis of the relationship between the two is needed so that formal requirements are met at the same time that the informal structure is used effectively. Neglecting either structure is likely to impede one's work.

Regardless of rules, positions in organizations are filled by people. All people need to feel appreciated and worthwhile, although the ways that enable them to feel this way vary. One important way is by the formation of *support systems,* networks of relationships with people who bolster one's sense of well-being and also facilitate one's work. Support systems may include personal friendships, but not necessarily; being professionally supportive of someone does not require being her or his friend, although it does require acting in a friendly way.

Keeping these ideas in mind, try addressing the following points:

1. Describe the formal organizational structure of your college or university. If you can, make a chart showing which offices (dean, advisor, and so on) have formal responsibility for what activities. To the degree that you know, rank these offices in terms of degree of power (the president has power over the deans, who have power over the faculty, and so forth).
2. Now modify your formal structure (in the previous question) to build in the informal structure. In your experience, who *really* has power over various decisions? Don't forget that people such as secretaries or even knowledgeable students often wield a great deal of power in colleges and universities.
3. Think about a situation in which you needed something at school (finding out about course requirements, getting a dorm room, and so forth). How did you go about getting it? Did you use the formal or the informal structure or both? Looking back, might you have gotten what you needed by using different tactics?
*4. What does the author mean when she says that she and David "edged nervously around the borders of a professional territorial dispute"? What "territory" is she referring to? Have you ever had this experience? How was it resolved?

---

*Questions notated with an asterisk are intended for advanced students who have had or are currently having some social work practice experience and who have made at least a tentative commitment to the profession.

*5. Thinking about a work situation in which you participated (or are presently participating), describe your support system. In what ways did (does) it help you?

*6. This chapter describes a work situation in which the formal organizational structure of the special education program did not work as it was purported to on paper. The director of pupil services did not direct the pupil services team or administer the program. How did the Orangetown school staff informally fill in the leadership gap? What were some of the leadership and administrative functions that simply did not get done in Orangetown?

CHAPTER 4

A No-Good, Low-Down Phone Call

or: Managing Personal Feelings in the Professional Setting

Concepts Covered in This Chapter

1. Professional behavior and personal feelings
2. Managing angry and defensive behavior
3. Using professional support networks
4. The importance of values on behavior
   a. Client values regarding the utility of social work and social welfare
   b. Worker values regarding professional commitment

Learning Objectives   After reading this chapter you should be able to

1. Describe the role of personal feelings as part of professional behavior
2. Define at least three reasons why users of services might act in an angry or defensive manner
3. List at least three strategies social workers can use to manage angry or defensive behavior from clients
4. List at least three circumstances under which social workers might want to use their professional support system
5. Discuss how the values of users of services can affect their use of services
6. Discuss the relationship between the values of social workers and the manner in which they do their work

I t seemed as though the whole world was conspiring to keep me from getting started. When it rains, it pours, they say. Well, there's something to that. It just wasn't fair, especially since I was trying so hard.

It began when I heard from David that a call from an angry father came right into the front office of the school one morning. The call came from the father of one of the students referred for ED evaluation and whom I had interviewed the evening before.

This particular father was a single parent, and I had secured the interview with him for a social history only after many fruitless telephone calls. I had finally made an agreement with him to meet him at school after his leisurely supper hour. This meant that I had to stay on at the school until after 8:00 at night to get that social history because I lived too far from the school to go home for my own supper and return again. Just so the man's sublimely indifferent son could have a chance to qualify for special education services. On the basis of his classroom observations, David felt the boy badly needed them.

Of course, Orangetown offered neither extra pay nor compensatory time for overtime work, and I often found myself working extra hours for one reason or another without recognition or remuneration. I felt alternately noble and stupid.

But anyway, to continue—the person who took the angry phone call reported gleefully to the entire front office, according to David, that the father complained that Ms. Wells had asked him a lot of nosy questions the night before, and he wanted to register an official complaint.

Neither the front office nor the person who took the call passed this message on to me, so apparently I was either shielded or considered too insignificant to inform.

But then another complaint came in. The husband of a woman with whom I had conducted a long, tearful interview (she broke down during the social history to tell me of her miserably unhappy marriage, and I suggested she might be interested in the services of the county guidance clinic) called to complain that his wife told him I forced her to tell me intimate things. I heard about that one, too, from David, who said he happened to be in the front office when the call came in.

Somehow, David managed to present these distressing reports in a way that seemed falsely sympathetic. He came across as if he thought I ought to know about my failures for my own professional development. There was an undercurrent of one-upmanship, it seemed to me, and so I could not turn to him for comfort. David seemed to be telling me that it was too bad I was so incompetent, but there, there, maybe I could learn to do better someday.

I held my own fort in the combined office–classroom in Orangetown, and I kept a stiff upper lip until I could flee home or to Kingston. I could, fortunately, unburden myself at home, enough to keep going, but there was no one even in Kingston whom I felt safe enough with to reveal my most intimate feelings of professional failure. With Constance Chase, I could share almost everything, but I felt it unwise to burden her with too many of my feelings of discomfort when they related to her husband.

Then, just to test me further, the fates descended once again. David told me about Mrs. Neatly one morning. Mrs. Neatly, he said, had come to school the day before to talk to him and Mr. Burr, the principal, about placing her son in a class for children with learning disabilities. She said her son needed special help in school and this was the kind she wanted him to have.

David said the boy had recently been referred for ED evaluation, not LD, because his teacher was having a difficult time controlling his behavior. David said he had explained to Mrs. Neatly that he suspected her son should be evaluated for ED, as well as LD, and that that would require a social history. David said the mother had agreed. David had told the mother to expect my call. Would I set up an appointment with Mrs. Neatly as soon as possible? Jimmy Neatly was more than a little unruly at school, and this might be an opening to work with the boy right away.

Since I had no immediate appointments that morning, I simply sat down, picked up the telephone, and dialed the number for Mrs. Neatly that David provided.

"Good morning, Mrs. Neatly," I spoke confidently into the telephone. "I understand that your son Jimmy has been referred for evaluation for behavioral difficulties. I've just learned that you came to school yesterday and that you are interested in having Jimmy evaluated for both learning and behavioral disabilities. I am the person Mr. Chase told you would be calling to set up an appointment with you to talk about your son's early development. Would you like to meet with me at school or at your own home?"

I had barely gotten these blunt, bulky words out of my mouth when my ears were treated to a far more eloquent tirade.

"Who the hell do you think you are!" the lady on the other end of the telephone hollered. "Just who the hell? I don't have no mentally disturbed child here. Nobody's mental here. No way I'm going to have you snooping around my house, asking stupid questions. You just want to pry into my life. It ain't none of your business. You ain't going to act like no busybody around me. So you think my boy is a mental case, do you—"This tirade went on for quite a while.

She didn't stop, but I managed to break in for a sentence or two. "Mrs. Neatly, nobody thinks your child is 'mental.' I don't think I used that word. The special education program just needs information from you to help us evaluate Jimmy's behavior and learning needs at school."

"I can't tell you when my kid took his first step, when he sat up, when he said his first word, and all the rest of that garbage. What does all that have to do with my kid? You're just a bunch of nosy people. I'm going to read my child's file down at that lousy school. I know my rights. You make a mockery of my child, acting like he's disturbed. You ought to be ashamed of yourself."

She actually stopped, and I meekly asked her whether she had any questions about the purpose of the required "developmental history" for her child.

"I got no questions to ask of you people, and don't you come snooping around my house!" *Slam!*

Shades of the warnings of Lou Bachus. They really were out there: angry fathers and even mothers now who didn't want any special education people "snooping" around their homes.

I sat still for a few moments, not even looking at David, who was working busily away over there at his desk a few feet from mine. He looked so very fresh and professional, as I glimpsed him out of the corner of my eye, writing away at his academic reports in such a very competent manner. There was not so much as a wrinkle in his clean tan shirt. He looked as if he hadn't heard a word of my awkward sputtering; he was so totally removed from it all. Damn his unruffled hide, anyway. So what. I can handle this. I took several deep breaths and thought I had calmed myself down pretty well.

I called Mrs. Neatly back in five minutes or so, hoping she had calmed down too. I still thought I had a chance of working her through it, of making the appointment with her that would help qualify her son for ED services.

This time, Mrs. Neatly didn't even wait for me to complete my first sentence.

"I don't want to have nothing to do with the county, young lady. Your county welfare, food stamps, and special education is just communist taxation taking away our freedom. What the hell have you been doing for the past five minutes, anyway? Who have you been talking to? I suppose you're writing all of this down in your files? I tell you, I'm going to tell that superintendent down there all about you nosy people in that county special education program that keeps pestering us—"

"Mrs. Neatly," I broke in. "Special education is entirely separate from county welfare. All the information you give us will be kept strictly confidential—"

"Don't you give me none of that, young lady. I know about them files. I seen them right next to that young man's desk when I was down there yesterday. You ought to learn when you ain't wanted, lady, and you ain't wanted here. You keep your dirty nose out of my business." *Slam!*

It should have been almost funny. I had never even met this woman, and surely, nothing I personally had said so far should have warranted this angry a response. Something else was going on here that I personally was not responsible for. And yet, when that telephone slammed down in my ear for the second time, I was literally shaking.

Was I angry? Scared? Frustrated? Probably all three and more, but I didn't know it. All I knew right then was that I felt absolutely miserable. This was much worse than hearing the secondhand reports of the other complaints about me through David. Suddenly I felt like the worst, most inept social worker in the world. And worse yet, I was crying.

Crying. Oh no, good Lord, not right in front of David, the coolest and most competent of breezy professionals. I'd never be able to face him again for the rest of my life.

But right then, right through my tears and my almost unbearable embarrassment, I could see him soften. That David, the impeccable, impenetrable Ivy League whiz kid, was softening. He got up from his chair with an incredibly concerned frown on his face, and he came over and gave me a hug. He told me it didn't matter, that that kind of thing happened to everyone once in a while, even to him.

I suppose I wish it had happened some other way. I wish David and I could have become friends and learned to trust each other both because he so admired my flawless competence and perfect professional demeanor and because I was strong enough to match his pride with my own. Actually, we became friends and learned to trust each other very probably just because I broke down and cried in front of him. Or at least, that helped.

It really seemed to me that from that time onward, David didn't bother to act the supremely cool and self-contained professional in front of me again. I guess he felt too good about rescuing the damsel in distress. And I, having hit rock bottom in terms of undignified behavior, didn't bother to set up my defensive hackles in front of him again, either. With David, I knew I didn't need them anymore.

I was grateful to be rescued, and it certainly felt one whole lot better to become part of an expanding support system in Orangetown.

DISCUSSION AND STUDY QUESTIONS

Many times social workers work with people who are frightened. When people are fearful, they often express their anxieties in indirect ways. In this chapter, Mrs. Neatly's fear that her son may have a serious behavior problem and that the behavior of the entire family unit may be the source of that problem leads her to attack the social worker. Other episodes in the book illustrate other instances of people acting unpredictably in situations that are frightening to them. When social workers are confronted with such behavior, they themselves may become anxious or angry. Obviously, however, angry exchanges between a social worker and a client are not usually productive. Therefore, an important skill for a social worker is understanding the feelings underlying behavior, his or her own and the other person's. Such understanding makes it easier to disentangle the multiple and often frightened responses people exhibit in life situations.

This chapter also addresses another aspect of a social worker's need to be aware of her or his own needs and behaviors. The author comments that she frequently works overtime hours without pay or compensatory time. She remarks that she felt alternately noble and stupid. This is a common dilemma for social workers. On one hand, they are committed to helping others and are motivated to do everything possible to achieve this goal. On the other hand, they are human beings with their own needs and their own personal lives, which also need their energy and attention. Each professional social worker has to struggle to find his or her own balance between working on behalf of clients and exceeding his or her personal energy and strength. The several examples of this struggle throughout the book are realistic examples of what social workers encounter in day-to-day practice.

1. Think about your behavior when you get angry. How does your anger affect the way you think about yourself? How does it influence your thoughts about others? How do you express your anger, directly and indirectly?

2. Can you think of a situation in which someone did something that hurt you even though you knew (or later discovered) they were angry at someone else? How did it make you feel? How did you act toward that person?

3. How do you decide when demands made on you are reasonable or unreasonable? For example, in courses how much reading is too much and what kinds of tests are unfair? When you encounter a situation in which you feel you are being treated unreasonably, what do you do? How effective are your behaviors? Can you think of others that might be more useful?

*4. Have you ever worked overtime voluntarily, knowing that you would not get extra pay or compensatory time? If so, why did you do it? Would you do it again? If you have elected not to work overtime in the past, why did you make that decision? Would you make the same decision again under similar circumstances?

*5. Sex roles always affect our personal and professional lives, yet we often don't recognize the depth of their effect. Imagine how the telephone scene with Mrs. Neatly and the subsequent "rescue" by David might have gone if the author had been male. If the author had been male and David female? If both the author and David had been female?

---

*Questions notated with an asterisk are intended for advanced students who have had or are currently having some social work practice experience and who have made at least a tentative commitment to the profession.

CHAPTER 5

Supervision

or: Coping with Ineffective Supervisory Styles

Concepts Covered in This Chapter

1. Understanding supervision and utilizing it effectively
    a. The functions of supervision
    b. Managing problems related to supervision
    c. Consultation and supervision
2. Developing a job description
3. Political skill in organizations

Learning Objectives   After reading this chapter you should be able to

1. Distinguish between the organizational and the professional purposes of supervision
2. Identify at least two organizational and two professional purposes of supervision
3. List at least three problems that can occur in the supervisory process
4. Distinguish between consultation and supervision
5. List at least three functions of peer consultation
6. List at least four elements of a job description (these should include activities expected as well as reporting and evaluation criteria)
7. List at least two advantages and two disadvantages of circumventing an organization's formal authority structure

Almost all social workers providing direct services to clients have supervisors. Certainly this is true in bureaucratic organizations, where most social workers are employed. Supervisors not only administer and coordinate the social work services; ideally, they also provide expert consultation to maintain and upgrade the quality of practice.

As an employee of the Emmett County special education program, I had a dizzying number of supervisors. First, I had been told in the county orientation session at the beginning of the school year that the psychologist in each local school system was the director of pupil services in each respective locality. This meant that Lou Bachus was supposed to be my supervisor in Orangetown and that Norman Werner, the more experienced of the two psychologists in Kingston, was my supervisor in that town. In addition, Martin Murdock was the liaison from the county to the Orangetown school system, and that made him my supervisor too. There was also a county liaison to the Kingston schools, a man named Dan Dwyer. I hadn't seen much of him yet, but he was also my supervisor.

Above and beyond all that, Dr. Knight, director of the Emmett County special education program, had announced at one of the county in-service sessions that she would be meeting with the social workers as a group, on occasion, to provide direct and specialized supervision. That would be interesting because Dr. Knight had no training in social work. But then again, none of my supervisors had any training in social work. Perhaps that was why, although I was loaded with supervisors, not one of them gave me the foggiest idea what I was supposed to be doing with my job (with the notable exception of the psychologist in Kingston, Norman Werner).

Now I not only wanted some direction; I also wanted some support. I knew I wanted to develop social histories for children referred with suspected emotional disturbance in Orangetown, but my local supervisor, Lou Bachus, had directly told me not to do them. I was going to need some assistance from somebody over his head. I had asked Martin Murdock whether he would talk to Lou about it, as Martin was our county supervisor and officially Lou's boss, and Martin had talked to me about the idea for quite some time. But he didn't get back to Lou Bachus to support my request. I had asked Lou about that shortly thereafter, and Lou had just looked blank for a few moments. Then he had gone into his "guns in the closet" routine again.

A bit disgruntled with the supervisors I had had contact with, I decided to try consultation—peer consultation, at that. So I took my questions and frustrations to Gertrude Baker, the full-time social worker in Kingston.

Gertrude and I worked in different schools in Kingston, and because our schedules were both heavy, we didn't see each other all that much. Most of the time, we were out interviewing parents or working with children or teachers at our respective schools. So I asked Gertrude one morning when we saw each other briefly in the open office room whether I could talk to her for a while after work. I explained that I had noticed some strange contrasts in evaluation procedures between Orangetown and Kingston that I wanted to talk over with her, and I expected I would be needing a good hour or so of her time.

Gertrude grinned and suggested a rendezvous in a local tavern. That suited me fine. Perhaps that is the reason why, by the time we got around to discussing social histories, Gertrude's response was so memorable. Gertrude was a rather big, husky woman, and her voice always packed a lot of wallop. But when I asked her whether she thought there was any way I could get the Orangetown pupil services team to permit me to do social histories on ED referrals, she let out a veritable war whoop.

Nervously, I sneaked little glances all around me to see whether we were about to be tossed out of the place, but then I realized I had gotten so caught up in the conversation at hand that I hadn't noticed the tavern had filled up since we arrived. The decibel level in the bar was already so loud that nobody in particular noticed Gertrude's incredible howl.

Gertrude laughed for a long time, and by the time she stopped, I had finished my drink and felt a lot better. "Would you mind telling me what's so funny?" I giggled.

Her next response startled me almost as much as the first one. "Carolyn," she shouted, "Carolyn, my dear, what you do is you go to Myrtle Knight and you say, *'Myrtle, I need supervision! Myrtle, I need supervision!'*"

"Ah," I replied. "Uh—I go to Myrtle Knight and I say, 'Myrtle, I need supervision'?"

Myrtle Knight was none other than the top administrator of the special education program at the county level.

"That's right!" hollered Gertrude.

"Whatever for?" I whispered.

Finally, Gertrude got down to business. She asked me had I by any chance noticed that I was asked to do social histories for absolutely all the ED referrals in my Kingston schools. I retorted that of course I had—how else did she think I had come up with such a brilliant idea to import to Orangetown?

"Well," she continued, "it just so happens that social histories are *required* by the county for approval of any M team [multidisciplinary team] recommendations for ED kids."

"Are you sure?" I gasped.

"Absolutely sure," she pronounced severely. "Sometimes," she went on, "it *is* true that parents won't cooperate. It doesn't really happen very often, but the county just will not approve M team recommendations for the ED kids without a complete social history. Those kids whose parents won't provide one just can't get served. That's a big problem, too, at times, in my opinion."

Could this be possible? If so, who was doing social histories now in Orangetown? Was I inadvertently trying to take over somebody else's claimed job territory? Was that why Lou Bachus kept telling me not to do them? Or more likely, was Orangetown somehow getting its M team recommendations for ED kids approved *without* social histories? In that case, could I persuade the county to extend the social history requirement to Orangetown?

And then the obvious suddenly occurred to me. Orangetown hadn't *had* an ED program before this year. The pupil services team simply didn't know about the requirement for social histories. They hadn't yet fully processed an M team report for an ED child.

This should be easy to get straightened out, I smiled to myself happily. I should just get the county to inform Lou Bachus about the requirement for social histories. How wonderfully simple—except for one slight problem. My immediate supervisor from the county was Martin Murdock. And so far, Martin hadn't been able to help me with much of anything. Gertrude was right, for reasons she wasn't aware of. I would truly have to go to Myrtle.

It was easy enough to make an appointment with Dr. Myrtle Knight, to my real surprise. Since Dr. Knight was head of the Emmett County program, I had expected that she would insulate herself severely. In fact, before I called to make the appointment, I discussed social histories for ED children once more with Martin. He remained unaware of any county policy and could not seem to remember to find out whether such a policy indeed existed.

So I called to make the appointment with Dr. Knight, sure that I would be diverted to Martin and prepared to insist on my request, if necessary. But I wasn't even asked to refer my problems to Martin. In fact, I got an appointment with Myrtle Knight for the next morning.

I arrived at her office, and before I knew it, the first words that popped themselves right out of my mouth were *"Myrtle, I need supervision!"*

She seemed a little startled, and certainly I was. I hoped my respectful use of the world "supervision" would gloss over my casual use of her first name. But she seemed quite at home with the use of her first name, and she quite comfortably used mine. I learned later that she did everything on a first-name basis. That felt nice and low key.

Myrtle Knight was young, dark-haired, and attractive. She was what some people would describe as "bouncy." Her basic energy level was high, and she talked and smiled a lot. She seemed very friendly and concerned, and when she focused her attention on you, you had the feeling that she was right with you. She was positively disarming, in fact. I felt very lucky to have such a warm human being at the top of the county administrative structure.

I explained to Myrtle about my desire to do social histories for ED referrals in Orangetown, as I did in Kingston. She was immediately sympathetic. I asked her whether it was true that social histories were required by the county for all ED referrals. She said they were. I asked whether they would be required for Orangetown, as well, and she said yes, definitely. I explained my difficulty in having the concept accepted by the Orangetown pupil services team and asked her whether she would be willing to communicate the requirement to the psychologist, Lou Bachus. And she said she would have Martin Murdock do so immediately.

Feeling relaxed and heartened by her response, I spoke to Myrtle as if she were a peer and not a top administrator. I said I had asked Martin about a lot of things in the past. He was pleasant enough, I remarked, but he seemed to be unable to follow through with any requests or suggestions. That was why I was in this office this morning. I had already talked to Mr. Murdock without results. In fact, I blurted out impulsively, I found dealing with him generally a waste of time. No, I didn't think communicating to the Orangetown pupil services team via Martin would get the job done.

I noticed her eyes narrowing then. She looked displeased. The conversation lost some of its zest for a few moments. I felt suddenly ashamed of myself. Not only had I not been kind, but also I had not been politic. But still, I did not become heedful enough.

Shortly thereafter, Myrtle changed the subject, and the conversation became warm and animated again. She was asking me whether I thought I would go back to the university at the end of the year or whether I thought I might stay on with the county. She seemed delighted when I said, honestly, that working in Kingston so far was more fun and more rewarding than teaching and that if things in Orangetown picked up, I certainly was going to have a tough decision to make.

As I left, Myrtle said that she would make sure that Martin Murdock knew about the county requirement for social histories for ED referrals that very day and that she would have him inform Mr. Bachus immediately. I wondered how this would work, but because I had already registered my concerns about Mr. Murdock, I felt more than enough had been said.

That day I went about my business as usual in Orangetown and didn't say a word about social histories. But when I returned to Orangetown two days later, I couldn't keep silent any longer. When I walked into the elementary school, there was Martin Murdock talking earnestly to Lou Bachus in the psychologist's office. It must be happening, then. Martin must be telling Lou about the county's social history requirement.

I swelled a little, feeling powerful and magnanimous. I wouldn't swagger as I walked into the office with the two men. I would just saunter in modestly. I would explain to Lou Bachus that I was aware that indeed he was right. There might truly be danger involved in gathering social histories. If he wanted to go along with me on the first few to check out the situation and make sure I was getting the information he wanted, that would be just fine. Yes, I would be careful to make Lou feel as if he were still in charge, even though he usually didn't want to be in charge. I was sure Lou would decline my invitation, but then it would be his own decision and he wouldn't feel like a loser. All this was running through my head as I moved into the office.

The psychologist's office in Orangetown was tiny, only about an eight-foot square, and it was mostly filled with an imposing desk. But the men apparently didn't notice me enter. I stood there just inside the doorway shifting from one foot to the other. The sense of power dripped out of me a little and then finally oozed away completely as I realized what they were talking so intently about—fishing. I hoped feebly, though, that perhaps prior to my arrival or sometime yesterday, Mr. Murdock had discussed the requirement of social histories with Mr. Bachus.

I cleared my throat a little after a few minutes. Then, I let out a little squeak. Finally, I began to babble about the canoe trip I had taken over the weekend, where the fish were jumping right up out of the water. That got their attention. They wanted to know what kind of fish.

For a brief moment I held the floor while they directed me their rapt attention—but I didn't know what kind of fish. I only know two kinds of river fish by sight—carp and catfish—and that never seems to impress anybody.

But I had my foot in the door. At least now they knew I was around. At a convenient pause in the conversation, I addressed Martin. "Martin," I asked, unable to suppress the excitement in my voice, "have you heard that social histories are required by the county for the evaluation of ED children?"

Now Lou Bachus would hear it from the horse's mouth, from the county's official representative, Mr. Murdock.

"Why, why, why—why, how could that be?" Martin mused. "Why, you know perfectly well that a lot of parents would refuse to provide social histories. Why, why— some farms have great big dogs that wouldn't even let you up the driveway. Lots of farmers around here keep guns in their closets, you know, and they wouldn't let you in their front door. Why, why—the county *couldn't* have a requirement for social histories. That would be impossible, quite impossible, don't you think, Mr. Bachus? For ED children especially? Why, those kids would come from the craziest families of all—"

DISCUSSION AND STUDY QUESTIONS

Since social workers usually work in bureaucratic organizations and are able to do their chosen work only through the resources of these organizations, they are generally subject to organizational rules and procedures. Among them is working with a supervisor. *Webster's* defines the verb *supervise* as "to superintend, oversee." This can, of course, take many forms, ranging from close control to helpful suggestions by a more experienced professional to a less experienced colleague. When properly used, supervision is part of the profession's responsibility to monitor its own practice by having the most competent social workers share their knowledge and skills with those who are working toward higher levels of competence.

Supervisory structures are generally mandated by organizations as part of their effort to monitor the quality of their services. The author notes that professionals also use consultation even though it is not necessarily required by the organization in which they work. *Webster's* defines the verb *consult* as "to ask the advice or opinion of, to deliberate together." Consultation is an important part of the collegial nature of a profession. Social workers work together to provide the best possible service to clients. When they need additional information or suggestions that will help them practice more effectively, the competent social worker consults with an appropriate colleague. Often, of course, a social worker will consult with a non-social worker—a nurse for specialized information about physical functioning, a psychologist for specialized information about psychological behavior, and so on. Whereas supervision is generally required by organizations, consultation is usually undertaken at the initiative of the social worker. Both can be important tools in the never-ending effort to help people as effectively as possible.

1. Have you ever supervised anyone? Consider such possible examples as washing a car or cutting the lawn with someone else or supervising someone who typed a term paper for you. What responsibilities did you feel as a supervisor? What skills did you try to use to avoid being "bossy"?
2. To what degree do you use consultation? That is, do you have certain people to whom you go for advice when you need it? Why did you pick those people? Do you always do what they suggest? Why or why not?
*3. Have you ever had a social work supervisor whom you thought was especially good? Try to identify as many things about that person as possible that

---

*Questions notated with an asterick are intended for advanced students who have had or are currently having some social work practice experience and who have made at least a tentative commitment to the profession.

contributed to her or his effectiveness as a supervisor, especially in terms of being helpful to you.

*4. Supervisors, being human, on occasion may do inadequate work, at least in the opinion of the social workers under them. What might be some useful tactics to try in dealing with supervisors who do not seem to be very informative, helpful, or competent?

*5. Analyze the possible relationship between a support system and the process of consultation. Illustrate the relationship you identify with reference to your own practice experience.

PART TWO

Practice Skills

INTRODUCTION

In this part of the book, the author focuses her attention on specific practice skills needed by social workers. Each chapter highlights specific skills, but it is important to remember that the author uses all these skills as needed in her practice. The use of a range of skills as needed to intervene in a variety of client life situations is called *generalist practice*. Every social worker uses many specific skills in his or her practice. However, the generalist practitioner's function is to have as wide a skill repertoire as possible in order to facilitate the interactions between people and the social institutions and situations in which they live. A new chapter for the third edition, Chapter 10, illustrates various skills involved in achieving change at the organizational and community levels.

The author, however, makes it clear that the generalist social worker does not do everything. One of the clearest examples is in Chapter 9, where she tries to engage the Emmett County Guidance Clinic to provide psychiatric services that would have been inappropriate for her to attempt. A very important skill of the generalist social worker is knowing when specialized skill is needed. The generalist, as the author demonstrates numerous times, needs to know *when* specialized resources are needed and *where* they can be found (if, in fact, they are available). The case of Rudolph Gonzales, in Chapter 12, shows how hard a task this can be. The actual provision of specialized services is done by other professionals with the necessary expertise. Such persons are commonly psychologists, psychiatrists, special education teachers, nurses, physical therapists, social workers with specialized training in some aspect of social work, and so on. Several instances of the work of such specialists are discussed.

A number of basic social work skills are illustrated in this section. Some of the most important concern relating to others in a caring and supportive way: communicating clearly and honestly, establishing supportive and helpful working relationships with colleagues, following appropriate organizational procedures, obtaining and assessing information, making referrals, following up on planned activities, providing information, and enabling people to express feelings. The author's use of these practice skills flows easily from her professional assessment of what is needed as well as her commitment to social work values. In her work with Mrs. Tabler in Chapter 6, the author works diligently to preserve the self-respect and self-confidence of a young mother in a difficult family situation.

Social work practice is a *problem-solving or planned change process*, which includes assessing problems, planning activities to alleviate problems, carrying out the plans, and evaluating results. The author's work beautifully illustrates this process. Social work problem solving involves mutuality, and we regularly see the author involving her clients, as well as her colleagues, in efforts to understand, plan for, alleviate, and assess problems and ways to resolve them. We can also see from her work that problem solving entails a great deal of trial and error. In any number of instances, the author develops a plan based on her best professional assessment; yet she is continuously open to modifying it as she proceeds. This flexible yet purpose-oriented approach is demonstrated today by her successor in Orangetown, as described in the chapter "Stretching Scarce Resources."

Social work practice takes skill and courage and caring. The social worker has individual skills that are used according to her or his professional judgment about what is needed and appropriate. As we see, this takes hard work, energy, and the strength to push forward in the face of resistance. Yet it also takes sensitivity and caring. Many times we see the author carefully nurture her clients' bruised feelings and help them overcome their sense of hopelessness and helplessness. We also see her own discouragement in the face of defeats made more painful by her caring for those she is unable to help in the ways she feels necessary. Ultimately, perhaps the most important practice skill illustrated in this book is the skill of being able to keep one's motivation and caring no matter how disappointed one may be (this is sometimes called "avoiding burnout"). In this, the author is indeed skillful.

CHAPTER 6

Another Welfare Mother
or: Assessing Client Needs and Making
Effective Referrals

Concepts Covered in This Chapter

1. Understanding teamwork and using it effectively
2. The concept of the person-in-the-environment
3. Using knowledge of specific social welfare programs in practice
4. Understanding confidentiality and practicing it effectively
5. The impact of program regulations on the implementation of social welfare policies
6. Understanding the feelings of users of services about their situation and about receiving social work services

Learning Objectives   After reading this chapter you should be able to

1. Define *teamwork* in social work and give an example of it
2. Define the concept of the person-in-the-environment
3. Apply the concept of the person-in-the-environment, using case material from this chapter
4. Distinguish between a presenting problem and an underlying problem
5. List at least five social welfare programs
6. Discuss how social workers make use of their knowledge of specific social welfare programs
7. Define *confidentiality* and list at least three factors that may make its use difficult
8. Discuss how application procedures and eligibility criteria sometimes make it difficult for people to gain access to needed services
9. List at least three things social workers can do to reduce the difficulty people have gaining access to needed resources
10. Discuss how the open expression of feelings by users of services can be both a positive and a negative element in social work

Over in Kingston, life was progressing busily and productively. Norman Werner, the psychologist in two of the schools for which I had responsibility, regularly made appropriate referrals to me, some for social histories and some for a variety of other services. One day he stopped by my desk with a concerned expression on his face. Now, a concerned expression was not unusual for Norman. A big, gentle man, he took his job seriously. Feelings of sympathy and compassion were readily acceptable to Norman, and his face often assumed an expression I can only describe as sweet, as long as I am safely out of earshot. Sometimes, however, referring teachers or our supervisors at the county level would ask him to do evaluations he considered incomplete, to get the papers moving faster. Then he would look stubborn and cloudy, decidedly unsweet, and he wouldn't comply. I liked and respected Norman.

So I felt good when he stopped by my desk one morning to ask for some professional collaboration. Norman had had a tearful phone call the afternoon before from a distraught mother, a woman named Mrs. Tabler, and he had made an appointment to see her this morning because she had sounded so upset. Norman wondered whether I could come with him. Some of the things Mrs. Tabler had said on the phone made him think a social worker's knowledge might bé useful in the interview. In particular, the young mother had said that she had been separated from her husband for some time and didn't have any income of her own. Norman didn't know whether Mrs. Tabler was qualified for or receiving any public aid, and he didn't know the details involved in applying.

Norman and I drove out together to the little country school where the appointment was to be held. Although this school was in the Kingston district, it actually was in a different town some 10 miles away. It was the smallest of my three schools in the district, consisting of only four classrooms. The principal of the school, a nervous but kindly woman who usually knew exactly what was going on with everyone in the little town, met us in the hallway and admonished us to be gentle with Mrs. Tabler. "Now you be good to that woman, you two," she said. "She's a good person, and she's had a terrible time of it. And there's nothing wrong with that little girl of hers that a happy family couldn't cure."

"Thank you, Mrs. Gilmore," Norman and I chorused in unison. We listened, because we were human and because Mrs. Gilmore usually knew everything worth knowing.

We were ushered into the little conference room between the classrooms, given a welcome pot of tea and a couple of cracked cups, and left with the promise that Mrs. Tabler would be with us shortly. Mrs. Gilmore said she expected her any minute, in fact. How Mrs. Gilmore knew all that when neither Norman nor I had as yet mentioned the purpose of our visit is one of those things that can only be understood by those familiar with the small town grapevine. Confidentiality in professional practice is an important principle, but it is certainly hard to apply (even if all the more important) in a small town. The client tells a little bit to one person in the morning, and by evening everyone knows everything and quite a lot more besides.

Mrs. Tabler was, indeed, with us in a few moments, and she entered the room already in tears. I looked quickly at Norman and saw that he was very moved by Mrs. Tabler's distress.

Norman took on the direction of the interview. "Mrs. Tabler," he began, "let me introduce you to Ms. Wells. She is our school social worker, and I thought she might have some useful ideas for you today."

Mrs. Tabler sniffed self-consciously and rubbed her eyes a little in my direction, trying to control her tears.

Norman continued. "When you called me yesterday, you were upset about your daughter. She had stolen something. Do you want to tell us about that again so we both understand?"

Mrs. Tabler nodded and even managed a hesitant smile. She explained that her own mother, her daughter Maria's grandmother, had discovered that her best pair of white Sunday gloves was missing. The grandmother found out that Maria had stolen the gloves and that Maria had also gotten them very dirty while playing with a neighbor's doll carriage. Maria was eight years old.

The grandmother, very angry, had spanked Maria, but she had also called the sheriff. Obviously, she had wanted to make an impression. I thought to myself that the grandmother herself must be quite a terror!

The sheriff had dutifully given Maria a lecture, but Maria wouldn't apologize. In fact, Maria had had a temper tantrum instead. Shortly after that, the sheriff had left. But not before he had warned Mrs. Tabler that she might have the makings of a juvenile delinquent on her hands.

Later that day, Mrs. Tabler decided to call Norman. Maria had been tested for learning disabilities by Norman last year, and Mrs. Tabler remembered that he was a psychologist as well as a very nice young man. She thought Norman might be able to tell her what to do about Maria. Mrs. Tabler didn't want her daughter to grow up to be a thief. She had finally made Maria apologize to the grandmother, but she didn't think that was really going to remedy the whole situation.

"The whole situation?" I asked then, my first contribution to the conversation. "Can you tell us more about the whole situation that you think affects your daughter?"

"Well," Mrs. Tabler continued, sobs frequently punctuating her explanation, "I have three other children, two, three, and five years old. Their father left us two years ago, just after the baby was born. I have had to live with my parents since then because I couldn't live on my own. My parents keep picking on all the children—they say they will grow up to be no-good bums like their father. They say they don't want the children around but are stuck with all of us because their father is no good. They used to treat Maria best, but lately they have been picking on her too. And I can't do anything about it." She began to sob in earnest. It was very emotional for a while. But gradually she gained control of herself.

"How did you get along with your parents before the children were born?" I asked.

"Not very well," she replied. "Sometimes I think I got married as young as I did just to get out of there. I tried to make it on my own when my husband left me, but he only sent money for a few months. I couldn't get a job with all the kids to take care of. When my mother invited me home, I was so grateful I forgot how hard it was there. I went back. That was almost two years ago, and things keep getting worse. It is hard for my parents to have all the children around, and they don't have a lot of money, either. They really don't want us anymore, but they are both religious. They keep saying we are their cross to bear. I just don't know what to do."

"Did you ever have a court order for child support or alimony from your husband?" I asked.

"No," she said. "We never got a formal divorce, but last week my husband wrote and said he wanted one. All this time I've kept hoping he would come back, but now he's found another woman and wants to marry her, he says."

At this point Mrs. Tabler began to cry again, and Norman looked as though he was going to dissolve with sympathy. I stepped back for awhile, and Norman did a terrific job reconstructing Mrs. Tabler's sense of self-worth. After all, she couldn't have been older than her late twenties; she was attractive and intelligent. With luck, she could still have a lot of worthwhile living ahead of her. That is, if she could gain some control over her life.

By now I had come to the tentative conclusion that the presenting problem, the stealing incident of little Maria, was secondary to the underlying problems in the living situation. If the living situation could be improved, somehow, it seemed likely that Maria's undesirable behavior would clear up on its own.

When Mrs. Tabler was smiling a little once again, Norman asked her the question on my own mind: Was Maria's stealing behavior an ongoing problem or was it a relatively occasional thing? Mrs. Tabler replied that the glove incident was the only time she was aware of that Maria had taken anything of the grandmother's without permission. She didn't know about any other stealing incidents, either, for that matter.

That made the sheriff's visit, solicited as it was by the grandmother, seem to be a particularly heavy-handed move, at least to me.

I asked Mrs. Tabler what she had thought about the sheriff's visit, and she was alternately indignant and fearfully approving if it would keep her daughter from becoming delinquent. She pronounced the world *delinquent* with such fear and awe that I had visions of eight-year-old Maria carting off all her grandmother's loot full speed ahead in her neighbor's unlicensed and stolen doll carriage!

I asked about the temper tantrum Mrs. Tabler had described. Was that usual behavior for Maria? Very rare, the mother replied.

About then I got into exploring options with Mrs. Tabler. Had she ever seriously considered moving away from her parents? "Oh yes, I would do anything to be able to do that. I think they are bad for the children. But I have no money to pay for a place of my own."

"Have you ever heard of a program called Aid to Families with Dependent Children?"

"You mean welfare?" Mrs. Tabler hit the dread word head on.

"Yes, welfare," I replied firmly. "Not everybody who needs it is eligible for welfare. But in your case, as the mother of four small children and separated from your husband, you would probably be eligible for the program called AFDC."

"But my mother and my father would throw us out of the house!"

"Let's talk about that," I said. "AFDC provides a pretty small budget to live on. The amount of money provided was never intended to make the families who receive it very comfortable. So since your parents are supporting you right now, you might want to keep things that way. How about if I describe the program to you, so you can think it over?"

"People around here think welfare is a disgrace," Mrs. Tabler said. "I always thought I might be able to get it, but I didn't even know where to apply. I've been afraid to ask my friends. They wouldn't know, anyway."

I explained to Mrs. Tabler the sort of thing that social workers usually tell reluctant but all-too-needy clients: that welfare programs are paid for by taxes, that her husband and her parents paid taxes, so that in an indirect way she was also contributing to the fund. After all, she was providing child care for offspring who were her husband's responsibility as well as her own.

I asked her whether she thought there was any way she could work to support herself and her children. She said there was no way, not at this time. She wanted to take care of the children herself until they were all in school, and she also didn't have a job skill that could bring enough money to pay for babysitting. She didn't want to leave the children alone with the grandmother. The grandmother had made it clear she didn't want the responsibility, anyway.

"Well," I went on to say, "lots of women are stuck just as you are—they don't have an income and they can't get a job because they have children to take care of. I myself am glad we have welfare programs because lots of people find themselves in situations such as this. I don't think going on AFDC is anything to be ashamed of. When the children are older and if you are able to find a job, then you can contribute to the program through your own taxes and help somebody else out."

"Do you have any idea how much money I could receive?" Mrs. Tabler asked. "I really would like to live in an apartment of my own, and if I could do that it would be important enough for the children that I think I might apply."

I took out my notebook and a pencil and figured out for her the approximate amount of money she would receive, given the number of children she had. I explained to Mrs. Tabler that the department of public welfare would probably require her signature to pursue legal action against her husband so that he would have to pay for part of the cost. But if she liked, she could authorize the welfare department to collect the husband's payments from the court. Then she could be sure of receiving the same monthly allotment from the AFDC program whether her husband kept up with his payments or not.

Mrs. Tabler was dry-eyed and almost excited by now. "I could live on that amount of money," she said. "I know because I used to pay all the bills when I was living with my husband. It would be awfully tight, but I think I could do it."

"There are a lot of things to consider," I warned, "such as where would you want to live, are there any apartments available if you decide to leave your parents' home, how will you tell your parents, how will you talk to your friends? Shall we make another appointment for next week, after you've thought this over a little?"

We did so, and the next week Mrs. Tabler was like a different woman. There were no tears now, only determination. She asked about all sorts of programs she had heard about via the grapevine: school lunches for reduced cost, food stamps, medical assistance. She was already checking out ads for apartments in the local newspaper. At the end of our meeting, I had her use the telephone in the school conference room to call the welfare department to make an appointment.

The visit to the Emmett County Department of Public Welfare was not a very pleasant experience. Because Mrs. Tabler had no car, I took her myself. The workers there didn't offer her any assistance in filling out the thick and complicated forms.

They were completely insensitive on the subject of her missing her husband. During the appointment itself, Mrs. Tabler became hesitant to sign the legal form that authorized prosecution of her husband for child support. Still wanting his love, she didn't want to antagonize him and drive him further away from her.

Mrs. Tabler and I had discussed this particular requirement before, and I was surprised to find that it didn't seem to bother her. But when she was actually confronted with the official legal document, she became upset and frightened. She worried about what her husband would think of her. Maybe he would never speak to her again. Her hesitation to sign, however, was perceived by her eligibility worker only as noncooperation. The worker impatiently threatened to throw out Mrs. Tabler's entire application for aid unless she signed the legal form immediately. The worker, after all, was a busy person. Mrs. Tabler signed. I was glad I was there to help her through moments such as these.

Now that the written application for aid was completed, Mrs. Tabler would have to have a home visit by another eligibility worker from the department. That visit apparently went very well. Rather than resenting any intrusion on her privacy, Mrs. Tabler seemed to welcome another opportunity to talk about her situation. The worker who visited her was polite and personable and left Mrs. Tabler feeling better about herself. She was now qualified to receive financial assistance from AFDC.

Now she could look for an apartment in Kingston, check out some courses at the vocational school to prepare for future self-support, and develop a new circle of friends. This was the kind of thing we had talked about in our counseling session.

That was a nice fantasy, but none of it came to pass. What did happen was that Mrs. Tabler's father suddenly had a stroke. He would require a lot of physical lifting and moving because he was partially paralyzed. The grandmother was not strong enough to provide the kind of care needed. The grandfather would have to go to a nursing home—or Mrs. Tabler would have to stay to take care of him.

At my last contact with Mrs. Tabler, this attractive woman in her late twenties was still living in her small rural township, caring now not only for her four young children but for her incapacitated father as well. It didn't seem to me that the wheel of fortune had given her a very fair spin. But at least she had an income of her own now to contribute to the family budget, and she could take that income and move on if she decided to. She was also clearly needed in her parents' home and no longer just a "cross to bear."

Her parents were treating her and her wishes with more respect, Mrs. Tabler said. That meant they weren't saying so many unpleasant things about her former husband or her children. And there were no more complaints from anyone about Maria's behavior. The little girl continued to develop as a normal eight-year-old.*

DISCUSSION AND STUDY QUESTIONS

Understanding people's problems requires a great deal of sensitivity as well as a lot of information. Often people approach a social worker with one problem, called the *pre-*

---

*The AFDC program that was so helpful to Mrs. Tabler is no longer available to assist needy mothers today. See Part V, Chapter 22.

senting problem. This is either the most immediate problem being experienced by the client or, in some cases, the only one the client feels comfortable or safe talking about. Often there are *underlying problems* that are related to the presenting problem. Identifying these requires patient, thorough information gathering. A *social history* is a commonly used framework for getting information pertinent to the possible physiological, psychological, social, and cultural aspects of the total situation that, in whole or in part, is being experienced as problematic.

People have feelings about themselves, their lives, and the opinion of others. When obtaining information and exploring problems, it is important for the social worker to acknowledge, respect, and deal sensitively with these feelings. Practicing *confidentiality* is an important part of the appropriate treatment of information. The social worker obtains information to assess the best possible service approaches, not to gossip or otherwise misuse the trust that a client has shown by providing the information. Respect for others is a basic social work value, and its use begins with the way information is obtained and used. As the author demonstrates many times, sharing information about clients requires their informed consent and/or the social worker's most carefully made decision to do so.

1. Have you ever experienced a situation in which information you shared with someone else in confidence was inappropriately passed on to others? What motivations did you attribute to the person who violated your confidence? How did you feel when you discovered confidentiality was not maintained? Did this incident affect your future relations with the other person?

2. The author says that "to go on welfare" carries a stigma in our society. What is a stigma? What effect did the threat of bearing a stigma have on Mrs. Tabler? What function does such a stigma probably perform regarding the number of applications completed for welfare assistance? Do you think this function is socially desirable?

*3. Social workers try to gather and assess all the information relevant to problem solving in a given situation. Where does the author first specifically utilize the "holistic approach" in this chapter? Can you think of any other kinds of information she might have requested that could have illuminated the problem even further?

*4. What factors do you suppose would make confidentiality difficult to maintain in small towns or even small agencies? Why does the author comment that confidentiality is probably even more important in those settings? What ideas do you have regarding how the author could best practice confidentiality in the situation described in this chapter?

---

*Questions notated with an asterisk are intended for advanced students who have had or are currently having some social work practice experience and who have made at least a tentative commitment to the profession.

CHAPTER 7

A Starting Plan for Orangetown: The Luxury of Children and Toys

or: Developing One's Own Job Description

Concepts Covered in This Chapter

1. The effective use of physical space in the delivery of social work services
2. Strategies for developing professional helping relationships with children
3. The use of counseling skills in social work
4. Understanding the use of group skills in social work

Learning Objectives   After reading this chapter you should be able to

1. Describe at least three ways in which physical space can be important in social work
2. Discuss why developing professional helping relationships is more difficult for children than it is for adults
3. List at least three strategies a social worker can use to develop effective helping relationships with children
4. Describe the difference between counseling and the use of groups in social work
5. List at least three reasons why social workers attempt to involve users of services in finding solutions to problems rather than finding all the solutions themselves
6. List at least three factors that social workers consider when they develop a therapeutic group
7. Define *self-concept* and describe why it is important in human behavior
8. Define foster care

As I think about it now, I don't know just why I didn't spend my early days in Orangetown asleep on the couch in the room I shared with David. While Martin Murdock did come around to check on both David and me at least twice every week, he never had any work he wanted either of us to do. He usually wanted to relax on the couch a bit and sip a cup of coffee or tea.

We took to scheduling anything we could come up with by 8:30 in the morning. Martin had a habit of arriving about 8:00, which must have made him feel quite diligent. I'm sure he was trying to do a good job. But his empty words at that hour of the morning drove us nearly to distraction, and we consciously began to develop expertise in limiting his time in the classroom. The early morning challenge had a very important positive function: it began to bring David and me together in an alliance against the common enemy.

The director of pupil services in Orangetown, the psychologist Lou Bachus, didn't have any work he wanted me to do, either; and he and Martin were my two immediate supervisors in Orangetown. If they didn't have any use for my services, surely I could justifiably enjoy my leisure. Hadn't I been looking for a job with less pressure, anyhow?

But I perversely refused to enjoy my free time in Orangetown. As I look back on it now, the other thing I could have done was to spend my whole week in Kingston. That would have been much more pleasant, as well as perhaps strategically canny, because then, surely, somebody in Orangetown would have complained. That would have forced the county to define my job function. But this simple solution, so obvious now, never even occurred to me at the time. No, I was bound and determined to work myself hard in Orangetown.

I must say for myself that I was eminently successful. There was a day when I discovered that I was getting behind in my work, that I could easily spend the entire week in Orangetown and still need more time. What the school system really needed was a full-time social worker and more, but that realization took a couple of months to develop.

As I was effectively blocked at the beginning of the school year in Orangetown from doing the kinds of evaluation work I was doing in Kingston (the social histories, in particular, although I was also doing classroom observations in Kingston on occasion), I thought I would let myself enjoy the luxury of working with individual children. Later on, I thought I might be able to identify natural groups and combine them in group counseling sessions.

The LD teachers got me going at first. There was an LD teacher for elementary school children, Mrs. Glass; an LD teacher for the junior high students, Mrs. Shasta; and a combination LD/ED teacher for the high school, Mrs. Chase. All these teachers suggested the names of children who they thought might benefit from regular counseling.

Getting started was a lot of fun. First came making finishing arrangements in the room to create the atmosphere I wanted. Luckily, David wanted an informal atmosphere too, so we cooperated in making a cozy corner around the little sink that conveniently came with the classroom. We brought in a pot that would heat water; a good supply of cocoa, coffee, tea, and powdered juices; and a variety of cups and glasses.

We got a bright cover for the ragged couch David had secured from the speech therapist and spent a few hours cleaning the ancient rug I had begged from the remedial reading teacher. David persuaded a young art teacher to paint colorful murals on the backs of our bookcases and on both sides of our room dividers. Before long, we had a place to be proud of. Makeshift, yes, obviously, and about as private as an open classroom with low room dividers can be—that is, not private at all. But the room provided a conversation piece for the young children we brought there and helped put them at ease. I bought an ample selection of games and toys myself, once I was certain Martin would be unable to locate county funds for supplies. I even requisitioned a duplicate dollhouse from a conference room in Kingston, along with an intriguing variety of broken furniture. Now we had a reasonable setup for play therapy.

David and I worked it out so that we often were able to schedule time alone in the classroom with our respective students, although we gradually found that it worked all right if we couldn't. In fact, at times we worked with students together. This would happen spontaneously, as when one of us joined in a game the other was playing with a counselee.

Students got so used to seeing us together in the same space that we rarely inhibited each other or our clients by our presence. This was not particularly advisable; privacy is an important concept in counseling. It was just a necessity. At times one of us would have no other place to work when our office mate had an appointment in the room. We stretched our concept of confidentiality to cover us both as a de facto corporate person. And it worked surprisingly well.

We had warm times in that room. Usually, when I brought a child of elementary school age into the room for counseling, I began by steering the child to my shelves of toys. The shelves provided a sort of grab bag of potential treats. Because it can be difficult for a young child to verbalize feelings, particularly to an adult and a stranger at that, I did a lot of relationship building with those toys and games. With few words passing between us, we would get to know each other by building huge towers of blocks, painting horrendously ugly pictures, or finding out how we responded to being the Old Maid.

Usually, this form of relationship building graduated into words. The LD kids who had been referred had low self-concepts because of their academic difficulties, and often this interfered with their relationships with other children too. Talking about it provided relief and direction.

One day, Mrs. Shasta, the LD teacher for the junior high students, referred to me an eighth-grade girl she described as a complete social outcast. Gunda had a learning disability and looked as if she might have a cognitive disability. She acted as if she were afraid of her shadow. She had only one friend, according to Mrs. Shasta, and that friend regularly picked on her in front of the other students.

When I first met Mrs. Shasta's referral, Gunda Schwartz, I wondered whether there would be anything I could do for her. She was tall and skinny, and her clothes drooped awkwardly over her knees and elbows. She stooped when she stood, and her various limbs bent out at funny angles. She didn't talk much, either, although she was not totally silent.

Her big brown eyes were attentive and serious, though, when I first brought her into my classroom, and she soon began coming down to see me by herself. She never said much beyond "hi," but she never missed an appointment. Although she didn't like to talk, she did like to play Old Maid, over and over, in fact. It seemed like a compulsion, a sad and homely female child's prediction of her future. Uncannily, she always lost the game at first. It was awful. Her eyes would droop, and I would see the tears begin to form.

I began to cheat. I lifted the Old Maid card a little higher than the others when I had it in my hand, just as my father had done for me when I was a little girl. I pretended that it was because I thought she would be more likely to take it that way. I looked truly chagrined when she learned my precious trick and avoided the unwanted card. Gunda began to lift up the Old Maid card, too, when she had it in her hand. I would usually take it. Not always; just enough to keep up the suspense. When I took it, Gunda would look animated and kind. She would try to make me feel better. And so we learned how to talk to each other. Not in great, lengthy conversations with lots of sentences and syllables, but with simple little phrases and asides.

Gunda eventually told me that she had lived in a foster home all her life and wondered about her real parents. They had never come to see her. She said that her foster mother made her pick up all her foster brothers' toys and clothes and made her cook the meals and clean the house. It sounded like some kind of Cinderella story.

I neither believed nor disbelieved the Cinderella aspects of Gunda's story. I figured that, facts aside, this was the way she perceived her reality. I noted that her clothes, which were always clean and pressed and might have looked nice on someone else, looked awkward on Gunda. It was as much Gunda's manner of wearing them, her slouched posture, as trouble with the clothes themselves.

When I got to know Gunda better, I asked her whether she would mind if I made an appointment to talk with her foster mother. She said she wouldn't mind but doubted that it would be possible because the foster mother worked full time.

In fact, Gunda's foster mother came to talk to me at school, and we also talked on several other occasions by telephone. I would have liked to make a home visit, because so often a home itself tells so much, but Mrs. Schwartz (Gunda had been with the foster family so long that she used their surname) preferred to meet with me at school.

Mrs. Schwartz came across as appropriately concerned about Gunda's self-image. She sounded as though she really cared. She said Gunda had been with them since a few months after she was born and probably would be with them until she became an adult. There had been no word from the biological parents in years, neither to her nor to the county social worker. She knew this bothered Gunda.

Gunda did do a lot of housework, Mrs. Schwartz admitted, because she herself worked full time and the other two children (Mr. and Mrs. Schwartz's natural sons) were boys. However, she said that Gunda often did more housework than she was asked to do. She thought that Gunda did this to feel wanted. She asked me whether I had any ideas that might help Gunda develop more self-confidence.

I was pleased at this question because it indicated genuine concern. But I didn't have any pat answers, nor would they likely have been useful if I had had any. Gunda's mother would probably have thanked me very much, and then she would have forgotten my suggestions because they were mine, not hers. What I did do was let Mrs. Schwartz know that her concern was very important and that she probably was the best person to know what might help Gunda at home. Would she share with me the kinds of ideas she might have?

Mrs. Schwartz did have some ideas to talk over. Perhaps, she suggested, if Gunda did extra chores at home, she could choose a reward for herself, such as a piece of jewelry or some new clothes. Perhaps that might help her develop confidence in her appearance. I encouraged her to try out some of these ideas and to talk them over with Gunda.

It was a little thing, but Mrs. Schwartz followed through. A week or so later Gunda showed me a new bracelet she had chosen as a reward for extra housework, and later on she proudly displayed a new blouse.

About all I did for Gunda was to provide her with a safe place to come and talk and a winning streak of Old Maid games. And I began to get different reports from Mrs. Shasta. First, Gunda got feisty one day when a student picked on her in class, and the other student actually backed off. Then, Gunda told her fickle friend that she didn't like it when she picked on her. Gunda began to court new friends, successfully.

She also began to take noticeable pride in her appearance. She began to wear shiny plastic belts so her skirts wouldn't sag and wore bright scarves so her neck wouldn't look so long and skinny. Somehow, her awkward arms and legs seemed to come more in line with her body. An occasional waft of perfume could be detected. Gunda honestly didn't look cognitively disabled anymore. The other students began to pay her some attention in a positive way.

By midyear, it was apparent that Gunda was more confident and self-reliant and that I could discharge her with a clear conscience. I was pretty busy by then and needed the time. What I did instead was to initiate a gradual weaning. I didn't want to risk a sense of rejection in Gunda.

We talked a bit about how things were going for her in school now and about the reasons Mrs. Shasta had originally referred her to me. Did Gunda think things were better now? Gunda said she wasn't letting kids push her around nearly so much anymore and she had new friends. But she didn't want to stop coming to see me.

From about midyear on, Gunda and I saw each other only about every other week, but she began to participate in a girls' club put together by Mrs. Shasta, Mrs. Hinkle, and myself. She was a joy to behold, as time passed. She could take care of herself.

The girls' club was an organizational miracle made possible by the reputation Mrs. Hinkle enjoyed with the school administration and by my own persistence.

As has been mentioned earlier, the elementary school guidance counselor, Isaac Jacobs, had attempted to organize a group of junior high students before and had been censured formally for his efforts because of some of the topics discussed by the group. All the school personnel knew about this, and so nobody was anxious to get back into developing any kind of socialization or discussion group for students who might benefit from that sort of thing. I thought Mrs. Hinkle might be able to make a viable group happen, however.

I thought this not because of any formal group work skills or training on her part but because of her reputation and personality. Mrs. Hinkle had lived in Orangetown her entire life, and she came from a highly respected family. She even lived in a beautiful old stone house that had been occupied by her ancestors for generations on a road bearing her maiden name. She had four grown children; yet she was still young in appearance and very attractive. She knew everybody and everything in town. This was part of the reason the school superintendent and the elementary school principal let her do just about anything she wanted at the school. As has been mentioned before, Mrs. Hinkle just ignored the job role for which she had been formally hired and functioned in a personalized combination of roles involving those of nurse, mother, and social worker.

On my own bad days in Orangetown, I would let myself hobble down to Mrs. Hinkle's friendly office for some of her soul-restoring warmth and attention. And when no one else in Orangetown would give me any ideas about what to do with my time, Mrs. Hinkle gave me referrals. Hence my first work in Orangetown was entirely informally arranged. I wasn't too proud to follow up on Mrs. Hinkle's suggestions.

Once Mrs. Hinkle realized the energy resource she had in me, she started giving me more informal referrals than I could possibly work with. Besides, by the time Mrs. Hinkle really got in stride, I had managed to persuade the bona fide special education staff that I could be of some use to them too. I began to get referrals from these more appropriate resources as well. Time began to be a problem.

Soon there was an identified core of students I knew needed attention, and I hadn't enough time to provide it. In addition, many of these students were not enrolled in special education and were not likely to qualify. So I approached Mrs. Hinkle with the idea of developing a group, the two of us together. I expected that with Mrs. Hinkle involved, the school administration wouldn't object and probably the parents wouldn't either. I was reasonably certain that with Mrs. Hinkle's natural social bent, she would be an asset in organizing and leading a group, even without formal training.

Mrs. Hinkle herself had thought about organizing a group before, I discovered, but she had already decided it would be too much work. So I promised to share the load and then solicited the support of two other teachers as well, the LD teacher, Mrs. Shasta, and the young art teacher who helped decorate the office–classroom for David Chase and myself. I then organized a few brainstorming meetings with just the interested teachers, Mrs. Hinkle, and myself to develop plans on how to go about putting a group together as well as how to make it acceptable to the school administration.

We discussed the purpose of developing such a group, tentative group goals, ideal group size, sex of the membership, and then a tentative list of children to include. We decided to give the project a try. We agreed to limit the group to girls because more of them seemed to need peer support, our main established purpose for the group. We didn't think a mixed-sex group would work very well given the age group involved, the junior high level.

And so it came to pass. We sent out permission slips bearing Mrs. Hinkle's name, which would reassure parents, and my name to acquaint the parents with it. Almost every student selected for the group obtained parental approval to participate. Group meetings began, and thereafter the meetings took place about every two weeks throughout the rest of the school year. About once a month I organized a separate meeting for the adult leaders to discuss and help resolve any problems. The adult leaders took turns arranging for meeting space and program content for the girls' group itself, and our young student members, initially selected as partial outcasts from their peers, evolved into their own in-group.

The young girls gained status and pride by their very belonging to something. Not one parent ever complained, nor did the school administration. And very probably, the girls individually and as a group gained more from their interactions with one another than each would have gained separately from counseling sessions with me alone.

DISCUSSION AND STUDY QUESTIONS

Gunda Schwartz provides a good example of *socialization* as the basic process through which people learn the behavior expected and acceptable in the social groups to which they belong. Her case is an especially good one for understanding sex role socialization—that is, the way we learn the different behaviors expected of men and women. In her case, her perception of what was expected of her was also influenced by the fact that she was a *foster child.* A foster child is one whose biological parents could not care for her or him and who has been placed with another family for child-rearing purposes. Usually foster home placements are temporary although in Gunda's case it seems to have become more or less permanent.

Gunda obviously had feelings about being a foster child. Many of her peers also had troubling feelings about themselves and growing up. These youngsters formed a natural grouping of people with shared concerns and shared interests. In a case such as this, forming a group makes sense. Groups enable people who do share concerns and interests to support each other as they explore those aspects of their lives. Although we most often see the author working with individuals or with families, we should note that social workers also work with groups when appropriate and feasible.

1. How did being a foster child seem to affect Gunda Schwartz? Do you think you would have similar feelings if you were a foster child? What factors would affect the kinds of feelings you might have?
2. Think about groups to which you belong. How do you act differently in a group than when you are with only one or two other people? What do you especially like and dislike about groups?
*3. Why did the author approach Mrs. Hinkle to lead the socialization/discussion group of junior high girls? When Mrs. Hinkle proved initially unwilling, how did the author manage to enlist her cooperation? How did the author go about developing group work skills in Mrs. Hinkle and the other two teachers she persuaded to help?
*4. Select two clients with whom you have worked or are working who are different ages. What kinds of socialization was each experiencing at his or her respective life stage? How was your work with these clients affected by their socialization?

---

*Questions notated with an asterick are intended for advanced students who have had or are currently having some social work practice experience and who have made at least a tentative commitment to the profession.

CHAPTER 8

Social Histories in Orangetown

or: Persisting in Performing One's Job
Under Difficult Circumstances

Concepts Covered in This Chapter

1. Social histories as part of social work practice
2. Initiative as part of job performance
3. Managing inadequate supervision
4. Informal communication and its effects
5. The right to accept or reject services
6. Recording

Learning Objectives   After reading this chapter you should be able to

1. Describe what a social history is and its purpose in social work practice
2. Discuss the potential benefits and risks of taking the initiative on the job
3. List at least three strategies for overcoming inadequate supervision
4. List at least three potential benefits and three potential risks of informal communication in an agency
5. Discuss at least three reasons why people should have the right to decide whether they want social work service
6. Identify at least one circumstance in which people should not have the right to decide whether they want social work service
7. Define *recording* and discuss its purpose in social work practice
8. Define *process recording* and identify at least two of its uses
9. Define *summary recording* and identify at least two of its uses

Hello, Mrs. Tolbert. This is Carolyn Wells calling for the Orangetown special education program. Your son John has recently been referred to us for evaluation for special services. I'd like to meet with you to talk over the reasons he was referred, and perhaps you would help me understand how he has been doing at home over the past few years."

I always began my telephone conversations in a general way such as that. I didn't use words such as *social history, social worker,* or *emotional disturbance* over the telephone when I could avoid them because these terms could be upsetting to rural parents living in a politically conservative community. The word *social,* in particular, seemed a little tainted, slightly pink.

And usually parents responded positively to my carefully worded requests for conferences. Most of them had been informed already of their child's referral to special education by the regular classroom teacher. That was supposed to be a county requirement, although not all teachers followed through.

Most parents seemed glad to be able to talk to someone in person from the special education program about their child. They usually had a lot to say about their child's development during infancy and up to the present time and about his or her behavior at home.

Sometimes parents chose to come and talk with me in my office—classroom, but more often they were pleased to accept my offer to meet with them at home. That was the arrangement I preferred, anyway, both because of the lack of privacy in my shared classroom and because of what I could learn about the home setting itself.

I started to do a lot of social histories in Orangetown a couple of months after I began to work there. I got started simply enough. It happened through my growing friendship with Constance Chase. She referred several high school students to me for counseling, and I knew from my colleagues in Kingston that I could not legally counsel children who were not yet enrolled in special education. Parental permission was required. And nobody was as yet formally enrolled in special education in the Orangetown high school because the school had never had a program before.

Constance wanted to evaluate most of the same students for either LD or ED services. Parental permission was necessary for that too. So we went to visit a few parents together, bringing with us the official parental approval form for special education evaluation. That form would permit both of us, as well as any other special education staff person, to work with the child for up to 90 days. By that time, an M team (multidisciplinary team) was supposed to meet and make final recommendations.

Parents seemed to welcome Constance and me. Certainly, nobody threw us out. The visits were enjoyable, helpful in developing plans to work with the students, and in fact, just plain energizing for both of us. They made the troubled children really come alive for us. We began to ask questions in greater and greater depth. Parents talked freely. I began to gather bona fide social histories for our own information and use.

At about that time, David also began to ask me whether I would visit the homes of some of the children he was evaluating. He was interested specifically in learning what techniques of discipline were used in the home and any other facts that might help him work more effectively with the children at school.

For David's first few referrals, he had preferred to make the home visits himself, but then for him, too, time began to be a problem. David preferred to invest his time consulting with classroom teachers and working with the referred children individually. Moreover, on several occasions he was unable to locate the parents of a referred child for the required signatures. David began to ask me whether I would try to find these parents.

Constance, David, and I discussed among ourselves the information I had been given by Dr. Knight concerning the county requirement of social histories for approval of M team recommendations for ED referrals. David confirmed this information for himself through a telephone call to the county office.

He also learned by telephone about another guideline the county used to decide whether to approve M team recommendations for ED placement. Evidence of disturbed behavior had to be demonstrated by the child under consideration not only in the school environment but in at least one other environment as well, the home or the community.

The given rationale was that evidence of disturbed behavior in a second environment would better determine that a child's behavior itself was disturbed. In other words, it would show that the child wasn't just being ineptly handled at school. In my opinion, that rationale was a good one. It also explained my presence on the special education team. Logically, my function would be to find out about behavior patterns within the home and the community.

The two ED teachers and I decided to distribute the necessary fact finding among ourselves. Constance and David would observe classroom behavior of all the ED referrals. Then, if a given child's behavior did indeed look disturbed in the classroom, they would ask me to make a home visit to develop a social history. As I learned about the child's behavior at home, I would also ask the parents about the child's behavior in the community.

We worked out this arrangement on our own, without clearing it with either Martin or Lou, because we knew already that they would not want any conferences with parents in the home. And when the time came for our first M team meetings for ED referrals, neither Martin nor Lou made any comment about my social history reports. They did include them in the final M team documents, however.

It was curious; I held exactly the same job position in Orangetown and in Kingston, and formally the supervisory structure was exactly the same. Only in Kingston, I got my referrals after they had been screened through a psychologist, just as the referral flow was formally diagramed on the official organizational charts (see pp. 6-7). In Orangetown, however, I got my referrals through the ED teachers; the referral mode there was one of collaboration rather than assignment.

In the long run, both arrangements worked. It took me some time, however, to figure out how to establish myself and my job function in Orangetown without using the formal channels.

I learned it was invariably ineffective to try to clear what I wanted to do through a supervisor such as Lou, who just wasn't happy with my presence, or through one such as Martin, who just couldn't figure out what was going on. It worked much better to do what I felt was necessary on my own and to wait for my supervisors to confront me. Lou never did.

But Martin confronted me on at least one occasion that I recall. That occasion was more funny and sad than intimidating. He stormed into my office one morning shortly after I had begun to produce social histories. "What's the idea," he sputtered, "what's the very *idea* of turning in reports as badly typed as these?"

I couldn't take Martin's verbal onslaught very personally, as I hadn't typed the reports, so I couldn't give him much satisfaction in terms of a humble or contrite response. In fact, I think I grinned at him.

But poor Martin managed to get the entire Orangetown secretarial staff on his sweaty back through this incident. Julia Green, the secretary for the special education staff, was overworked and underpaid, as is common for secretaries. She was rightfully proud of her work. Even compared with the secretaries in Kingston, she did a thoroughly professional job. She rarely got compliments, but she was surely open to them. She cared.

The problem was that once I had discovered I was in the wholesale report business, I had begged Mrs. Green to let me dictate my social histories rather than type them. That would save me a lot of time but would surely make more work for her. Blessed Julia had reluctantly acquiesced.

I had gleefully brought in my own portable tape recorder and proceeded to rattle off a number of reports as fast as I could. Since Julia was the only full-time typist for some half-dozen members of the special education staff, she couldn't really keep up with all our reports. So she decided to break in her new assistant with my dictation.

Julia forgot to proofread the results of the new worker's efforts. I did, in fact, see a copy of the social history that so infuriated Martin, and I saw it before it was sent off to the county. So I really was guilty. But the report was basically coherent, and I felt the misspellings and uneven margins and strange capitalizations were tolerable, given the work load of the staff. There was nothing in the report that could lead to misunderstandings, in my opinion.

Martin not only hollered at me about the typing—he bawled out the entire secretarial staff in the front office of the school and informed the county office about it as well. I was even asked whether I had sufficiently upgraded the quality of my reports by Dr. Knight, the director of the Emmett County special education program, at a social work supervisory meeting later on.

Martin did have to supervise something, but he lost ever so much through his efforts. Word of his impending presence in the school began to spread like electricity up and down all the hallways the moment he even drove up to the schoolyard, and he became the butt of numerous jokes. He could have had the most brilliant ideas in the world after that, and nobody would have listened to him.

But back to Mrs. Tolbert, the woman I called on the telephone for a social history interview. Mrs. Tolbert wasn't an ordinary run-of-the-mill parent. She was a phantom. I called her house at all hours of the day and even from home on several evenings and weekends, and still I couldn't reach her. But her little son John kept coming to school on the bus, so I figured she must be out there somewhere. John had been referred to special education because of his temper tantrums in the classroom and his frequent physical fights with other children on the playground, which he usually instigated.

And then one morning Mrs. Tolbert answered her telephone. Now what? How could I gain her cooperation? I used the blandest words in my vocabulary to explain the purpose of my call, and she actually agreed to have a conference with me. Only she didn't want me to come to her home—she'd meet me at school.

I was all keyed up with anticipation the day she was scheduled to come to the school. I knew that David wanted especially to work with her son. In fact, David *was* working with little John. We all wanted to make his efforts legal. David could have been hauled into court by the wrong parents, and the county would not have defended him. He was bending the rules. Special education staff were legally required to have written permission from the parents to do anything with any child referred, no matter how needy.

To make a long story short, Mrs. Tolbert didn't show up for her appointment. I wasn't too surprised, but my repeated phone calls again brought no response. However, off and on I tried a telephone number that was listed in the school files for her husband at work. One day, to my surprise, a pleasant male voice answered the telephone at the work number. It turned out that the voice belonged to Mr. Tolbert.

"Oh, don't be surprised if she doesn't answer the phone," Mr. Tolbert said amiably of his wife. "She's around and she hears the ring, but she just won't answer. She's shy. Why don't we just make an appointment for you now to see her at home, and I'll let her know when you're coming?"

"That would be fine," I responded gratefully, and we set a date and time. "Do you want me to check back with you to find out whether the time is all right? And would it be better if you were there too?" I asked.

"Oh no," came the response. "My wife is always home, and she can tell you everything you need to know. I do appreciate your concern for my son." He gave me directions to get from the school to his farmhouse residence.

I was astounded by the man's articulate manner of speaking. His grammar was impeccable. His voice tone sounded so calm and so competent. And yet I had heard via the grapevine (some powerful instrument, that) that Mr. Tolbert had been in and out of jail for drunken driving and that he ran around on a motorcycle. In fact, I had even heard that he was recently hospitalized after running headlong into a tree.

No matter that some of my most highly principled friends have also been thrown bodily into jail more than once and that some of them have also been injured riding motorcycles. I visualized Mr. Tolbert as a regular hoodlum, and I had expected a harsh, ungrammatical response if I ever connected with him.

When I arrived at his farmhouse on the day of my appointment, I really expected that after a few awkward words with his wife, everything would be all right. I was that reassured by the measured and modulated tones of Mr. Tolbert's voice. The place looked deserted, but I didn't believe it. Hadn't I made an appointment with such a nice-sounding man?

The driveway down to the farmhouse was a good quarter of a mile long. The ruts fanned out to avoid some boggy-looking places, and I had to maneuver my car around piles of old bricks and some rusty old cans and broken farm equipment.

But the sun was shining brightly that day, the sky was blue, and I was in a happy frame of mind, anyway. The drive out had been absolutely beautiful, the road winding among picturesque farms and through dark, planted forests. I like old farms and old farmhouses, and I was curiously anticipating what I would find inside. Would I find a timid but heartwarming country recluse who had made a comfortable home in these rough surroundings? I usually get along pretty well with recluses, having some of that inclination myself.

Then I saw the big dog leaping around down by the farmhouse door. It was quite a big dog, a German shepherd. Just how was I going to get out of the car and up to the house? Maybe somebody would see me and call the dog.

But no one did. The wind howled around the house and over and between the silo and the barn, and the dog began to growl at me from between a fine set of large yellow canines. He was now quite close. When I parked the car, he had loped right up beside it. As I began to open the car door, he began to bark with great, powerful sounds. The huge shepherd had a very angry, deep, and authoritative voice. I was impressed but optimistic on this gorgeous day.

Well, that should do it, I thought cheerfully to myself. Mrs. Tolbert will have to know I'm here now, and she'll come to the door, and she'll call the dog.

But she didn't. The dog continued to bark and growl at me, and as I peered out at him through the open window of the car, he seemed to stand nearly as high as a horse. But I thought to myself that Mrs. Tolbert was surely inside that house. She was probably very shy, as her husband had said, and now that I was here, she was afraid to show herself. Maybe if I got out of the car and let her get a good look at me, she would be reassured. After all, I fancied myself to be a decent-looking person. And I wasn't carrying a club or even a briefcase, just a pad of yellow paper for my notes.

But if I got out of the car, I would be eaten. No doubt about it. None. But wait a minute, I reminded myself. I like dogs, and they generally know it. Usually I can win over a mean animal. But then, of course, not always. Should I risk it? I just couldn't imagine going back when I was so close to my goal.

Still certain Mrs. Tolbert was inside that house, I decided to brave the dog and get out of the car. I talked gently to the big animal. I flattered him shamelessly. I told him he was a big, fine, handsome fellow and that he had the makings of a champion. But even I thought I was being terrifically courageous to take my chances with the great animal. I thought of Lou Bachus and his warnings about farm dogs. I probably wouldn't get any sympathy at all if I came back with only one hand or short a leg.

The dog didn't let me by. He stood bodily in my way as I climbed out of the car and continued to growl in a horrible, menacing manner. He even pressed against me as I gently but firmly pushed my way closer to the back door. After what seemed like a few years I reached the door and knocked. I looked through all the windows I could reach and knocked on them too. No luck.

I can't believe what I did after that, under the circumstances. With the dog trotting circles around me and snarling in great, angry gasps, I cased the house, walking all around it, even climbing up a fire escape to peer in some upstairs windows.

What a disappointment. Unless Mrs. Tolbert was hiding in a closet, there really wasn't anyone home. I went back to my car, wrote both Tolberts a note, returned to the house, and slipped the note under the door. Then I eased my way back to the car through the grumbling dog, patting him a little by then. He seemed embarassed, and I was starting to breathe again.

But now what? No answer either on the Tolbert's home phone or on Mr. Tolbert's work phone. I decided to talk about it with Polly Hinkle, the Title I teacher turned nurse, mother, and social worker all in one. Polly was a veritable grab bag of information about the community. She had been born and raised in Orangetown, and she had raised her own children within a block of the school.

Polly shouldn't have known as much as she did about all the special education referrals, for reasons of confidentiality. But she sat in on all the special education staff meetings and contributed her own information. Lou Bachus, formally the director of pupil services, had no policy of limiting special education meetings to special education staff. No one else enforced any such policy, either, or seemed even aware such a policy might be advisable. I didn't have the guts to object. I figured I could do the right thing for the right reasons, and I could run myself right out of the school that way.

Besides, Polly was always willing to help me, and heaven knows, I needed help at times. She meant good things for everyone, and she really did seem to spread "information" rather than just "gossip." Actually, I got a lot of both from her, and where is the fine line? I used Polly's knowledge as everyone else did when we reached the end of our own resources.

It was Polly who told me about the grandmother. This grandmother was Mr. Tolbert's mother. She, said Polly, would be able to get me an interview with Mrs. Tolbert to obtain a social history for John if she were convinced there was an important reason. Polly even gave me the grandmother's name, which wasn't Tolbert, and shared a couple of good ideas concerning the best way to approach her.

It worked. The grandmother sounded as articulate on the telephone as had her son. And she also promised to arrange a meeting for me with Mrs. Tolbert. When I arrived at the farm the next time, Mrs. Tolbert was there. She granted me a useful interview which wasn't even particularly awkward, as first interviews go. She even signed the slip authorizing a special education evaluation for John. Her farmhouse was pretty rough inside, though, and some of the stories she told me about John's early years were frightening. I figured the little fellow was growing up fending largely for himself.

And the big German shepherd put on a new personality for me. He almost smiled. Mrs. Tolbert told me he was very dangerous, however, unless she was there to control him. I let her believe it.

DISCUSSION AND STUDY QUESTIONS

As noted earlier, organizational procedures are an important part of professional social work practice. Record keeping is a basic task of organizations. To keep records, workers must have a systematic way of keeping track of their activities. As the author demonstrates, note taking is a commonly used procedure. Notes enable the worker to provide information in the form required by the organization. Two common forms are *process recording* and *summary recording*. Process recording involves a detailed account of the interaction that occurred between the social worker and the client. Summary recording provides a summary of the major points discussed, agreed on, or acted on, but it does not attempt to describe the interaction through which these actions were accomplished.

Translating notes into organizational records requires the help of support staff, such as typists, secretaries, and office managers. As the author notes, obtaining the cooperation of these personnel is an important part of the social worker's management of organizational procedures. Support staff are colleagues and should be treated accordingly. They are also part of both the formal and the informal organizational structures, as this chapter describes. Although Mr. Murdock may have had the formal authority to criticize their work he probably lost a great deal of his informal influence with them by doing so.

1. What type of record keeping do you use in your daily life? For example, do you keep an appointment book? A diary? A checkbook? Why do you keep records? Have you ever needed some type of record that you didn't have? How does it feel when your system of record keeping proves to be insufficient?

2. Think back to an instance in which a secretary or another support staff member was helpful to you. Had you expected that person to be able to help? Did this person act differently toward you than a person with more formal authority? Did you act differently toward the support staff member than you would have toward someone with more formal power?

*3. Thinking about where you are working now or have worked as a social worker in the past, have you ever asked a secretary for a favor? What kind? Why didn't you go through formal channels to get the task done?

*4. In your current or former agency, do (did) you use process or summary recording? What are the advantages and disadvantages of each? Which do you prefer? Why?

---

*Questions notated with an asterisk are intended for advanced students who have had or are currently having some social work practice experience and who have made at least a tentative commitment to the profession.

CHAPTER 9

Emmett County Guidance Clinic Offers You Everything
or: Confronting the Reality of Scarce Resources

Concepts Covered in This Chapter

1. The problem-solving process
2. Community social welfare resources
   a. Rural and urban communities
   b. The functions of community resources
   c. The availability of community resources
3. Biological factors in people's need for social work service
4. Referrals
5. Spina bifida

Learning Objectives After reading this chapter you should be able to

1. Define the problem-solving process and discuss why it is used
2. Identify at least six community social welfare resources mentioned in this chapter
3. Discuss why there are likely to be different social welfare resources in rural and in urban areas
4. List at least three factors that may limit the availability or use of social welfare resources in rural areas
5. Define foster care
6. Explain why an adult might need foster care
7. List at least three biological factors discussed in this chapter that affected the need for social work services
8. Define *referral*
9. List at least three aspects of the referral process that affect whether it will be successful
10. Define *spina bifida* and discuss the social work services that people with this condition might need

A
s a school social worker for the Emmett County special education program, I was responsible for providing direct services to students enrolled in some seven schools. All together, my potential caseload involved almost a thousand students.

Students were referred to me for myriad problems, some appropriate for special education services and some not. But all referrals had to be reviewed and assessed initially to determine whether they might qualify for services from the special education program. This process is sometimes referred to by social workers as "gathering and assessing information" and "defining the problem."

Once information is gathered and assessed, a plan or plans of action must be formulated. Then, somebody has to carry out the plan(s). For students who were determined to be eligible for special education services, I liked to carry out some of the intervention plans myself if they involved counseling. I liked to counsel students.

But often, even for students who were found to qualify for special education services, the M team recommendations involved services none of us could actually provide in the school. Because of the constant need to evaluate new referrals, time was an important reason for this dilemma. Early in the school year, for example, I myself became unable to accept new referrals for ongoing counseling because of lack of time. But even more important, the school system itself often simply lacked the resources needed to help resolve the problems identified in the assessment and planning phases of the intervention process.

Moreover, many students referred for special education evaluation were found to need ongoing services, yet they did not meet the criteria that would make them eligible for services from special education itself. So it was essential to find responsive, responsible agencies and programs to refer our needy clients to when we couldn't provide the needed services ourselves. And Emmett County had very few resources for referral. A rural county, it believed its citizens should pull themselves up by their own bootstraps, and besides, it didn't have vast hoards of funds to divert into social program development.

But Emmett County had one major agency that openly solicited referrals from the school: the guidance clinic.

My first contact with the Emmett County Guidance Clinic occurred in a special education in-service session, only a couple of weeks into the school year. The director of the clinic and several of the social workers came to the special education office to conduct an informational program for an hour or so to alert the special education staff about the resources available through the guidance clinic.

The news they told us seemed just too good to be true, and so it was. This is why I still feel a little angry at the clinic. Were the staff more honest with themselves and the community professionals, perhaps something might have been done to improve the situation. But what they told us at the meeting was that the clinic had the staff and services available to meet just about every emotional need of just about every person in the county.

The director of the clinic, who conducted the in-service session, and the social workers who came with him were young and personable, attractive and energetic. They told us that the clinic had consulting psychiatric services and counselors of all types available and that clinic policy reflected infinite concern for the mental well-being of the population.

Because one of the towns in which I was working happened to be at the other end of the county (Orangetown, of course), I asked the spunky young speaker whether or not workers from the guidance clinic could make home visits if prospective clients lacked transportation. Without hesitation, the answer came resoundingly in the affirmative.

Everything seemed so cheerful and sophisticated, and everybody looked so smart and stylish that I thought perhaps my own generation had finally made it out of the schools and into the real world to staff the backwoods with savvy and service. The very existence of the Emmett County Guidance Clinic filled me with a sense of well-being.

Constance Chase and I, early in the year before our schedules got hectic, decided to check out the actual facilities ourselves. We arranged for a tour and an interview at the guidance clinic with one of the social workers.

We were treated to an inspection of a clean and hospitable facility—somewhat slick and cold, to be sure, as "health" facilities so often are—but quite within the realm of the acceptable. The friendly staff member we interviewed was very similar in personal characteristics to the social workers who had conducted the in-service session—young, energetic, clearly "with it" in garb and vernacular.

She gave us a somewhat more realistic assessment of the potential for home visits by clinic workers, however. She said that although home visits were permitted and did occur on occasion, usually the schedules of the staff were just too crowded to allow many appointments of this sort. Clients from a place as far away as Orangetown would probably have to come to the clinic to obtain the benefits of its services, she informed us.

She was right. Staff from the clinic just didn't have the time to come to Orangetown. Yet we surely needed access to clinic resources, and often. But that's what scarce resources are all about—they are scarce. And they tend to be consumed where they happen to be located.

The first time I knew I needed the resources of the clinic was in the case of Don McHenry. A small, dark, slender, and wiry guy, he was continually picked on by the six-foot monsters that inhabited the hallways of the high school. Don was a junior in the Orangetown High School, and I might have taken him for a sixth grader if Constance hadn't told me about him before I met him.

Constance told me that Don was one of the students who kept coming into her classroom looking for help. But he didn't fit into any of the obvious categories of disability, as far as she could see. He didn't have a learning disability—she had tested him for that—and he didn't exhibit any obvious emotional disturbance. His teachers told her he was quiet in the classroom and usually completed his assignments at a low but passing level. Thus nobody in particular noticed Don at school except the bullies who liked to torment him.

Constance asked me whether I would talk with Don to see if I thought there might be any advantage to making an ED referral for him even though he wasn't a behavior problem at school. She said that sometimes he didn't make sense when she talked with him. Perhaps a counselor was what he needed more than a special teacher.

Constance had good instincts. When I finally got a private place to talk with Don, I knew I was in over my head. (Finding that private place in the Orangetown High School required, each time, consultation with the main office to locate a classroom that might be temporarily empty. Then usually the rooms scheduled to be empty did in fact have occupants who were using them to hide, smoke, neck, even study on occasion. It was an endless nuisance to try to find counseling space in Orangetown. When spring came, I used a side lawn. That solution was chilly and rather damp but reliably available.)

Don began his counseling session by telling me how immensely strong he was. He bulged his tiny biceps in truly macho fashion. He said he had to keep himself from killing his tormentors by constant concentration. Don said he could just stare hard at a spot in a wall, concentrate "away," and hypnotize himself.

Don said that through his magic concentration he could also handle any amount of pain. But he sometimes put his fist through the wall at home when he failed to hold his temper. And he told me he hated his stepfather so much he was afraid he might kill him. Don had even made getaway plans. During his concentration sessions, he had made friends with the captain of a spaceship who was going to help him escape when the time came.

Oops. It did take me another session to become fairly sure that Don was living deep in his fantasies and that he wasn't having a bit of fun with the social worker. In those sessions he took me to places I'd never been before.

I called Don's mother and went to talk with her. Yes, Don did put his fist through the wall in his bedroom. The room was a shambles. Don had temper tantrums so violent the family just didn't know what to do with him. And sometimes he just seemed to sit and stare at the wall for hours. It was worse lately, now that his real father was calling him occasionally and making promises for a visit, which he never kept.

Here, then, was the common mix of psychological disturbance and family pain. I suggested to Don's mother that ongoing services at the county guidance clinic might be helpful. She sounded interested. I then talked to Don about the idea. Would he be interested in talking with someone regularly who might be able to help him feel better about things? Don was interested, but he wanted to check the clinic out first, without his mother and stepfather along. His mother agreed, and so I took him myself for the first appointment.

I specifically asked for a first appointment with both a psychiatrist and a social worker present, if at all possible. I was afraid Don suffered from a psychosis, as his talk entered such realms of unreality. Because of that, I felt psychiatric consultation was a must. However, I wanted a social worker present as I expected a social worker would deal with Don's case on an ongoing basis. And the family interactional aspects of the case, I felt, could best be assessed and altered by a member of that profession.

I was impressed. The first session at the clinic did indeed include a psychiatrist and a social worker, and they had the courtesy to ask Don and me, prior to the session, whether I wanted to take part. Don chose to have me present, and so I got the chance to observe the clinic team at work.

Dr. Way looked just as a psychiatrist should. He had thick, bushy, gray eyebrows, a thatch of silver hair, and steely gray eyes. I really couldn't quite believe it. Everything at this clinic seemed to look the proper part. The social worker, Mr. Glick, looked concerned and bright, just as he ought to.

The social worker and the psychiatrist did a very good job with Don. Don was willing to return for another session, with his parents the next time. He was given some mild medication by Dr. Way to help him sort out the barrage of stimuli he had to cope with every day. Don and his family went to the clinic for ongoing counseling with Mr. Glick over the next several months.

The family had to pay the guidance clinic a moderate fee (the clinic offered fees on a sliding scale, and Don's parents had a steady, working-class income), but they felt the service was worth the cost. Besides, because of the medical supervision of the psychiatrist, their union insurance policy paid for most of it.

Don's mother told me later that she hadn't known services such as these were available. She honestly didn't know what the family would have done without them. According to both Don and his mother, things at home began to go a lot better for all of them after the family went into counseling.

Don's relationship with students at school didn't improve quite so much, unfortunately, but he did make it through the school year. He frequently sought haven with Constance informally in the ED classroom.

Things didn't usually work out so smoothly with respect to the guidance clinic as they did in Don's case. What was required for potential clients to utilize the services of the clinic was an organized family that could make decisions and that had the motivation and the resources to get themselves there. They had to be willing and able to pay for the services.

Most of the clients who badly needed the services of the clinic simply lacked the qualities required to use them constructively, especially the organization and the motivation. Money, or the lack of it, was really not the greatest barrier preventing people from using the clinic, as the very poorest clients could be served free or have their fees paid by medical assistance.

Consider the case of Chad Rothberg. Chad was a victim of spina bifida. He was wheelchair-bound. He was, fortunately, not hydrocephalic, that common companion to the crippling birth defect, but he was severely depressed. For this reason, although Chad's intelligence was normal and unimpaired, he was unable to exercise his mind effectively in the academic setting and he was flunking most of his subjects at school. He was eighteen and only in his sophomore year.

What chance would a high school dropout with spina bifida have to earn a decent living as an adult? Chad's only chance to win any advantages in life lay in his achieving academic success and a desk job, where he could use his head to support himself. At least, that was how I saw things.

Chad had a lot to be depressed about, and although he didn't talk a whole lot, he would certainly tell me what was bothering him: he could only watch the local baseball games, never participate in them; no one wanted to spend time with him after school except the two four-year-olds down the street; no one wanted to hire him for a summer job, so he never had any spending money.

Chad's family was theoretically intact, but his father spent all his evenings out entertaining women other than his wife, clearly and obviously to everybody in the little town. He chose to entertain his ladies right in the local tavern. Mrs. Rothberg had several tearful discussions with me about this when I dropped by her home to try to make something work out for Chad.

Because I never met Mr. Rothberg, and because Mrs. Rothberg was so unhappy, hurt, and alone, I might have been tempted simply to judge Mr. Rothberg as "at fault" for most of the family's emotional pain. But I felt compassion for the man as well. First, he had built a heartrending rendition of a playful little bar in the corner of his tiny kitchen. The faded, tawdry thing was buried under canning jars and dust. Second, it was a fact that Mrs. Rothberg was a whining, unattractive, and dreadfully overweight woman. Third, Mrs. Rothberg's ill, ancient mother occupied the living room of the house, using the couch as her bed. The house itself was so small Chad had to sleep on the enclosed porch.

The family, for whatever set of historical reasons, was now simply painfully short on energy investment for each other and painfully short on sources for hope and joy. Chad and his entire family needed regularly scheduled counseling. Ongoing intervention by a professional therapist might help resolve some of the constant tensions in the home and thereby release some personal energy for problem solving. The Emmett County Guidance Clinic offers you everything—except transportation, organization, and motivation. Mr. Rothberg wouldn't go to the clinic. He wouldn't even meet with me. He had a car and he could drive, but he used it to go to work during the day, and he wouldn't use it to take his family all the way across the county to the clinic the one evening a week it was open for service. Mrs. Rothberg couldn't drive, but her husband always kept the car keys to himself, anyway, I was told. A most supportive, organized, and together sort of family.

I took Chad and his mother to the guidance clinic for one counseling session, and the county nurse took them for a second. A clinic social worker made one home visit to Mrs. Rothberg during the day—and that was that. The clinic knew the family badly needed help, but the staff just didn't have the time to make regular home visits. Certainly they didn't have the time to try to chase down Mr. Rothberg. But heaven knows, that family needed help.

I ran into the transportation roadblock again with another resource I located for Chad—the county sheltered workshop for the disabled. The workshop did have a program for young adults. I took Chad over for an evaluation, and the workshop accepted him for a summer program that would start at the end of the school year. But the workshop also sponsored an evening group session every week for young people with disabilities.

That special group probably would have been a motivating experience for Chad. But there was no way to get him there. His father wouldn't take him, and his mother couldn't. Some of the neighboring towns had volunteer organizations that provided drivers for special need situations. I tried all the ones at that end of the county. But none had services for Orangetown. And none would have taken Chad regularly, anyway. These services were for emergencies.

I set up an impressive staffing session for Chad at the sheltered workshop involving the guidance clinic, the workshop staff, myself, Chad, and his mother. The idea was to try to develop some kind of plan for the boy that would provide him with new hope and resources. It looked as though the key might be to find him an alternative living situation in Kingston, the town where the workshop was located. Chad had told me on a number of occasions that he was eager to get out of the home situation. I had been told by the Social Security office that since he was already eighteen, he would qualify for Supplemental Social Insurance once he left home and that he would also qualify for medical assistance. These programs would pay his basic expenses.

The staffing meeting recommended foster care and ongoing services by the sheltered workshop for Chad, as I had hoped. With supportive services from the workshop, maybe Chad would be able to finish high school. There was also a branch of the state technical school in Kingston, which might have appropriate courses for Chad. His mother was willing to let him go.

Finding a foster placement was the job of the guidance clinic, which had a purchase-of-service arrangement with the welfare department to locate and supervise foster homes and other living arrangements for hard-to-place, special needs children and disabled adults.

Chad was enthusiastic about the idea of a move, and he really perked up for a couple of weeks after the staffing meeting. I called the clinic foster care supervisor several times and made suggestions for her regarding possibilities for alternative living situations. I believed that at this point, even nursing home care for Chad in Kingston, if supplemented by programming at the workshop, would be preferable to the home situation in Orangetown.

But the guidance clinic didn't make a placement, not during the rest of the year that I worked with Chad. It is true that foster placements of any kind were in limited supply, and Chad was definitely a hard-to-place young man, needing constant physical assistance and medical care.

Chad limped through his school year in body, but he flunked all his subjects. He was as depressed at the end of the year as at the beginning. I could only hope that the summer program scheduled at the workshop might offer him new hope. A neighbor who worked near the workshop had promised to transport him for the daily activities.

And then there was the case of Cindy Reinhart. Cindy was unfortunate enough to get pregnant "out of wedlock." She was seventeen years old. The father of her child denied his involvement. She had no emotional support from anyone. Her parents were furious at her and wanted to send her away.

By this time, I had been told by the director of the Emmett County Guidance Clinic that the clinic was particularly interested in working with unwed mothers. The clinic had a purchase-of-service contract with the county welfare department to counsel pregnant girls and to recruit foster and adoptive homes where required.

It looked to me as though Cindy might need foster care for herself during her pregnancy because the atmosphere in her own home was so negative and tense. Also, I felt that Cindy needed ongoing counseling, probably more than I could offer, because she was so alone.

So I took Cindy over to the guidance clinic and participated in an initial counseling session in which the worker promised to give Cindy all the help she needed and to visit with her in her home for the next appointment, as Cindy had no means of transportation.

When I brought Cindy back to her home, I felt I had made the right connection. I relaxed in her case, satisfied that the clinic worker would carry on in the area of counseling and child placement. (Cindy thought she would probably surrender her child for adoption.)

Cindy stopped coming to school a couple of weeks later, and I called her to see whether she was interested in homebound instruction. She was, and she promised to return the required medical form (which I had previously given her) as soon as she went to the doctor. I then convinced the M team, which authorized homebound instruction.

A week after the M team's authorization, however, I still hadn't received the medical form, so I called Cindy about it. She said she had a doctor's appointment in another week and would send the form then. But she also told me she hadn't seen the worker from the guidance clinic since our original appointment. I was surprised about that and suggested she contact the clinic worker to find out when she would be coming for an appointment. Since Cindy was seventeen and seemed quite capable, I expected she would be able to do that by herself.

A few weeks passed. Still no medical form came. I called Cindy again and learned that she hadn't kept the doctor's appointment and hadn't seen the worker yet from the guidance clinic. Upset by now, I called the clinic worker and asked her to please schedule an appointment soon. I explained that in addition to counseling regarding her plans for the baby, Cindy needed to be motivated to see a doctor and that the special education program needed to have the medical form completed before we could authorize homebound instruction.

The worker apologized for her delay in getting back to Cindy and promised to make an appointment right away. When I checked back with Cindy, the appointment for the home visit had been scheduled. I relaxed again.

A couple more weeks passed, and it struck me that I still didn't have Cindy's medical form. I still hadn't heard anything at all from her, in fact, nor from the clinic social worker, nor from the doctor. I called Cindy again.

What I found out from Cindy this time resolved the problem for all of us, but it wasn't what I wanted to hear. The scheduled appointment with the clinic worker had been canceled because of a winter storm. The worker had rescheduled the appointment, but not for a couple more weeks. In the meantime, Cindy's mother had decided to send her off to a home for unwed mothers. Cindy was leaving in a few days. Everything was all arranged.

There was also the saga of the Eckhardt family. The Eckhardt girls stopped me in the hallway of the high school one day. That was my first contact with them. For some reason, they wanted to talk with me, a stranger, about something that had already happened. One of the girls had almost had her parents arrested the night before. The parents regularly beat the children, she said, and last night after they beat her she had run down to the police station and had told the police officer on duty. She had some visible bruises on her arms and face, which she showed me.

The police officer threatened to arrest the parents unless they agreed to go to counseling as a family. This was a most unusual police officer. I had made a point to go and meet him at the beginning of the school year, as it is not uncommon for a social worker and a police officer to work with the same people, especially in a small town. The police officer was new to Orangetown, and, unfortunately, he left after only one year. But while he was there, he tried to introduce some progressive ideas into the law enforcement establishment there, and I had a lot of respect for him.

The Eckhardts agreed under pressure that counseling might be helpful—but alas, the parents said, how unfortunate it was they didn't have the time or a means of transportation to travel all that way.

Obviously, the Eckhardt parents had no interest or motivation to go for counseling. And motivation is perhaps the greatest single barrier preventing people from seeking help. The Eckhardt parents didn't think they needed help. They were just disciplining their kids. On the practical side of things, they didn't have a car.

This case had a happy ending. The police officer himself recruited the minister of the family's local church to take the family to the guidance clinic for the next several weeks. The parents could hardly refuse to cooperate with their minister, particularly with the police officer's threat of arrest as an alternative hanging over their heads. That took care of the motivation, the organization, and the transportation!

Future reports from the girls indicated that they were enjoying the counseling sessions very much and that they looked forward to going. The parents, at least for the time being, were afraid to hit them because somebody would know about it right away.

Little George Jacobs was another problematic case handled by the Emmett County Guidance Clinic. In his case, personal tragedy resulted from the inadequate services the clinic provided (or was able to provide because of scarce resources). George was a foster child who had been brutally beaten for his first five years of life in his natural home. Everybody knew about it, but proving child abuse can be a tricky business. Physical evidence and courageous witnesses are required.

When George was discovered, by a police officer, wandering bruised and bleeding down the street one night, unable to remember his own name because of a severe concussion, he was removed to a foster home. He lived in his foster home only a few miles from the guidance clinic, and he was enrolled full time in a self-contained ED classroom in Kingston.

George was a real terror when it came to his behavior in the classroom. He needed constant supervision and required an incredible amount of ongoing attention from his teacher. He was well known by the Emmett County Guidance Clinic, which had selected and supervised his treatment foster home. George was supposed to be getting weekly counseling sessions at school and at home from one of the clinic psychologists. But he wasn't.

George blew up regularly in the classroom, attacking children and making himself generally unbearable. Almost every other week the foster mother would cry out to George's teacher or me that she didn't know whether she could cope with his behavior at home one minute longer. She needed help with George to make a go of it, and George needed ongoing psychological services desperately.

George was supposed to be receiving these services from the guidance clinic, and his foster mother was supposed to be receiving regular consultation from the clinic as well. For that reason, I couldn't work with George or his foster mother regularly myself; it is professionally unwise and confusing to the client to mix counselors and agency auspices. George was seriously enough disturbed, anyway, that I did not feel qualified to work with him as his primary counselor.

The psychologist from the Emmett County Guidance Clinic, however, didn't provide George or his foster family with ongoing services. He showed up periodically for the emergency special education staffing meetings that we held on unnervingly frequent occasions. Each time he came, he promised to follow through more regularly with his prescribed role. And he really meant to do so; that seemed real enough. The clinic psychologist was an intense, serious young man. The problem was, he said, that he was swamped with psychological evaluations that were assigned to him from the courts. He had legal deadlines to meet for his paperwork, and that had to come first.

Scarce resources. Little George became a casualty. He made it through the school year in his foster home, but I learned later that he was finally rejected and had to be moved to another family. And for how long this time?

DISCUSSION AND STUDY QUESTIONS

A primary focus of this chapter concerns scarce resources. Any society produces limited goods and services. According to an American cultural belief, people are supposed to pull themselves up by their own bootstraps. This means that they are supposed to earn access to our society's goods and services by means of their own efforts or those of their family. Rural areas in America tend to be particularly "conservative," which means, in the general positive sense, that they treasure the old values of individual achievement and individual responsibility. It also generally means that they do not officially recognize, or at least, they do not officially respond to, the fact that some people through no fault of their own will be unable to obtain the goods and services they need.

Because social service agencies are not strongly supported in many American communities, as they provide service to people that much of the public considers inadequate, undeserving, or undesirable, they are often understaffed. In other cases, needed services simply are not available. And in still other instances, services are provided in such restrictive, difficult, or unpleasant ways that people will avoid using them unless they are completely desperate. When resources are unavailable or provided in unappealing ways, problems are created for social workers. Meeting people's needs is difficult enough even when resources are available. When they are not, the social worker's creativity and commitment are sorely tested. In addition, people who resist needed services (called "resistant clients") become even more resistant when they sense that services are provided grudgingly by society. This, of course, makes more difficult the social worker's helping efforts.

1. Have you ever needed a service that was not available to you—perhaps financial help to go to school or a summer job? How did it feel to lack something that you felt you legitimately needed? How did you finally get what you needed or find an alternative way to meet your need? Do you feel being in need made you a stronger person?

2. What *one* group of people in our society do you think gets more than its share of socially provided services? Do you resent this unfair distribution? What effect does it have on you? On others?

*3. The author mentions that the Emmett County Guidance Clinic had a "purchase-of-service" agreement with the county welfare department to find foster homes for hard-to-place persons and to counsel unwed mothers. Be sure you know or find out what a purchase-of-service agreement is. Does the agency you work in (worked in) have any? What kind? If not, discuss with your supervisor why not.

*4. The author states that clients who most need clinic services are least likely to get there to obtain them. Why? What qualities does she feel potential clients must already possess in order to utilize a guidance clinic? Are these same qualities needed to utilize the services of the agency in which you work (or have worked)?

---

*Questions notated with an asterisk are intended for advanced students who have had or are currently having some social work practice experience and who have made at least a tentative commitment to the profession.

CHAPTER 10

Stretching Scarce Resources

or: Practicing at the Macro-level to Meet
Large-Scale Needs

Concepts Covered in This Chapter

1. Scarce resources
2. Levels of generalist social work intervention
    a. Micro-practice
    b. Macro-practice
3. Using macro-practice techniques to stretch scarce resources
4. Funding sources
    a. Competitive grants
    b. Documentation of need
    c. Surveys
5. Program development

Learning Objectives   After reading this chapter, you should be able to

1. Discuss the levels of intervention involved in generalist social work
2. Define *micro-practice* and *macro-practice*
3. Describe the concept of preventive social work and discuss the levels of intervention involved
4. Discuss why macro-level practice skills are emphasized in preventive social work
5. Understand how macro-level practice skills can help stretch scarce resources
6. Discuss the role of funding in program development, and the skills involved to secure it
7. Discuss the use of volunteers in community-based intervention
8. Describe the reasons for partnership between private organizations and professional social workers in program development for contemporary communities

Resources for children and families with special needs in Kingston and Orangetown have remained scarce since the first two editions of this book were written. In preparation for the third edition, I returned to Orangetown to talk with the social worker employed there today. Thomas Monroe, MSW (not his real name, of course), turned out to be a big, tall, energetic and outgoing man. He was clearly a person not easily discouraged, and was willing to share ideas and insights even when short on time. The information he provided is furnished below.

Thomas Monroe's position as school social worker in Orangetown today is full-time. Thus he has the major advantage of not needing to spend half of his week in another school system such as Kingston. However, the workload with which Thomas finds himself confronted still far exceeds the time he has available. He is expected to work with all children from kindergarten through high school, not only those in special education. He deals with the myriad problems of children in regular education *and* special education, problems such as truancy, misbehavior, eating disorders, and substance abuse, as they arise. He also does all the family liaison work and social histories for children referred to special education with suspected emotional disturbance.

Soon after Thomas took his position in Orangetown, he realized that the number of hours in the day was simply insufficient to allow one-on-one work with all the children experiencing problems. He recognized a strong need to stretch scarce resources. Thomas decided to invest a significant portion of his time doing preventive work, rather than intervention after problems had already occurred. Preventive work would require him to use every level of generalist social work intervention, including "micro-practice," or work at individual, family, and small group levels, and "macro-practice," or work at organizational and community levels. However, it would require a shift of emphasis toward the macro-practice level.

A concerned parent as well as a social worker, Thomas' two young children attended Orangetown public schools. Thus he had a personal as well as professional interest in making improvements in the situation in Orangetown as a whole, both inside and outside the school setting. Rather than risk frustration and burn-out trying to solve problems after the fact with few resources, which would negatively affect both his work and his family life, Thomas began to think about ways he might be able to help make Orangetown a better place, a more cohesive community where fewer problems would occur in the first place. His generalist social work skills provided a primary resource.

Using the intervention process of his profession, Thomas carefully assessed the major needs of youth in Orangetown. He soon realized that the children of the town had little to do outside of school. Their boredom tended to get them into trouble, all too often involving alcohol and drug abuse. Thomas then looked into community resources that might help improve the situation. He began with the churches. He soon learned, however, that the churches in the area were waning, providing only limited Sunday School programs for the children. The clergy were experiencing scarce resources themselves, and didn't have any extra time to devote to developing new programs for children.

Thomas decided then to talk with the town chairman. He hoped to interest him in developing new programs for local youth, but Orangetown's town chairman expressed no interest in such an endeavor. Since this man was very successful in developing new business opportunities for adult entrepreneurs of the town, however, he seemed sure to keep his position for many years to come. So the town administration seemed like an unlikely place for Thomas to find help for the children.

The social worker could identify no other resources in Orangetown that might be willing to invest in children. Given these conditions, he decided that the most logical local institution to persuade to develop new programs for children was the school. But what new programs were most needed? How could new programs be organized, funded, and staffed?

Thomas began to develop a plan of action. He determined that of all the different age groups of children in the town, the teenagers were most at risk. Due to their tendency to get into trouble during leisure hours, the teenagers strongly needed some kind of recreational program where they could learn positive social skills. A recreational program would keep teens off the streets and, hopefully, out of trouble.

Thomas went to talk with his immediate boss, the director of pupil services, about his idea. He hoped this man would become excited about the possibility of developing recreational programs for teens, and become involved, perhaps in a leadership position. But Thomas' boss, a psychologist who worked half-time for the schools in Orangetown, simply wasn't interested. That was a great disappointment. Thomas refused to be discouraged, however. He made appointments to talk with other school administrators, the vice-principal, principal, and superintendent. He suggested developing a teen drop-in center to these higher administrators. They were generally supportive; they even offered space for such a program but said they couldn't provide any funding.

Funds were essential if a teen center were to be developed. Money was needed to staff the center and to purchase equipment (for example, a stereo system, sports equipment, prizes, and the like) and refreshments. Thomas began searching for a source of funds. The persistent social worker learned that his state's Department of Public Instruction (DPI) offered competitive grants for the development of alcohol and drug-related programs in selected schools. Grant applications, however, required painstaking documentation of need. Undeterred, Thomas conducted a formal survey of children in the Orangetown schools. He found that six teens had died in the previous four years from alcohol-related causes, five through automobile accidents and one through suicide. That seemed like serious documentation of need indeed. Thomas then spent many days writing up lengthy, detailed application documents. He won his grant.

About the time the grant was secured, Thomas happened to read in a newspaper that a local Optimist Club was being formed; new members were being actively solicited. Thomas was delighted. He thought that an Optimist Club might be a good resource for himself and his family. He had met some Optimists in a neighboring town, and knew that the organization had energetic members and was youth-oriented. Thomas joined the developing local group primarily for the sake of his own children and family.

Once involved, however, the social worker soon realized that the club could become instrumental in helping develop a teen drop-in center for the town. Thomas brainstormed with other Optimists about ways to involve parents in the endeavor, since the grant he had received was not large enough to pay for any staff. Members of the club helped Thomas advertise the project and solicit a number of volunteers.

With a volunteer staff, space in the Orangetown elementary school, and DPI funding for equipment and snacks, the new teen program began. It was an immediate success. Thomas had expected that about 20 or 30 of the local youth would attend the first session, held on a Saturday afternoon. But over 85 children came! In addition, several parents who had not been specifically asked as volunteers appeared as well. Three of these parents later became members of the Optimist Club, to Thomas' great satisfaction. After the first two sessions of the teen center, it was clear that the space the school had allocated was too small. Administrators permitted the program to move to a large, air-conditioned gym in the high school.

Finding volunteers to staff the teen drop-in program, held every other Saturday afternoon, required hard work by the Optimist Club and by Thomas personally. Thomas volunteered at every session, assisted by a dedicated teacher. Other volunteers came and went, but the program was able to operate throughout the school year. Thomas was extremely pleased. His venture couldn't have been more successful. He would have liked recognition and praise from his boss, the school psychologist, but no congratulations or support came from that direction. However, children flocked to the school every Saturday afternoon that the program was offered. That was reward enough for Thomas to continue volunteering his time.

As if Thomas didn't have enough organizing work on his hands, he also decided, as a result of the needs assessment he conducted early on in his career with the Orangetown schools, that parenting classes were needed. Thomas found to his distress that the primary form of discipline used by many parents was physical punishment. Children then cleverly demonstrated what they learned at home by attempting to resolve disputes at school with other children (and sometimes teachers) using physical persuasion as well. That, of course, frequently got them into trouble.

One by one, Thomas counseled various children and their families whenever he could find the time, introducing them to nonviolent methods of discipline and dispute resolution. However, there was simply not enough time in the day to do all the counseling needed, and not enough resources in the area to make appropriate referrals. Thomas decided he wanted to undertake a preventive approach. If parents could learn better ways to discipline their children, he reasoned, then children could learn better ways at home to control themselves and resolve disputes. New, appropriate negotiating skills could very possibly transfer to the school setting and elsewhere.

More money was needed. Thomas envisioned two types of parenting classes, one for parents of younger children and one for parents of teenagers, because very different types of discipline are required for children of diverse developmental ages. Thomas wanted to hire a parenting expert to teach these classes. He also wanted to attract parents to the classes, and he doubted that the presence of an expert on child rearing would be sufficient motivation for many parents to attend! Thomas knew that people who needed to learn better child-rearing techniques often were unaware of the need, and might even get angry if such a need were suggested to them. If, however, a special incentive could reel them in—. Thomas decided that the best incentive to bring parents to parenting programs would be a good meal, served to entire families before class. That way Mom would get a break—she wouldn't have to make dinner! Free babysitting while the class was in session was also important, he believed. Funds were needed for both purposes.

Thomas was forced to embark on another search for funding. He investigated private foundations that had a special interest in child-rearing techniques. He conducted another survey to document the need for parenting classes in Orangetown, and then wrote a proposal to the foundation that seemed most appropriate. Once more, Thomas was successful and obtained the funding he needed. He organized three six-week sessions for parents of children under 12, and one session for parents of teens. Thomas had hoped to hold more classes for parents with teens, but interest was much stronger among those with young children. The teachers told him they were not surprised at this result. Teachers said that parents of young children came much more frequently to parent-teacher conferences than parents of teens. They wondered if parents of teens were not a bit "burned out."

Thomas took a survey of results of the parenting classes and found that they were excellent. Parents indeed learned new options to help maintain discipline, all nonviolent, and they expressed strong satisfaction with both the classroom experience itself and how the new methods were working with the children. Again, Thomas' boss provided no congratulations or support, but Thomas' encouraging results alone were enough to motivate him to want to continue.

Given the remarkable results of his programs, both the teen drop-in center and the parenting classes, Thomas hoped they would be funded for another year. He had been careful to develop and maintain linkages among parents, the school, and community resources, factors which were theoretically important for funding considerations. Attendance at the teen center and the parenting classes was high. However, to everyone's great disappointment, both grant applications to renew funding were denied!

In retrospect, Thomas ruefully reflects that the DPI grant application required information on contingency plans if the grant should be denied. Thomas fears that his alternative plans appeared too plausible, so that the DPI realized he was determined to carry on his programs even without additional money. Thus, limited DPI seed money may have been invested in a less established endeavor. Thomas is less sure why the grant for the parenting classes was not renewed.

Ever the "Optimist," Thomas Monroe is currently making plans to solicit the local Chamber of Commerce for funds to continue his teen center. He has been asking everywhere he can—at school, at the Optimist Club, wherever he encounters parents—for names of people who might volunteer to staff the center. Members of the Optimist Club have agreed to telephone potential volunteers to obtain commitments. Thomas has written up a protocol for each telephone call, including duties required, time involved, and a pitch for membership in the Optimist Club! Thomas is considering asking the Club to put on a fund-raiser as well.

As far as the parenting classes are concerned, Thomas is determined to continue these as well. At this point he is considering writing to a major sports figure who has an interest in public service. He has already persuaded the school food service to provide meals free of charge for the classes next year.

Thomas Monroe, with his dedicated, determined zeal, is an excellent example of an authentic, generalist social worker—committed, hard-working, effective, persistent, and able to work at a variety of levels of intervention, including individual, family, group, organizational, and community levels. He continues his work despite setbacks. He pays careful attention to the interests of the entire community in which he lives and works, especially its children, as he goes about his daily labors. Thomas is the kind of professional who makes social workers proud of their profession.

DISCUSSION AND STUDY QUESTIONS

Many community needs are indicated in this chapter, in particular the lack of resources to meet children's ongoing developmental requirements for positive socialization experiences. The social worker tries to involve both the area churches and the town administration in developing new programs for children, but these institutions indicate little interest. Undeterred, he finds a way to secure grant funding from resources outside Orangetown. He solicits volunteers to help staff the new programs that he develops himself. The skills required to achieve these results involve every level of social work intervention, but in particular, skills working at organizational and community levels, or macro-practice skills.

The social worker uses his macro-practice skills to secure additional funding to develop parenting classes as well. These classes are also successful. However, when outside funding runs out and is not renewed, the social worker is left with the task of carrying on without funds or exerting more effort to gain new funds. This is a problem frequently encountered by social workers today. Community needs are not met via regular, ongoing tax levies that can provide permanent programs to meet predictable needs, such as recreation for the children. Instead, committed individuals, professional and nonprofessional alike, must struggle to meet the needs on a temporary basis. The continuation of these programs, regardless of their merit, is never secure.

1. Think of the town or city in which you grew up. What major needs of the children or families did you perceive? What programs were available to help meet these needs? What other resources do you think could have made your home community a better place to live?

2. Was the school you attended involved in serving your community in ways other than as an educational institution? If so, were you involved in any of the additional services or programs? What was your assessment of their value? Why?

*3. How were programs such as those you identified above funded in your community? Was the funding source long-term and ongoing or based on short-term, competitive grants?

*4. Imagine your future career as a social worker. What do you think you might enjoy about engaging in macro-level practice skills? What concerns do you have?

---

*Questions notated with an asterisk are intended for advanced students who have had or are currently having some social work practice experience and who have made at least a tentative commitment to the profession.

PART THREE

Human Diversity and Human Behavior in the Social Environment

INTRODUCTION

Social work practice rests on a knowledge foundation (as well as a value base, of course). To understand the complex life situations that clients encounter, social workers must understand the biological, psychological, social, and cultural foundations of human behavior. This knowledge enables the social worker to "tune in" to the many sources of people's behavior as well as the ways in which they express themselves. A dramatic example is provided in Chapter 11, where a biological problem generates extremely difficult social behaviors that in time become enmeshed in other problems with social origins.

Human behavior is complex and integrated. We act as biological-psychological-social-cultural beings, with each part affecting the others. Any social worker who ignores the integrated totality of social behavior is doomed to miss the forest for the trees. For example, in Chapter 15 the author's work with the Hosmer family illustrates a number of individual problems, some biological, some psychological, some social, and some cultural. Yet she wisely attempts to understand the way their interaction creates problems for the young Hosmer girl, and her intervention effort is a multi-faceted one that reflects the complexity of the behaviors involved.

Understanding the multiple sources and the multiple modes of expression of human behavior enables a social worker to respect human diversity. The case of Rudolph Gonzales in Chapter 13 is the clearest example of the need for social workers to respect the varied ways different groups of people meet their basic human needs. In this example, the author recognizes how culture is fundamental to our sense of well-being and how it undergirds our efforts to participate in our surroundings. Her search for culturally appropriate resources for Rudolph was a key element in the successful conclusion to his story. However, it took persistence and creativity to overcome the culturally insensitive environment in the county as a whole and the school system in particular. A new chapter for the third edition, Chapter 16, illustrates some of the complications of addressing issues concerning sexual orientation in a nation that strongly discriminates against many minorities.

Social workers are frequently in the position of working on behalf of diverse groups, be they unmarried parents, racial minorities, homosexuals, people with physical or emotional disabilities, or others. Their concern for diverse groups grows in part out of the values and ethics of the profession. However, it also comes from a knowledge base that helps them understand the unique needs, strengths, and obstacles encountered by members of these groups.

CHAPTER 11

A Little Person of Value

or: Understanding the Interaction of Factors That Affect Human Behavior: Biological, Psychological, Social, Cultural, and Economic

Concepts Covered in This Chapter

1. The biopsychosocial whole
2. The life cycle
3. Families as systems
4. Economic factors in human behavior
5. Concept of the least restrictive environment

Learning Objectives After reading this chapter you should be able to

1. Provide an example from this chapter of how the biological, psychological, social, and cultural factors in people's lives interact and affect their needs
2. Define the life cycle and list at least five life cycle stages
3. Define a system
4. Explain why the family can be best understood as a system
5. List at least three ways in which economic factors can influence human behavior
6. Define the concept of the least restrictive environment
7. List at least three populations for whom the concept of the least restrictive environment might be relevant

Harvey Holcolm didn't get a fair shake in life. He was born with an embarrassing physical handicap. He was also poor. To make things even worse, he was born to elderly parents (he was a "change-of-life" baby). His parents were not well educated. Talk about strikes against him—he had a number of them, except that he was actually a handsome little guy and quite appealing in his general personality when he first came to Kingston.

Harvey had been born without an anal sphincter. He had been born with a few of his vital organs mixed up inside him as well, but these had mostly been straightened out by extensive surgery during his infancy. Modern medicine was unable to supply him with a sphincter, however. And as a result, he continued to wear diapers well into grade school. The day came when he refused to wear his diapers, but he still needed them.

When I first met Harvey, he was in the fifth grade, newly transferred into the Kingston school district and living with his adult sister and her husband. He was doing well in his new class, and his teacher liked him. That seemed wonderfully fortunate. According to the Kingston school nurse, Grace Conway, the nurse in Marlboro, where Harvey had come from, had said that Harvey had accidents in class every hour on the hour.

The entire school system in Marlboro had allegedly breathed a big sigh of relief when Harvey moved to Kingston. Children of his own age wouldn't associate with him in Marlboro, according to the Marlboro school nurse, and Harvey was considered in every way a pathetic brat. He talked back to his teachers and smeared his feces on the walls and the desks. He threw handfuls of the stuff at the principal when that good gentleman tried to correct him. And he smelled, and so did everything and everybody he got close to by the end of the day.

Grace Conway didn't tell the gory details to the school principal in Kingston, nor did any of the rest of the special education staff. We all hoped fervently that a change of scene would make a difference in the little boy's behavior. The classroom teacher, of course, had to be informed about the nature of Harvey's physical problem, and Harvey was allowed to go to the washroom anytime he wanted.

Grace instructed all of us that a child of Harvey's age should be able to anticipate "drainage" and that if he "strained" properly on the toilet a number of times each day, he should be able to avoid involuntary "soiling"—even without a sphincter. I thought that was pretty amazing.

For five weeks Harvey proved that Grace was right. A little boy without an anal sphincter can indeed remain quite clean and ordinary-appearing to others.

But then it was all over. The way the story goes, Harvey was attending a ball game with some of his new friends from Kingston when some thoughtless young acquaintances from Marlboro caught sight of him and began to make all sorts of unsavory comments. Whatever happened, the results were spectacular.

When Harvey began to "soil" in his new classroom, he didn't do it occasionally or even develop a gradual crescendo to test the local response system by degrees. Instead, he began to demonstrate, with gusto, exactly the same performance Grace had heard about in intimate detail from the Marlboro school nurse.

The classroom went into an uproar. The school went into an uproar. The principal went into an uproar. And the next thing you knew, Jim Atkins, the psychologist for that school, and I were being hauled into the principal's office. Just what were we going to do to put an end to this outrage? For god's sake, pull the kid out of school and send him to an institution, howled the principal.

For all the principal's fearsome rhetoric, he was a professional and caring man. He had the power to suspend Harvey indefinitely, as a disciplinary action, and he didn't do it. But something would have to be done to alleviate the situation, and quickly. Jim and I were shaken enough by Harvey's dramatic behavior and the impassioned pleas of his classroom teacher and the orations of the principal that we even experienced fleeting desires of our own to pull little Harvey out of school and send him away to an institution. But, fortunately, under special education law we couldn't do it.

Special education law requires a complete evaluation of the needs of each child referred and a detailed set of recommendations from a multidisciplinary team geared to meet those needs. Moreover, the child's special needs must be met in the "least restrictive environment" possible. That meant that ideally every child's needs would be met in the regular classroom. If that were not possible, then the child should remain in the regular classroom but receive special services from appropriate special education staff (LD, ED, speech therapy, or the like). If necessary, the child might spend a few hours each day in a special classroom. Only if that were not enough should the child be scheduled to spend full time in a special classroom. And only after placement in a special class failed could a child be recommended for institutional placement.

This was Kingston, and so the evaluation for special education services was planned properly and thoroughly. Grace, the nurse, was asked to find more information, if possible, about the medical details of Harvey's problem. Jim, the psychologist, was asked to do in-depth psychological testing. I was asked to gather social and developmental histories from the perspectives of both the adult sister presently caring for Harvey and Harvey's parents. Usually, an evaluation team would also request records from the school of prior attendance. A parental signature was required for that, and it was often my job to secure it. But in Harvey's case, we already had the most recent school records available.

Grace, Jim, and I, however, made a trip in unison to talk informally with the school personnel in Marlboro. That was the fastest way we could think of to get the breadth of information we needed to help our own school personnel cope with the immediate situation. Truly, this was an emergency. And the quickest special education evaluation possible would take a few weeks at minimum. We needed some ideas for stopgap action.

The school personnel in Harvey's previous town didn't have a whole lot of ideas to share with us. They told us that they had had the parents send Harvey to school with three changes of clothes each day and that they had frequently sent Harvey home to shower anyway. Luckily, in both towns Harvey lived within walking distance.

But Harvey frequently abused the privilege of showering and stayed home a good deal longer than he was supposed to. That didn't bother the Marlboro school staff much, though. They got some peace that way. Harvey's mother wasn't any good at exerting discipline, they observed, and his father didn't care about schooling. Harvey's father had recently died, they told us. That was certainly an important new piece of information.

We returned to Kingston with our ideas regarding clothing changes, and Jim began to work out a rudimentary program of behavior modification with the regular classroom teacher. We hoped this practical approach could hold things together until we had completed our evaluation. It did, just barely.

I went to interview Harvey's sister and brother-in-law. These energetic and appealing young people were both in their early twenties. They worked days in a canning factory, and they liked to enjoy various sports activities after work. They liked Harvey and had strong opinions about how to get him to control his behavior. Fortunately, their ideas made sense. The brother-in-law, in particular, was articulate about his behavior modification plan, although he didn't call it that. He made Harvey spend regular time in the bathroom, and he took him to various recreational activities only if Harvey controlled himself for certain fixed periods of time. Harvey's behavior at this foster home wasn't ever as good as it had been at school during the first five weeks, but it was tolerable.

The sister said that Harvey's mother had never had any disciplinary standards for him at her home at all, and she felt that was why Harvey's behavior was so bad. The sister said she had volunteered to take care of Harvey after their father had died a couple of months before. She didn't think her mother would be able to cope with Harvey by herself. She said Harvey's deliberate smearing behavior was relatively common in the mother's house but never occurred with her and her husband.

The young surrogate parents had one gripe, however. Harvey's mother had promised to give them the Social Security check that Harvey was entitled to as his father's surviving minor dependent. Instead, the mother was keeping the check. This made the daughter and her husband angry, as Harvey had a good appetite and went through new clothes with amazing speed. They were finding their stint at foster parenting to be expensive in terms of money as well as time and energy.

I naturally suggested they talk over this problem again, more firmly, with Harvey's mother. I could see that keeping the youngster on as a member of the household with no financial remuneration might lose its appeal rather quickly. I said I would be willing to meet with all three interested adults jointly, if the family thought my presence might be helpful in mediation.

But I wondered out loud whether it would be worth the effort just yet. Did the young couple really think they could continue to keep Harvey with them for a long period of time? The school was finding his behavior quite difficult to cope with—how about them?

The two young people asserted that they could cope with Harvey's behavior indefinitely and that they wanted to keep him with them. They felt that they could give Harvey a fair chance to live a normal life.

The opinion of Harvey's sister and her husband was also that if Harvey couldn't seem to make it in a regular classroom at school, he would be able to survive very well in a special classroom. They certainly didn't believe Harvey needed to be institutionalized. When I explained the behavior modification approach used in most ED classrooms, they correctly perceived that the classroom procedures for behavior control were very similar in principle to the ones they were using at home.

I left this family interview feeling encouraged. If Harvey could have a consistent and stable living situation such as this one promised to become, I thought that he could make it in a special classroom. A specially trained teacher for the emotionally disturbed would be sure to confer regularly with Harvey's sister and brother-in-law. Behavioral goals and reinforcements could be mutually developed so that they would be consistent at home and at school. It looked as if this story might have a happy ending.

Next, I went to talk to Harvey's mother, Mrs. Holcolm. She startled me with her frail little body and stooped shoulders. She looked very old, much older than her actual years, with her white, limp, and thinning hair. Her manner of speaking was almost tearful, her voice undulating between a whine and a sob. She talked of her difficult life and her terrible time making a go of it with such a dismally disabled son, who had been born just at the time she hoped to be free of child-rearing responsibilities.

Mrs. Holcolm described for me the details of Harvey's complicated early operations to correct some of his physical problems. She also described how the family had coped with all the stress, emotional and financial, and how Harvey had related to his parents, brothers, and sisters. According to her description, Harvey's behavior had been pretty erratic all his life—just as provocative at its worst as it customarily was at school. She explained how Harvey's behavior had led to family fights. Mr. Holcolm wouldn't discipline the boy at all because he felt so sorry for him, and Mrs. Holcolm wouldn't because she thought discipline should be the father's responsibility. When she tried to assert herself with Harvey, the boy wouldn't obey her, anyway.

The elderly mother described how her husband had insisted that Harvey be kept at home and how she had allowed it because Mr. Holcolm had loved Harvey so very much. She knew the death of her husband had been a terrible blow to Harvey, but she felt it had been much worse for her. She was now left alone to cope with a frustrating son with disabilities and all her other problems as well.

I asked Mrs. Holcolm, of course, what other problems were pressing her at this time. She explained that her deceased husband had never worked at a job long enough to qualify for a pension. She herself had never held a paying job outside the home because she had had so many children to raise. Now, because she was only 58 years of age, she couldn't qualify for Social Security survivor's benefits on her own. She would have to wait until she was 60 to receive even reduced benefits for herself. Meanwhile, survivor's benefit checks were sent to her as Harvey's custodian; she qualified for part of his benefit checks as his caretaker. That didn't give her much money to live on, but it was something. She was always struggling to make ends meet, with no end in sight.

She didn't mention the fact that she shouldn't be collecting the money from Harvey's checks unless she was actually taking care of the boy, and I didn't bring the subject up until later in the interview, when our relationship felt more established. What I did ask Mrs. Holcolm at this time was how she felt about Harvey's move to Kingston. She brightened up for the first time in the interview. "Oh," she exclaimed, "that part is wonderful. It's not Harvey's fault, but he's such an impossible boy. I get so tired of trying to make him behave, and he makes me so upset all the time. It's much better having him live at his sister's. And besides," she offered shyly, "my new boyfriend can't stand how he smells."

Her new boyfriend? "Oh, yes," she said, and then suddenly a cautious smile curved her features. She looked younger. "Well, he isn't really a boyfriend, just a friend. A body has to have her own life, doesn't she?"

She certainly does. I was happy to know that Mrs. Holcolm had some positive emotional input from somewhere.

But the sister's home did seem like a much better arrangement for Harvey. He was wanted there; he was disciplined in a consistent, predictable way. And by comparison, Harvey behaved like an angel for his sister and brother-in-law.

Before I left the interview with Mrs. Holcolm, I talked with her a little about the Social Security check problem. I explained that legally the money should be sent to her daughter to pay for Harvey's care. I sounded Mrs. Holcolm out on her ideas regarding potential employment for herself to earn her own living. But I didn't push the matter. It seemed as though this might be one of those situations where there just wasn't enough money to go around. Could this frail and unfortunate woman really learn to support herself at her age? I personally doubted it.

The M team meeting was held shortly after my visit with Mrs. Holcolm. She didn't attend, but Harvey's sister and brother-in-law did. They actively contributed their ideas.

The special education team determined that Harvey should be placed full time in a special classroom for the emotionally disturbed until his "soiling behavior" came under control. The school nurse still insisted from her research that missing sphincter or not, Harvey should be physically capable of controlling his soiling behavior if the emotional barriers could be overcome.

The regular classroom teacher and the principal of the school preferred a recommendation for institutionalization because of the severity of the behavior they had been coping with, but they agreed to go along with the majority plan. After all, a transfer to an ED classroom removed Harvey from their own school, and that fact surely helped sway their consent to the majority opinion. Their particular school did not have a special classroom for ED children of Harvey's grade level.

The move to the new school was approved by the county the next day. Dan Dwyer, the county liaison for Kingston schools, took care of that most efficiently. Approval of an M team plan by the county often took weeks, but not in this situation. Harvey moved to a classroom in a school where Gertrude Baker was the social worker and Norman Werner was the psychologist.

Jim Atkins and I didn't worry very much about a transfer of Harvey's case to a new pupil services staff. We knew that both Gertrude and Norman were as competent, or more so, than ourselves. We worked closely with our co-workers, and we felt satisfied with our case debriefing. To be certain of a smooth transition, Gertrude and I met with the foster parents and Harvey together at their home.

Harvey's actual transfer went well. According to Gertrude and Norman, although his behavior in the new classroom was far from perfect, it was much improved over his behavior in the regular classroom. The ED teacher and Gertrude worked closely with the sister and her husband to coordinate goals between the classroom and the home.

Whew, a relative success, or so we thought. What happened next was totally unexpected, but perhaps it shouldn't have been. Somehow, the importance of the relevant predictive information had gotten lost in the transfer between Gertrude and me. I had told Gertrude about the financial situation and the feelings involved, but I had not stressed the problem, perhaps as I had not known what to do about it myself. So I bore a part of the responsibility.

One day Gertrude came rushing into the common office room and dashed over to talk to me. "Can you believe it?" she exclaimed. "Harvey has been abducted by his mother!"

Abducted? By his mother? But she didn't want him—

It was true, and they were both gone for good. None of us ever saw Mrs. Holcolm or little Harvey again. We pieced the immediate tragedy together later. The problem, of course, was money—the Social Security check.

Harvey's sister had called the Social Security office in a huff one day. She had demanded that the Social Security personnel send Harvey's check to her. Harvey's sister had explained that she was caring for the boy and so she thought she ought to get the money for his keep instead of her mother.

The Social Security staff began to investigate. When the officials determined to their satisfaction that Harvey was indeed residing with his sister and not with his mother, they called Mrs. Holcolm and threatened to prosecute her for fraud.

Mrs. Holcolm must have panicked. At any rate, she nabbed her son back to requalify herself as his custodian and moved away from the jurisdiction of the original Social Security office to discourage an actual suit. A pretty smart move for an old lady, in fact. Perhaps she made it okay. She was a survivor. And that was that.

DISCUSSION AND STUDY QUESTIONS

Our biological functioning is a basic component of our social well-being. Because of our physical characteristics, we are included in or excluded from various social situations. No one finds it desirable to be excluded from groups to which she or he wishes to belong, regardless of the reason for the exclusion. Biological bases for exclusion can often lead to social isolation of various kinds. Harvey's case is one example, but persons with severe physical handicaps or learning disabilities frequently suffer the same social isolation.

The concepts of "least restrictive environment" and "normalization" refer to efforts to reduce the degree to which persons with biologically based disabilities are excluded from ongoing social life. Both attempt to limit the disabled person's social participation only in those areas required by the disability. In Harvey's case, for example, his average intelligence should not have excluded him from the regular school classroom. Only if his incontinence could not be controlled and if others found this behavior objectional would there be a basis for putting him in some kind of alternative learning environment.

Keeping people in their regular environment as far as possible generally reduces their feeling of being undesirable. It also maximizes their exposure to the kinds of social stimulation that facilitate life cycle development. Thus, the need for remedial services is reduced in two ways. Mental health services are avoided by enabling people to feel accepted and productive. Special educational services are also unneeded. However, normalization is a relative concept. Persons with severe physical handicaps may need very special kinds of environments, but even then, there may be areas of living where they can function like most other people. They should be allowed to do so in these areas.

1. Have you ever known someone with a severe physical disability? How did you feel about this person? How did others treat him or her? Was there any effort to "normalize" this person's environment?
2. What physical disability would you find most troublesome, were you to have it? Why would you find it undesirable? Try to separate your feelings into those relating to limitations on your activities, reactions of others to you, and your feelings about yourself.
*3. The author briefly mentions that a behavior modification program was set up for Harvey to reduce his soiling behavior. What are some of the basic principles of behavior modification? Given the limited information you have, what types of reinforcements do you think might have been effective with Harvey? Why?
*4. Transferring clients from one social worker to another can be a delicate business. What are some potential negative effects of transfer? What measures can be taken to help minimize the negative effects? What did the social workers do in this chapter to help reduce the potential negative effects? Have you ever used any of these in your own practice? Have you used others?

---

*Questions notated with an asterisk are intended for advanced students who have had or are currently having some social work practice experience and who have made at least a tentative commitment to the profession.

CHAPTER 12

Serving Bar with Mrs. Casey

or: Dealing with Clients Who Perceive a Different Reality;
Issues in Power and Social Control

Concepts Covered in This Chapter

1. The social perception of reality
2. The importance of religious values in social work practice
3. The working poor
4. Laws and deviance
5. Power and social control
6. Social institutions
7. Public welfare and private charity
8. Status offense

Learning Objectives   After reading this chapter you should be able to

1. Explain the importance for social workers of the social perception of reality
2. List three situations in which religious values might be important determinants of behavior
3. Distinguish the working poor from the poor
4. Explain the relationship between laws and deviance
5. Discuss the limits of power and mechanisms of social control as illustrated by the Casey family
6. List at least three social institutions in American society
7. Define *status offense*

Mrs. Casey was a professional. She could have taught courses in how to get around school officials and the public health department. She didn't quite manage to get around the welfare department on one important occasion, but she certainly did defy a court order requiring school attendance for her children, and she got away with it. Her tactics, actually, were quite simple and available to everyone.

To get around public officials, one should simply act as if one isn't there. But if these same officials should thrust themselves on one's hapless person, one should simply smile in a friendly way and pretend to understand and agree. One should indicate that one intends to comply with any and all official requests as soon as possible and then totally forget about those requests. If that doesn't work and the officials begin to initiate a court case, one then moves to a different county.

This way of life can get a little inconvenient, of course. It requires the effort of frequent mobility. For example, in the eight months I knew or knew about Mrs. Casey, she first moved into Emmett County, fleeing from a welfare fraud conviction and a pending child neglect court case in neighboring Hickson County. Mrs. Casey had to leave Emmett County, too, before the end of the school year, to avoid another court case. But nobody would be on her back again until the next fall at least; that much was certain. And perhaps the officials in her new county of residence wouldn't bother with her.

That was unlikely, however. She had nine children, eight of school age, and her oldest daughter, a junior in high school, was pregnant. Because eight of the children were supposed to be going to school and none were attending regularly, school officials would be likely to get around to complaining. The compulsory education law automatically brought the family into the public domain. Besides, pregnant girls of school age may be referred for special education evaluation and services.

There was a husband involved with Mrs. Casey. I never saw him, and, according to her, he worked in another town during the week and only came home on weekends. Mrs. Casey worked in a bar in the evenings and on weekends, so she and her husband didn't get to see each other much. That was good, she said, because it helped them get along better.

The welfare fraud case was unfair, she volunteered, when I interviewed her for a social history. That was an interesting contribution, as I hadn't asked her anything about the fraud conviction. Mrs. Casey was clearly preoccupied by her court conviction, concerned about my opinion of her, and eager to put her case in a better light for me. I did know about the fraud case already, through the professional grapevine, in this case the Kingston school nurse and the full-time social worker. Grace Conway's colleague in public health in Hickson County and Gertrude Baker's friend who worked in the Hickson County Welfare Department told my two colleagues, who in turn informed me.

Mrs. Casey explained that when she applied for welfare in Hickson County, she and her husband were actually separated and intended to stay that way. She had applied for AFDC and gotten it. But then her husband had come home, more or less. He began to contribute to the family budget again. Mrs. Casey "forgot" to mention this fact to the welfare department. When they found out, they got upset.

But everything was straightened out now, Mrs. Casey said. She and her husband were paying the money back in monthly installments. Of course, that didn't leave anything left over to buy little Robert's glasses. Robert's glasses, or lack thereof, happened to be one of the reasons I made my first visit with her.

The other reason I was visiting was because Robert had been referred for an ED/LD evaluation. His third-grade teacher in Kingston said that Robert had a tremendous need for attention in the classroom, couldn't get along with any of the other children, was far below grade level, and couldn't read the blackboard. She thought he probably needed glasses, among other things.

Mrs. Casey didn't tell me about the neglect case that had been pending in the Hickson courts when she left the county. That I knew about from Gertrude Baker. Gertrude's social worker friend and colleague in the Hickson County Welfare Department had been working for the prosecution in that case. The Hickson County worker believed the Casey children were entirely inadequately cared for by their natural parents and was professionally invested in securing foster care for them.

Under these circumstances, I didn't exactly expect the Caseys to rush out to buy their little son Robert a pair of glasses just because I happened to remind them he needed some. In fact, where glasses were concerned, I talked to Grace Conway, that infinitely kind and humanitarian school nurse in Kingston. Grace had an inside pull with the Lion's Club. The Lion's Club considered provision of glasses to the needy to be one of its charitable missions.

When I reviewed Robert's school records as part of my initial investigation into his ED case, I read in the transcripts, forwarded by Robert's former school, that he had been truant most of the school days the year before. Mrs. Casey had insisted the absences were for reasons of health, so the school had referred the case to the public health department. A public health nurse had visited the family regularly for a while, but she had terminated the visits when the mother never carried through any of her suggestions.

The school had finally taken the case to court as a truancy matter. They won a court order requiring medical verification for every absence. The school was to report absences to the Hickson County Welfare Department, which included a child protective unit. This unit was to investigate any violations of the court order. That was the point at which Gertrude's friend had become involved.

Robert's school attendance didn't improve, and the welfare department took the case back to court as a child neglect matter. The Caseys were not only failing to get any of their children to school but also were not providing acceptable supervision at home. The children were running all over the neighborhood at all hours of the day and night, according to documented evidence. Moreover, the parents were failing to meet their children's basic health needs. The health department had documentation of severe dental deterioration and inadequate nutrition for all the children.

The Hickson County Court initiated the neglect case; what probably loomed ahead was the removal of the children to foster care. But the family moved to a different county before the case could be completed.

The Hickson County Court should have transferred the case to the Emmett County Court, but it neglected to complete the paperwork by the proper filing date.

Gertrude's friend, who had been working with the case, was tremendously upset about this because the children's need was so evident and so much painstaking work had already been done to document the inadequacy of the parents.

The neglect case was dropped by the Emmett County Court without review.

And that was the situation when I became involved with the Caseys. Not having met them and having been thoroughly warned about them through the grapevine and the school records, I expected to meet a monster in Mrs. Casey.

I was unable to reach the Casey residence by telephone. My first attempt resulted in the information that the Casey telephone number had been disconnected.

According to the school records, Mr. Casey worked in a town some 40 miles away, so it seemed fruitless to try to reach him. Mrs. Casey, however, worked at the Paradise Valley Tavern in a neighboring town. Maybe I would be able to reach her there.

I could reach the Paradise Valley Tavern by telephone, and a man there who knew Mrs. Casey promised to give her the messages to call me. But she never did call. Tactic number one: Ignore the "authorities."

I mailed her the permission form that would allow the special education team to conduct an ED/LD evaluation for Robert and included a note asking her to call me. I included a stamped, self-addressed return envelope with the permission slip for evaluation.

No response.

I sent another inquiry by mail, setting a date for an initial staffing for Robert. I explained in my note that we would need parental permission to conduct the staffing and that Mrs. Casey and her husband were welcome to attend. I included another stamped, self-addressed return envelope with the second permission slip.

Again, no response.

I'm a little slow. But eventually, it occurred to me that Mrs. Casey was avoiding me. I had a brainstorm and called the tavern on a weekend. I figured she'd never suspect that a phone call she received on a weekend would be from the school.

I gave the man who answered the telephone only my first name. I think I tried to make my voice sound a little tipsy and rough. It was almost fun, except I do hate to think about work on weekends. I wouldn't have done it had I not been getting a little peeved myself under the professional veneer. Good gracious, I was being ignored. Moreover, Robert's school attendance and his performance in class were continuing to deteriorate, according to his teacher.

Mrs. Casey herself actually came to the phone. When she found out who I was, her voice didn't betray the slightest hint of surprise or dismay. Tactic number two: don't get rattled; be smooth.

She hadn't received the permission forms I had sent her, she said, and she couldn't make the meeting I was suggesting on the date scheduled. She would like to reschedule for after Christmas, only a few weeks away. No, it was too soon to reschedule today. Please call back after Christmas. Tactic number three: lie a little; delay things as long as you can.

Because the special education program had to have that signed permission form to begin to conduct the evaluation for Robert, Mrs. Casey had me over a barrel. I had to humor her or lose what chance we had to work with the boy.

When I called the tavern again shortly after the Christmas vacation, Mrs. Casey herself answered. She agreed verbally that a staffing should be set up for Robert the next week. She would attend and sign the proper forms to continue the evaluation, if the staffing meeting came to the decision to do so—that is, if I would provide her with a ride to the meeting.

That sounded quite encouraging. I begged Mrs. Casey the humble favor of allowing me to transport her to the meeting.

I arrived at Mrs. Casey's address a little early on the day of the staffing meeting, expecting anything. The anything I expected came true. There was no one home. At least, there didn't seem to be anyone at home. The place looked thoroughly deserted. The paint was peeling off the ancient farmhouse in long, forlorn strips; the back door hung ajar at a funny angle; and the remnants of faded curtains drooped along the edges of the kitchen windows in limp little curls. There was no furniture at all on the lumpy bare floor in the kitchen, at least as far inside as I could see.

I banged on the swinging back door, producing only weak, hollow rattles. But lo and behold, a pregnant girl came out from another room to greet me. She was almost nicely dressed, and her fresh face and flowing youth stood in stark contrast to her decrepit surroundings.

I had heard about Mrs. Casey's pregnant daughter before from Gertrude, who was working with her in the high school. Gertrude thought the daughter was quite intelligent and had the potential to make it through high school. Gerturde was encouraging her to try to remain in school to keep up with her studies. But the girl was home today.

The daughter explained very nicely that her mother was out working. She gave me directions, and I drove down toward the Paradise Valley Tavern, the mother's place of employment. It was only a mile or so away from the house. The tavern was certainly an ugly little place, set back down a long rutted driveway. I was a little afraid to head down that driveway all by myself, but I took a deep breath and steered my car along the ruts toward the tavern's forbidding entrance.

The bar looked very dark inside, and a knock on the outer door brought no response. I couldn't hear anybody inside. I opened the door cautiously and tried to peer in. It took quite a while for my eyes to adjust. Finally, I could just distinguish a large, heavyset woman standing behind the bar.

She looked at me in surprise and then smiled in a friendly way.

"Mrs. Casey?"

"Yes, dear. What can I do for you?"

Tactic number four: look friendly and agreeable.

"Oh, my goodness," she said. "I forgot all about the meeting at the school today."

At that point, I was absolutely sure she wouldn't come to the meeting with me. And just in case that sort of thing should happen, I had brought along a copy of the form that would allow the special education team to carry on its evaluation without her. Would she sign? Hardly a chance, I guessed quickly. Poor little Robert. We wouldn't be able to offer him any special services.

But to my astonishment, Mrs. Casey asked me to sit down and wait for a few minutes. She offered me a glass of soda. She said that she expected her boss to come in shortly, and if he did, maybe she would be able to attend the meeting with me.

And her boss did arrive, and Mrs. Casey and I drove together to the initial staffing meeting for Robert. My conversations with her were pleasant both to and from the meeting. She participated in the conference. She said all sorts of concerned and sympathetic things about her son. I couldn't believe this was the neglectful mother described in the former school records. But, of course, I was still in the stage where I was trying to elicit cooperation by positive means. And she was still using the tactic of being friendly and agreeable.

Oddly enough, our relationship never got very far out of this stage. Mrs. Casey seemed incapable of saying a nasty word. I wondered whether she might be cognitively disabled. Maybe that was why she took such haphazard care of her children, while honestly seeming to love them, or why she was always so friendly, while never following through on a single suggestion I made unless I was personally present to push her. Not, I hasten to add, that a cognitively disabled mother must take haphazard care of her children, be continually pleasant, or ignore suggestions. But Mrs. Casey was a woman I liked; she seemed to like me, and I got absolutely nowhere with her in terms of stimulating an improvement in her child-care habits. Of course, realistically, any mother who has to work full time and care for eight children may be a bit haphazard in her child-care habits.

Three of the children came down to the bar on the day I interviewed Mrs. Casey at length for the social history. They all seemed to feel affectionate and easy with her. The teenage daughters, one the pregnant girl I had met before, were taking care of Mrs. Casey's three-year-old, after a fashion.

In the social history interview, Mrs. Casey told me all about the pointed comments that her neighbors and friends had made about her letting her children run wild, like animals. She seemed hurt and curious, as if the reality of the accusation was inconceivable to her. And yet right before my eyes, two of her daughters were truant and she was using them to babysit for her toddler.

Although the purpose of this interview was to obtain a social history and not to intervene in the Casey living situation to bring about change, I had to point out the contradiction. I had to point out that her daughters were truant today and wasn't this evidence that her neighbors might have a point? Perhaps Mrs. Casey wasn't properly supervising her children?

"Oh," she replied, apparently surprised. "They're not truant today. They weren't feeling well this morning, and so I gave them permission to stay home. Besides, you were coming, and I needed somebody to watch the baby for me."

I let it drop for then. I needed cooperation for my social history more than I wanted to make a point.

When the social history was fairly complete and Mrs. Casey and her daughters and I began to chat relatively informally, I asked them all whether they were aware of the services of the Planned Parenthood agency in Kingston. But none of them were interested. They were Catholic, they explained. Their pregnancies usually were unexpected, but that was how things were in life.

I also referred the family to the Emmett County Guidance Clinic for services relating to the oldest daughter's present pregnancy, although I was sure Mrs. Baker would already have done so. She had. But the family wasn't interested in services from the clinic, either. They felt they could handle things themselves. It was clear that Mrs. Casey didn't want to seek the services or attention of any public agency unless she was forced to. I suppose that related to the recent court cases she had faced in Hickson County.

Robert's school attendance didn't improve because of my attention. In fact, it deteriorated to the point that he rarely came to school at all. Norman, the psychologist, could not complete his psychological evaluations, the ED teacher could not complete her classsroom observations, and the LD teacher could not even begin to conduct her tests. The special education team was stymied as far as evaluating Robert for special education services was concerned, unless we could get the boy to school more regularly. He came off and on, to be sure, but the various professionals concerned could not just drop their planned schedules to work with him alone on those rare days when he did come in.

I went out and talked at length with Mrs. Casey, explaining the necessity of getting Robert to school more regularly. She promised faithfully to get him there. But he was so ill all the time, she complained; and of course, he couldn't read at school without glasses, so he didn't like to go.

Tactic number five? Pathetic but plausible excuses?

So I sighed, thinking this was probably what had happened in Hickson County last year. Still, I got the public health nurse to visit and the school nurse to complete her arrangements for glasses. They duly performed their roles. In fact, when they met with Mrs. Casey at home and discovered the three-year-old, they made an immediate referral I should have thought of myself: to the Head Start program. But Mrs. Casey didn't follow through with the referral, even when I reminded her, and she still didn't get Robert to school. Back to tactic number one: ignore the "authorities."

This was a situation in which I would have liked to involve the county guidance clinic. In fact, I talked to the clinic director about the Caseys. I thought the only possible new resource that might bring some positive changes into these children's lives would be ongoing, active outreach by a family-oriented treatment agency. But the clinic staff wasn't interested in working with a family that wouldn't seek its help. Clients without motivation won't change, they said. Our doors are open, but Mrs. Casey will have to ask for our services first. Besides, we don't have time to make home visits, especially to people who don't request our help.

Mrs. Casey wouldn't ask for help, of course. She wasn't interested in services from a guidance clinic. In fact, she would prefer it if outsiders would just leave her alone. Outsiders always made demands that she change herself or her children, or else they threatened to take her children away.

I talked with the protective services unit in the welfare department, hoping they might get involved. That was probably the referral that was most theoretically correct. Protective servcies is supposed to investigate family situations where child neglect is suspected, and poor supervision, lack of health care, and inadequate nutrition constitute grounds for child neglect.

But protective services in Emmett County was inactive. The supervisor was a depressed victim of alcoholism himself, and his entire unit was thoroughly demoralized, having no support or direction. My referral there brought no action.

Finally I knew I had run out of things to do—except initiate truancy proceedings. I didn't like getting involved in truancy proceedings. Truancy is a status offense; that is, it is an offense for which only children and not adults can be convicted. I had no desire to convict little Robert Casey of a crime in court.

But I knew of no further way to bring pressure on the family for change. At least, a court order for Robert to attend school would force the involvement of authorities such as protective services and/or the police. It looked as though force of some kind was going to be required if the Casey children were to receive anything like an adequate education or a minimal home environment. Perhaps foster care would have to be ordered, eventually. Things had almost gone that far in Hickson County, and I could see no realistic alternative in Emmett County.

The elementary school principal in Kingston wasn't eager to initiate truancy proceedings. Contrary to my perspective from the other side, that of a child growing up, I was finding as an adult that schools weren't eager to leap into a fracas in court to punish a wayward child. If only I had known that in time to have a little fun while I was a kid!

In fact, the principal pointed out that truancy proceedings would require a great deal of time and energy from the school staff. He suggested we wait awhile to see whether Robert's attendance might show some improvement in time.

During the wait, I threatened Mrs. Casey with a truancy case if she didn't get Robert to school. I didn't threaten in a dramatic, frightening way. Except under extreme circumstances, I seem incapable of dramatic threats. What I actually did was to tell her clearly that I didn't believe she was serious about getting her son to school. She had told me she would too often without results.

And I told her that if I didn't see a change, I was going to recommend truancy proceedings. I told her I was sure the school would initiate truancy proceedings on several of her children, in fact, if she didn't see that they attended regularly and right away.

Mrs. Casey remained invariably pleasant and friendly! She continued to promise to improve. I almost believed her at some level. I continued to encourage her by saying that I was sure she could get her children to school if she really would just try. We talked over 101 ways to get them out of bed in the morning and onto the bus. But she had a sad little reason why each and every idea wouldn't work (although, of course, she would try). We got hung up in a "yes-but" game, and I couldn't see the way out of it myself.

And there was no improvement in Robert's school attendance. Finally the elementary school principal decided to initiate the truancy complaint. He had a system where he sent three warning notes. Then he got down to business and went to court.

The principal sent Mrs. Casey warning notes on all four of her children of elementary age. All had been missing school regularly, although Robert was the only one I was personally dealing with as he had been the only one referred to special education.

At the third and final warning note, Mrs. Casey and her family left the county. They hadn't stayed long enough yet to have any more court convictions to travel with them to their new location. They would arrive unheralded. Heaven help the new school system and those poor children.

DISCUSSION AND STUDY QUESTIONS

This chapter addresses two especially difficult circumstances for social workers: client fraud and client noncooperation. Fraud, although relatively rare, does occur. Sometimes it is unintentional, created by confusing and conflicting rules and programs. Other times, it is intentional but often motivated by needs barely met or still unmet by existing programs. The cumulative effects of marginal resources and borderline intelligence are reflected in Mrs. Casey. She seems to be unable to understand what the authorities feel is so self-evident and too unmotivated to deal with what she does understand. At least from her point of view, the realities of her life are different from what the authorities perceive.

As a result, she is noncooperative with those who—from their point of view—are trying to be helpful. Reading between the lines, one gets the sense that she is trying to be cooperative, but within her own frame of reference. This is a good example of the difficulties that arise when values are different. All parties may be operating in good faith yet doing different and contradictory things. Who is right? Because certain groups in society have been given the authority to make certain kinds of decisions, people such as Mrs. Casey become defined as wrong. A chapter such as this one should alert us to the fact that human life is made up of many different points of view. However troublesome some of them may be, we must exercise great care when we go about deciding which are "right" and which are "wrong."

1. The Casey case is probably fairly typical of a welfare fraud situation. Overall, what do you think society gained by prosecuting this family for welfare fraud? What might society have lost? On balance, do you think the net social gain for prosecution for fraud of the Casey family was worth the cost? Consider probable net monetary balance as well as less tangible factors and give specific reasons for your answer.
2. How do you think social class or social worker and client family values might have affected the interactions in this chapter? For example, do you think Mrs. Casey and the author held the same values toward education? Toward the use of birth control? Toward child rearing? Why or why not?
*3. How does this chapter illustrate the reality of the "working poor"? How do biology, religion, and social class values interact in this case to perpetuate the situation?
*4. What connection might there be between the alcoholism of the supervisor of the protective services unit in the Emmett County Welfare Department and the type of work he was involved in? What insight does this possible

---

*Questions notated with an asterisk are intended for advanced students who have had or are currently having some social work practice experience and who have made at least a tentative commitment to the profession.

connection reveal to you about the importance of regular, conscious self-care?

*5. Have you ever worked with a problem in which your best efforts could not overcome resistance to change? What do you think were the sources of the resistance? How did you respond to this situation? In hindsight, are there other things you now think *you* could have done, or was the situation beyond any one social worker's solution?

CHAPTER 13

Rudolph Gonzales

or: Should a Little Boy Disturbed by Cultural Differences
Be Diagnosed as Emotionally Disturbed?

Concepts Covered in This Chapter

1. Migration
2. Culture
3. Hispanic (Latino) culture
4. Cultural disorientation
5. The broker role of social workers
6. Bilingual education

Learning Objectives   After reading this chapter you should be able to

1. Define *migration*
2. List at least three groups that are currently experiencing large-scale migration
3. Define *culture*
4. List at least five aspects of behavior that are affected by culture
5. Define *Hispanic* (note that an alternative term for *Hispanic* is *Latino*)
6. List at least five Hispanic (Latino) groups
7. Define *cultural disorientation* and list at least three ways it can affect behavior
8. Discuss the broker role for social workers
9. Give an example of the broker role from this chapter
10. Describe bilingual education and discuss why it is controversial

When I first met Rudolph, it was several months into the school year in Kingston. Norman Werner, the school psychologist with whom I usually worked in Kingston, showed me the referral slip the day he received it.

"I don't like this," he said. "I knew something like this was bound to happen sometime. We don't have the resources to work with this one. I don't like the look of this at all."

Norman had just received an ED referral for a fourth grader whose primary language was Spanish. Neither Kingston nor Emmett County as a whole had any bilingual staff.

Kingston had a small Spanish-speaking population. It didn't have a small Spanish-speaking community exactly; Hispanics were distributed thinly throughout the town, mostly in cramped apartments over garages and department stores. There were as yet no special shops, cafés, or services geared to help bring Spanish speakers together.

The Hispanic settlers generally came as migrant labor for the larger fruit, potato, and carrot farms in the area. Most of the laborers left when the autumn declined and agricultural work disappeared.

But every year a few more migrants became "immigrants" to Emmett County. They sought temporary work in the canneries in the fall and then did what they could to secure permanent work for the winter. Some succeeded in finding jobs; some failed and left. But some also failed to find jobs and stayed nevertheless, applying for public assistance. These became targets for disapproving comments by the older residents of the region.

There weren't many Hispanics in Kingston, but those that were there were looked on nervously as potential rivals for scarce jobs or else as freeloaders. Everybody knew who the outsiders were on sight because their coloring was a little darker than the largely Scandinavian and German population that originally settled the region. They spoke Spanish in the supermarkets, to the annoyance of the Kingston-born townspeople.

Rudolph Gonzales was Norman's and my first Spanish-speaking ED referral in Kingston. There had been a Spanish-speaking ED referral already in Orangetown, and we had dealt with the special circumstances there by borrowing the talents of a Spanish-speaking teacher's aide for translation and consultation. That wasn't legal, and we knew it in Orangetown; we should have come up with at least a bilingual psychologist to administer and interpret the psychological tests that were used to help determine evidence of psychological disturbance.

But the county didn't come up with any means to obtain the services of a bilingual psychologist or a bilingual social worker, for that matter. We decided not to make a recommendation for ED placement, anyway, in that case, and the little boy began to do better in the classroom because of David Chase's consultation with his teacher, so the issue never really had to be met head on.

But the initial referral slip describing Rudolph Gonzales made it look as though we would not get by so easily here. Rudolph exhibited violent behavior on the playground, and he was described as a "very large, tough fourth grader." He banged his fists and slammed his head on the walls of the classroom. He threw his chair and his desk against the wall on the day his teacher made the referral. He couldn't read, and this seemed to frustrate him just about as much as his unsuccessful relationships with other children.

In general, Rudolph was operating academically on a first-grade level, and socially, he was pretty much an outcast, according to his teacher. It sounded as though he really had problems.

Norman and I knew we had no access to bilingual staff. But we did believe we needed bilingual expertise to evaluate properly and make recommendations for this young boy.

The reason a bilingual evaluation should be provided, in our respective professional opinions, was to protect Hispanic children such as Rudolph. If their primary problems were language and cultural disorientation resulting in confusion and isolation because of an all English-speaking environment, then the primary cause (cultural disorientation) and not the resulting disturbance (bad behavior) should be specifically addressed.

Instead of being separated from his peers in a special classroom for children with emotional disturbance, we thought that perhaps Rudolph's normal environment should be enriched by bilingual services. Then Rudolph would have something familiar he could understand and relate to in his regular classroom. Possibly in a partially Spanish-speaking environment, Rudolph would not be so frustrated and would not behave in such a violent way.

So Norman and I decided we would take it on ourselves to refuse to make an M team recommendation for ED placement, regardless of the severity of Rudolph's behavior in school, until the county managed to supply us with bilingual consultation.

Norman and I discussed our beliefs with Kingston's liaison from the county special education offices, Dan Dwyer. Dan, a competent but busy man, often disagreed with our initial assessment of problem situations. He usually wanted us to hurry up and get things done, regardless of the circumstances. But if we could get him to see things our way, Dan could and usually would manage to help us.

Unfortunately, in this case we could not get Dan Dwyer to agree with us. Dan told us to get on with our respective roles in carrying out Rudolph's evaluation and that if the M team then recommended services by special education, the county administration itself would decide whether further evaluation by bilingual staff was needed.

Norman called the state special education office on this one because he believed it was a state requirement to provide bilingual evaluation for predominantly Spanish-speaking children. And, indeed, the state office duly informed Norman that the services of a bilingual psychologist were legally required in a case such as this. But the state didn't supply any personnel to meet its own requirement. They told Norman to inquire at the county level.

Norman had already inquired at the county level, of course, without response, and he didn't get any better response when he went back to Dan Dwyer to inform him of the state requirement. Dan didn't believe the state would enforce its regulation. "Be realistic," Dan argued. "If this boy needs help, he's going to get it a lot faster if we prescribe it ourselves. The county doesn't have any funds for bilingual evaluation, and if the state doesn't provide any staff to help out, you can be sure it isn't likely to have any staff to investigate violations."

"But, Dan," Norman and I insisted in unison, "we don't feel competent to make any recommendations for Rudolph when there is such a strong cultural component to his referral. We don't think we are going to be able to decide by ourselves whether

Rudolph is emotionally disturbed or whether he is just acting crazy out of frustration because nobody talks or thinks the way he does."

"Go talk to his mother, Carolyn," Dan ordered. "Find out about his behavior at home. That should give you some clue. And Norman, get at those psychological tests. Then let's see how you two feel about an ED placement."

Well, Norman and I did perform our respective roles. My own first home visit remains etched clearly in my mind. I had to go to the Gonzales's apartment building several times before I could rouse anyone. Making an appointment by telephone was not possible; the family had no telephone. Written notes didn't bring any response.

The family lived upstairs over a store, and so they could not hear my knock on a downstairs door. But by chance one day, the downstairs door was unlocked, and I happily ran up a long, narrow staircase to a dark hallway on the second floor. I knew the apartment number from the school records, and so I was able to knock on the appropriate door. A large, heavy woman opened it and greeted me in Spanish. Fortunately, I know a few words and was able to greet her in her own language. My accent must have been terrible, however, because she grinned kindly and invited me in, in halting English. We were beginning to communicate.

Mothers usually like to talk about their children, and Mrs. Gonzales was no exception. Rather than treating me like an intruder, she seemed to welcome the chance to talk. Her apartment was clean but gloomy because the place had very few windows. She was all alone except for a TV set and a baby. Adult companionship seemed more than welcome.

Mrs. Gonzales told me the language spoken in the home was entirely Spanish. That was all her husband spoke, and she knew Rudolph felt strange and scared at school. But she also told me Rudolph didn't like his stepfather (her present husband) much and had tantrums at home. Rudolph stayed out later than he was supposed to at night and had fights with neighborhood children. Mrs. Gonzales said she would be quite willing to have Rudolph placed in a special class, if I thought that would help him.

The responsibility of a trust such as that, so freely given with so little basis, weighed on me. I told her I didn't really know yet what I thought about a special class, and I explained how the evaluation team hoped to gain the consultation of a bilingual psychologist. We left it that I'd get back to her as the evaluation progressed.

So I clearly had evidence arguing for disturbed behavior in more than one environment, and Norman's tests, from what he could determine, indicated disturbed thinking patterns and emotional upheaval. Norman and I knew that if we convened the M team, we'd have to recommend ED placement. But we didn't want to do that without resolving the bilingual issue. We kept insisting to Dan that the county supply bilingual input before we would agree to make recommendations. Time passed. It turned into a waiting game.

Then Rudolph had another major violent episode in the classroom. He threw chairs, pounded the walls, banged his head, sobbed, and knocked several of his classmates onto the floor.

Furious at what she was putting up with and at the slowness of the special education evaluation, Rudolph's teacher wrote a nasty letter to the county special education office. She lambasted the inefficiency of the Kingston psychologist and social worker, poor Norman and me. We were taking entirely too long in our evaluation of Rudolph Gonzales, the teacher asserted. Her letter was co-signed by some other teachers.

The teachers were right, in that Norman and I surely were slow in getting anything done about Rudolph. But we had told Rudolph's teacher specifically what the problem was. Rudolph's teacher didn't think bilingual input into the evaluation process was nearly as important as getting the boy out of her classroom. She had a point. And as clearly as Norman and I had tried to explain our own point of view, we had obviously failed to enlist the support or understanding of the teaching staff.

So now our professional credibility was being questioned. Norman and I weren't sure what to do next. Our county supervisors certainly weren't behind us, and the teachers in Kingston wanted immediate placement of Rudolph in the ED classroom. There wasn't any doubt about that!

I went to talk to the Kingston superintendent, Mr. Sorensen, about Rudolph. Mr. Sorensen was the man with whom I had originally interviewed for the job in Kingston and who had impressed me so very much. I thought if Rudolph couldn't get the help he needed from the state or the county, maybe the local school system would be willing to fill in the breach. Maybe Mr. Sorensen would hire a Spanish-speaking aide for the regular classroom, at best, or a bilingual psychologist to help with Rudolph's evaluation, at least.

Mr. Sorensen, a superb superintendent, was still his warm, caring self. But even he honestly didn't know what the trouble was.

"America is a melting pot," he told me sincerely. "All foreign children must learn to be American, and that involves learning to speak English. This little boy will have to learn to adjust to his new environment. Maybe it'll be hard for him in the short run, but it's just what he needs in the long run. I can't see trying to provide this boy with education in Spanish. Why, that would slow down his learning to be a real American."

"But," I demurred, "some people believe in teaching their children to swim by tossing them into the deep end of a swimming pool too. I suppose a lot of those kids make it, but a few drown. Rudolph seems to be one of those kids who are drowning."

"I know you mean well, Ms. Wells," the superintendent replied. "But one thing I believe in is the American way. The faster these Mexican children learn what this country is all about, the better. This boy may be upset now, but he'll learn the language and customs here fastest if he has to make it on his own like everybody else."

"But Mr. Sorensen, Rudolph isn't making it. The way it is now, his teacher wants him out of her classroom."

"Well, if he can't make it in the regular classroom, then special education is the place for him. I believe very strongly in your program, you know, Ms. Wells."

The subtle difference between a little boy with emotional disturbance and a little boy disturbed by cultural differences was certainly difficult to explain. Mr. Sorensen, too, remained unconvinced by my arguments. He said he wouldn't be willing to spend scarce dollars on bilingual classroom staff or a bilingual psychologist. Money was tight, he reminded me. In fact, his own dream of a new high school building had been voted down that very year by the citizens of the town. Everywhere, the major concern was cost containment.

Perhaps it was time to give in. Norman and I talked to Rudolph's teacher again, as well as a few of her closest colleagues who had signed the complaint letter, and decided we were beaten. Rudolph was hurting himself and scaring everyone. In fact, a special placement in an ED classroom seemed the only option available. It really didn't seem likely that, in the event a bilingual evaluation determined Rudolph *not* to have emotional disturbance, the regular school system would hire Spanish-speaking personnel to help him cope in the regular classroom. That seemed like a veritable pipe dream, in fact, after my conference with the superintendent.

So Norman and I decided to bow to the real world and convene the M team. But just before we did so, Dan Dwyer, our supervisor from the county, changed his mind. Somehow he became convinced of the logic involved in securing a bilingual evaluation and he hired a Spanish-speaking psychologist from a neighboring county. It came as a complete surprise at the time, as Norman and I felt so defeated by then. But as I look back on the situation, I imagine the county became nervous that the state might refuse reimbursement on this case if an ED placement were made. Norman and I had certainly made the case visible at the state level, and the state reimbursed the county for many of the costs of the special education program. The state also had the right to refuse reimbursement for cases it felt were improperly evaluated.

The Spanish-speaking psychologist duly performed his tests, and he, too, recommended ED placement. That was something of an anticlimax, but at least it helped Norman and me feel better about such a placement. We had done all we could to examine the situation from all sides. Rudolph, the bilingual psychologist said, might primarily be frustrated by his language and cultural barriers, but the situation had gotten so bad the psychologist didn't believe the boy could make it in a regular classroom. The ED classroom was the only other option available. Why not try it?

Rudolph's entry into the ED classroom was not a smooth event. As I got the story later, he kicked and screamed all the way down the hallway to the special class. Then a few days after he was placed in the room, he really blew.

"Fuckin' pussy!" he yelled, in potent fourth-grade English. "Fuckin' pussy, I'm a mental! I'm a Mexican! I hate Mexicans and mentals! Mexicans are mentals! I hate Mother! Mother hates me! I'll kill the teacher! Kill me!" He hurled his body into his classmates, his teacher, and the wall; he pulled his own hair and everybody else's, until it flew about in great gobs.

Rudolph didn't speak perfect English, but he surely could speak lucidly. His biggest problem seemed not to be an inability to use the English language but rather something different but intimately related—his sense of not belonging, of not being like other kids.

Clearly, the placement in the special classroom had made him feel even more unlike other kids. That was, of course, the reason I'd hoped to meet his needs another way.

But from an administrative point of view, Rudolph's tantrums could be handled better in the special classroom. It was smaller, and the students enrolled were all used to outbursts. There was a little "quiet room" in the back to which Rudolph could be taken for a cooling-off period by the teacher and her aide, if he wasn't totally wild.

But when Rudolph really blew, the teacher and her aide together couldn't hold him down. One of them had to run for the principal, and the principal had to get the boys' gym teacher to help him haul Rudolph home bodily.

Well, the M team recommendations had included counseling for the boy and his family. The recommendations had even suggested bilingual counseling and bilingual tutoring.

Where were these services to be found? There was no chance that Rudolph's family would take him to the guidance clinic. They hadn't even a telephone, much less a car. Rudolph's mother and his stepfather would have been unable to use the guidance clinic's services anyway, if they had had the desire or ability to get there. That slick-walled Anglo facility would have scared them right back to Texas. And nobody would have spoken their language at the clinic.

Of course, I had been looking around for bilingual resources for Rudolph ever since he was first referred. The problem was that resources were virtually unavailable. There were indeed two agencies for Hispanics in two different neighboring towns. One was the Spanish Farm Workers Cooperative; the other was Hispanic Services.

Both these agencies had said they were unable to meet the particular need of counseling or tutoring for a fourth grader in the school or to counsel with a family in the home. They said they could provide job counseling for adults at their offices and urged me to refer Rudolph's parents. I did tell them about the services, but Mr. Gonzales was already working and neither parent was looking for a new job.

Both agencies shared my perception that bilingual services in the schools were a growing need. Hispanic Services even solicited a letter from me to that effect later, which they planned to use in negotiating with the county to develop these services. Staff in both programs were articulate and concerned. But they didn't have the staff or the policy to work with a child such as Rudolph, and they didn't have any suggestions to make about where to look next for help. In fact, there just weren't any other resources, as far as anybody knew.

I made a minor breakthrough by consulting with the Spanish teacher in the high school. I thought she might know of some students who might be able to tutor Rudolph in Spanish. She didn't know of any students who could speak that well, but she had a neighbor who came from Spain. The neighbor was fluent in English, as well as Spanish, and might be willing to serve as a classroom volunteer.

I contacted the neighbor, Mrs. Lopez, and she willingly agreed to tutor Rudolph. That seemed to help him a bit, but Mrs. Lopez spoke Castilian Spanish, which was considerably different from Rudolph's Texas dialect. She could help him somewhat in his academic studies, but her individual attention didn't seem to reach his aching guts. Her Spanish language might be intelligible to Rudolph, but her cultural orientation was as different from his as was that of the Anglo. Rudolph continued to have his tantrums pretty regularly. I continued to look for new resources.

During a home visit, Rudolph's mother suggested that Rudolph might behave better if he were prouder of his appearance. She mentioned that her husband's paycheck from the canning factory covered basic needs but didn't leave anything for school clothing. It was true that Rudolph had a motley sort of look about him, which was not assisted much by his short trouser legs and tattered shirt sleeves.

Rudolph's natural father was in prison in Texas because of some long-ago infraction and had never contributed to the boy's support. Rudolph's present family should thus qualify for stepfather aid.* I took Mrs. Gonzales to the welfare department myself, as she had no car, and I expected she would be overwhelmed by the place. As I expected, there was no assistance offered to help a Spanish-speaking mother read and fill out forms in English. I did it for her. Eventually, Mrs. Gonzales began to get a monthly check for $60 or so.

Rudolph got new winter clothes, but that wasn't the key. He still acted absolutely awful.

I found a small new program for migrants that ran a bilingual school and clinic in a neighboring county. The possibility of Rudolph's transferring into this program excited me for awhile. But it didn't work out. The staff was interested in Rudolph and sympathetic about the boy's problems, but the boy lived in the wrong county and didn't really qualify as a migrant anymore.

And then the special new resource himself appeared, Juan Salazar. I met him at a party hosted by a mutual friend. Shortly after I walked into the party, I spied the young man, and I determined immediately to talk with him.

Juan had a large, heavyset body, a wave of thick black hair, and expressive dark eyes. He was dressed almost formally and caught up in animated conversation with our hostess. The hostess was a person I knew fairly well, so I didn't think she'd mind if I joined them. Perhaps this stranger might know something that would be useful for Rudolph.

I threaded my way around the forest of plants behind which I had hidden myself (being normally quite shy at parties) and sauntered up to my hostess and her friend as casually as I could manage. I just about hit the jackpot.

It turned out that Juan and I had several mutual acquaintances besides our hostess that evening. Just by chance, he came from a town only a few miles from a place in New Mexico where I'd once served as a VISTA volunteer. We swapped yarns happily all evening.

Then, when Juan was quite mellow with good wine, I mentioned that I knew this poor, dear little boy who was so unhappy and needed counseling in Spanish. It turned out that Juan thought he might like to counsel professionally someday. He was not professionally trained in counseling, but he did have a B.A. in psychology and a liking for children.

He worked for Hispanic Services. No, he said, Hispanic Services did not usually have time for home visits, school visits, or counseling with children. But maybe, if he asked his boss in just the right way, he could get permission to work with this child occasionally at school.

It certainly wasn't a reliable or a professional proposal. But it might be better than nothing. I decided to risk it and urged Juan to approach his supervisor to see whether he could get the time.

---

*Stepfather aid is no longer available to help needy families today.

Hispanic Services was a small agency, and it turned out that Juan's supervisor was one of the office staff to whom I had already spoken. So he knew of the case. Because Juan wanted to try out his counseling wings, the supervisor gave his consent.

I went with Juan to meet with the Gonzales parents and Rudolph early one evening. Juan explained the role of Hispanic Services and explored his interest in working informally with Rudolph. Rudolph looked at Juan out of the corner of one eye, but both of his eyes gleamed.

Juan was at that stage in life where boyhood was just shifting into the solid adult. He exuded warm energy and a kind of gutsy machismo. It was clear he radiated something which filled Rudolph with admiration. He was young enough that Rudolph could feel somewhat like him, yet Juan was clearly a grown-up as well.

If Rudolph could just identify with a positive Mexican role model, maybe he wouldn't hate himself so much anymore. So often in class he said, "I'm a mental, I'm a Mexican, I hate Mexicans, Mexicans are mentals." Maybe Rudolph could achieve an A in a logic course with his linguistic connections, but he was killing himself in the process.

Juan probably visited with the Gonzales family together only two or three times and with Rudolph over the course of the rest of the school year only a half-dozen times more. But his presence was electric. The class was awed by him. Rudolph's teacher gave Juan the floor when he visited. She had him talk about New Mexico, about Texas, about the Spanish-American heritage. And then, when the class was at rapt attention, she let Rudolph go off and have private, coveted walks and talks with Juan.

Juan told Rudolph's classmates that he and Rudolph had something special that they shared between them—they could speak *two* languages, not just one. The status of bilingualism soared.

Juan also spent some time in private conference with Rudolph's teacher, explaining to her what he saw as differences in behavioral norms between Texas-Mexican children and the average Anglo child. One example the teacher passed on to me concerned eye contact. She had always thought Rudolph was shifty-eyed and therefore sneaky. Juan told her that children of Rudolph's background were taught at home to avoid direct eye contact with adults as a sign of respect.

Rudolph didn't exactly turn into a model student, but he calmed down a whole lot. If he started to go into a tantrum, the mention of Mr. Salazar's name was enough to redirect his attention. His attack behavior on other children, the teachers, and the wall ceased completely. He stopped saying he hated Mexicans.

At the M team meeting at the end of the year, the ED teacher recommended that Rudolph be allowed to take some of his nonacademic subjects, like art and music, with the rest of his regular class at the beginning of the next year. She felt it wouldn't be long before Rudolph would be able to make it in the regular classroom on his own.

DISCUSSION AND STUDY QUESTIONS

Culture is the knowledge, values, and behaviors practiced by a racial or ethnic group that are preserved and transmitted from generation to generation. It is an integral part of our sense of self, of a feeling of rootedness in a group. Such everyday things as

speaking the language that everyone else speaks or valuing the same kinds of interpersonal relationships occur among people who share a culture. In a world charac-
terized by multinational corporations and jet planes, people move about a great deal.
This leads to the juxtaposition of more than one culture in the same geographical
area.

Different areas cope with the presence of more than one culture in varied ways.
Cosmopolitan cities, such as New York or San Francisco, may accept it as a matter of
course, developing special services as needed (such as bilingual education, for example). Other areas, such as Emmett County, are less willing to adapt to the needs of
members of different cultures. Obviously, the existence of culturally relevant services
facilitates the work of social workers. A more basic point, however, is the need for social workers to understand that people have to have a cultural identity if they are
going to feel whole and secure. This chapter is a good example of this basic fact. The
social worker's persistence in working for recognition by the county of the integrity
of Rudolph's culture paid off in his moving from feeling worthless to worthwhile.

1. Do you think the Hispanic people had a right to find jobs in Emmett County,
   even if they competed for those jobs with local residents? Do you think they
   had a right to apply for financial assistance? Be sure to provide specific reasons for your opinions.
2. The author mentions that the Emmett County Welfare Department provided
   no special assistance for Spanish-speaking applicants. What effect would this
   have on the number of applicants who would actually be able to get themselves certified for aid?
*3. Had you been the author in this situation, would you have held out as long
   as she did to secure the bilingual psychological consultation? Why or why
   not? What problems did the "waiting game" present? What were some possible positive results of the whole affair?
*4. Have you ever practiced social work with a member of a different culture?
   What special issues arose, if any? How did you familiarize yourself with the
   nature of your client's culture? If you have not yet practiced with someone
   from another culture, how would you plan to learn about your client's culture?

---

*Questions notated with an asterisk are intended for advanced students who have had or are
currently having some social work practice experience and who have made at least a tentative
commitment to the profession.

CHAPTER **14**

Clarette Emalina Jones and Jeffrey Redcloud

or: Psychological, Ethnic, Socioeconomic, and
Cultural Factors Influencing Behavior

Concepts Covered in This Chapter

1. Socioeconomic standing as a factor influencing life styles and life chances
2. Ethnicity as a factor influencing life styles and life chances
3. Homogeneity as a source of social cohesion
4. Difference as a factor in social conflict
5. The interaction of cultural, family, community, and organizational factors in the creation of social problems
6. The interaction of self-concept and social behavior
7. The roles of professional social workers in addressing problems created by intergroup differences

Learning Objectives   By the end of this chapter you should be able to

1. Define social class
2. List at least five ways social class influences life style
3. List at least three ways social class influences life chances
4. Distinguish between race and ethnicity
5. List at least five ways ethnicity influences life style
6. List at least three ways ethnicity influences life chances
7. Discuss at least three sources of intergroup conflict
8. Using one case example from this chapter, discuss the interaction of cultural, family, community, and organizational factors in the creation of problems
9. List at least five different systems with which the social worker in this chapter worked (or should have worked) to address the problems of either Clarette or Jeffrey

When I was considering how best to revise this book for its second edition, colleagues suggested that ethnic and cultural minority content be added to increase the usefulness of the book in teaching social work in a multicultural society. Although I considered this an excellent suggestion, I was stymied at first because Emmett County, rural area that it is, has very few ethnic or cultural minorities. I worked with only one or two persons of this background besides the Rudolph Gonzales family described in Chapter 13. However, in an area where minority persons are few, it is perhaps even more important for the social worker to respect and understand diversity since few other people have such experience. In seeking appropriate additional materials for this book, I consulted with various members of the special education staffs in Kingston and Orangetown. The following case examples illustrate work of the Kingston special education team.

Clarette Emalina Jones was a darling little girl with big black eyes and lots of curly black hair, which tumbled in attractive ringlets about her head. Her skin was also black, or rather, it was a rich, smooth brown, different from almost everybody else's in town. Clarette Emalina lived with her grandmother in the poor section of Kingston, in a small wooden house with thin walls and drafty windows that let in too much of the winter cold. Clarette's grandmother kept the household immaculate, what little household there was. There was no carpet on the floor, only bare linoleum, which was kept scrupulously clean. The house boasted no comfortable furniture—just a few wooden chairs and a small card table for eating, all kept carefully free from dust by a practiced hand. Cherished black and white photographs of distant family members adorned the walls, along with various religious articles such as pictures of Jesus and the Last Supper. Both grandmother and child slept on a lumpy double mattress on the floor of the only bedroom. The entire house was covered with tar paper on the outside, which helped protect it from the weather but did nothing to enhance its status in the town.

There was a reason why Clarette Emalina slept right with her grandmother, a reason that went beyond the fact that the little house contained only one mattress. Even if there had been another place to sleep, Clarette would have snuggled as close to her grandmother as she could. She had night terrors. She would awaken screaming almost every night, frantic that she and everyone in her nightmare were being shot at by a madman with a gun.

Was Clarette another child exposed to too much TV violence? Not exactly. Young as she was, only seven, Clarette had lived through the reality of what she dreamed. The madman with the gun was her own father. Clarette's father and mother were divorced when the little girl was almost five years old. The relationship between her parents was troubled even after the divorce, and Mr. Jones became jealous of every new boyfriend of Clarette's mother, real or imagined. One night, in a rage, he broke into the house and began shooting wildly at everyone in sight. Those persons happened to be only Clarette, her mother, and her brother. Clarette was slightly injured. Fortunately the others escaped physical harm, but all were scarred emotionally, very deeply. Clarette's father went to jail for his crime. Still, Clarette remained terrified of her father and feared that he might return some day.

After the shooting, Clarette's mother sent her to live with her grand mother. She thought a new environment might help the little girl forget her frightening experience. To an average middle-class white person, sending a frightened little girl away to live with a grandmother might seem like an odd way to help her overcome her fears. But then, the average white family rarely depends on grandparents for ongoing shelter and major financial support throughout many years of development. Also, the average white child probably has never actually lived with a grandmother over long periods of time, thus having the opportunity to know her almost more intimately than the mother herself.

For black families, however, survival is more difficult than it is for whites. The following comments should be viewed as generalizations, not true for all African Americans but reasonably true for many. Jobs are harder to get and keep for blacks than for whites. Also, they don't usually get paid as well as whites. So the extended family becomes crucial for survival. It is very common for grandparents, aunts, uncles, and parents to live together in one small home or apartment, where they can share expenses for rent and food. Often a grandmother cares for a grandchild while the mother works; grandmother thus provides free day-care services, which enables the mother to bring money into the home. The extended family provides great strength and stability for African Americans in an often hostile environment.

Clarette thus was not sent to live with a grandmother whom she hardly knew. She was sent to live with a grandmother with whom she had lived for years before, when her own mother was experiencing hard times. Clarette and the grandmother loved each other and had a good relationship. Clarette's mother decided not to stay with the grandmother herself at this time because she had a job in a neighboring city.

Clarette entered second grade in Kingston, where the other children teased her because of her brown skin, her black ringlets, her threadbare clothes, and her different accent. It wasn't long before the little girl was falling behind in her studies, fidgeting constantly in her seat, and occasionally hitting out in anger at her provocative classmates. She was referred to special education for evaluation with suspected emotional disturbance.

Children didn't tease Clarette because they were innately mean or unkind. Rather, they had rarely seen anyone like her, and they had learned that black people were "inferior" from their general social environment: for example, from comments, sometimes subtle, made by relatives, neighbors, friends, and even parents. The only ethnic minority people the Kingston children had had a fair amount of experience with were the migrants, normally Hispanics; and migrant children were by definition transient, only in school for part of the year. Kingston children were uncomfortable around Clarette because she looked and sounded so different from everybody else, and they didn't know what to make of her, and because they had vague notions that she wasn't as "good" as they were. So they giggled, pointed, poked, and teased.

Had Clarette remained in the inner-city neighborhood school she had attended prior to the shooting, she would probably never have been referred to special education. According to the Kingston team, Clarette's disruptive behaviors in the classroom were so mild that they probably would have warranted little attention in her original urban environment. But in Kingston she stood out like a sore thumb. Her second-grade teacher didn't know what to do with her, so why not try special education?

Because of the mildness of Clarette's disturbed behavior in school, mostly simple distractibility, neither Jim Gottwald, the social worker assigned to the case, nor

Norman Werner, the school psychologist, initially considered her to be special education material. But Norman's initial psychological tests, especially his projective tests, identified a high degree of emotional disturbance. Therefore, upon consultation together, Norman and Jim decided to carry the evaluation further. Jim Gottwald went to visit the grandmother to learn how the child behaved in the home and community.

Information that Jim learned from the grandmother helped explain a great deal. Through his home visit and assessment of the new information, the social worker was able to interpret for the rest of the staff what life was like for Clarette. He explained about the ordeal Clarette had recently experienced, her current night terrors, and her ongoing poverty. In addition, he helped the staff understand that the grandmother's health was poor; that although she loved the child, the responsibility of caring for Clarette overwhelmed her at times. Jim explained that the grandmother felt alone with the heavy responsibility of rearing a scared and very unhappy little girl. The grandmother herself was nearly 80 and partially crippled with arthritis. Clarette's screaming every night kept them both from sleeping, exacerbating the grandmother's health problems.

The special education team now had evidence of disturbance both at home and at school. They determined that placement in an ED classroom might be helpful to Clarette and to the grandmother as well. Clarette would have a more structured, protected classroom environment and the grandmother could benefit from regular supportive consultations and visits from special education staff. Clarette was indeed placed, and her behavior in the classroom improved.

Counseling with Jim helped diminish Clarette's constant fears. Children in the tightly controlled classroom were not allowed to tease her, and she gradually began to make friends. Her attention span for her studies improved. The staff took care to visit the grandmother, and occasionally they were able to bring donated toys and clothes to help the meager household budget. The grandmother was the classic ideal client: she openly appreciated everything that was done for her and thanked everyone involved to an almost embarrassing extent.

All in all, this was a pretty successful case while it lasted. Eventually, the grandmother died and Clarette's mother took the little girl back to the city. In all likelihood, in her urban environment Clarette would be enrolled in regular education classes as a matter of routine. Her behavior and physical appearance would more nearly approximate the mean there. She would no longer look and sound so different that other children would tease her, and, in addition, the considerable attention from the special education team that she had received in Kingston had helped her to become more consciously aware of her own needs and feelings, including ways to deal with anger besides hitting out at others.

Jeffrey Redcloud also stood out like a sore thumb in Kingston because of his different appearance. Jeffrey was a Native American boy, adopted into a family new to Kingston. The family moved to Kingston because of a job transfer of the husband and father. They brought with them three biological children and one adopted child, Jeffrey. The adoptive family was white, not Native American, which made life more difficult for Jeffrey. Ideally, the boy would have been placed with a family from the same ethnic and cultural background as his own, to help him develop a clear sense of personal and cultural identity. But a Native American family must not have been available at the time Jeffrey needed a permanent home. Although names have been changed in this case to protect people's privacy, ethnicity is portrayed as it was in the actual case.

The biological children all melted into Kingston without evident difficulty. Jeffrey, however, endured various taunts and teases because of his different appearance. His hair was thick, black, and straight, and he wore it long. His eyes were black and his skin a light reddish brown. He clearly looked different from most children in Kingston. In addition, Jeffrey came with a psychiatric diagnosis of schizophrenia. This was not known to the school at first. He suffered from attention deficit syndrome as well, and needed to take Ritalin, a drug that helps children with this diagnosis keep "on task," or concentrate on what they are trying to do. All these difficulties made Jeffrey seem quite different indeed.

Jeffrey's behavior in the regular classroom was almost immediately disruptive. In addition to the fact that he was goaded toward misbehavior by the teasing of other children, he himself had a very hard time concentrating on anything for long enough to know what he was supposed to do, part of the symptomatology of his attention deficit syndrome. He wouldn't listen, not to anyone. He often forgot to take his medication. He fidgeted in his seat, broke pencils and pens, tore pieces of paper into tiny strips, and threw them all over the floor and wouldn't pick them up. He snapped at the teacher frequently, with such provocative phrases as "I won't," and stole from his classmates. A referral to special education with suspected emotional disturbance was made.

Again, the special education team evaluated Jeffrey's symptoms and needs very carefully because a label of ED and assignment to a special classroom would be just one more difference Jeffrey would have to endure. But upon investigating the home situation, Jim Gottwald, the social worker assigned to the case, learned that the boy frequently beat up his adoptive mother. He was a large boy of junior high age, and when he lost his temper he became uncontrollable. The father often was not home to protect the mother because of his job, which required a good deal of travel. Hence the social history documented clear evidence of difficult behavior at home as well as at school. Jeffrey was diagnosed as emotionally disturbed and placed in the ED classroom.

In the ED classroom, the specially trained teacher strictly supervised the taking of medications and utilized a highly structured program of behavior modification. As a result, Jeffrey's behaviors changed. His language at school remained occasionally objectionable, but he listened and generally followed instructions. He no longer stole or broke his pencils and pens into pieces. Paradoxically, however, Jeffrey's behavior at home worsened. Even with coaching from the special education staff, Jeffrey's mother became less and less able to handle the boy. Periodically, he beat her nearly to the point of hospitalization. She rarely got angry about the beatings, as she felt so sorry for Jeffrey; she understood that he felt different from everybody else. The special education staff got more upset about the physical attacks than the mother did; no one could really understand why the behavior modification techniques developed for the home weren't working, and the staff began to become seriously concerned about the mother's physical safety.

Finally, after a particularly damaging beating, the special education team sat down with Jeffrey's mother and reviewed with her once more other resources she had to help in coping with Jeffrey's behavior. This time the mother chose to file charges in court. In that way, the special education team explained to her, Jeffrey could be ordered temporarily into a county-run group home, where he could be counseled regarding his behavior and put on a strict behavior modification program. It was hoped that later on Jeffrey would be able to return to his own home with a better understanding of all that home had to offer, and with more desire to protect his place within it.

The mother took the giant step of pressing charges against her adoptive son. Jeffrey duly appeared in court. But the judge did not order placement in the group home. That was understandable because the group home was full, and there was nothing else to offer. Less understandable was the fact that the judge did not order Jeffrey into detention until a place in the group home should open. He simply gave the boy a short lecture and released him into the custody of his mother. Norman Werner's comment afterward was a pained "Justice is blind until you get a dollar bill." In other words, without adequate funding, foster or other custodial care simply is not provided despite evident need.

Jeffrey went home and proceeded to beat his mother up again; this time the mother called for help in the middle of the beating. She was able to reach the boy's pediatrician, who arrived at the home to declare the boy dangerous to himself and others. The pediatrician called the police, who took the boy into custody. Jeffrey was then commited to the state hospital. It should be noted that the expense of in-patient hospitalization for a boy such as Jeffrey is much greater than the cost of supervision in a group home. The "economy" of saving dollars by withholding needed services is often false economy indeed.

How are the cases of Clarette Emalina Jones and Jeffrey Redcloud similar? Both children suffered from the fact that they stood out physically and culturally in an environment where almost everyone else was white. The special education team hesitated to make a placement in the ED classroom in both cases because they hesitated to label the children as even more different. In the case of Clarette at least, the little girl probably would never have been referred to special education in a situation in which she did not stand out as so physically different. However, combining the children's personal problems with the environmental circumstances and the resources available in Kingston, a special education placement was determined appropriate, after careful evaluation. In the case of Jeffrey, it was lack of additional supportive services from the community that eventually led to his full-scale hospitalization as a danger to himself and others.

DISCUSSION AND STUDY QUESTIONS

Like Chapter 9, this chapter involves scarce resources and some of their effects. However, it primarily examines the effects of racial and cultural minority status on young children. It discusses two children who stood out in a white rural environment because they were nonwhite. In the case of one of the children, Clarette Emalina Jones, not only did she look different but she *sounded* different as well. Her accent and her appearance opened her to ridicule and rejection by her peers.

Rural people are not intentionally more cruel than any others when it comes to responding to people who are different. But they have had less exposure to difference, and hence less practice in dealing with it. The children of Kingston rarely saw anyone who wasn't white, with hair that ranged in color from blond to dark brown, from straight to wavy. None of the children born in Kingston had black hair or black eyes, and certainly they didn't have natural tightly curled ringlets. More than that, the accents of all the Kingston-born people were almost exactly the same, making an urban black dialect sound quite peculiar. People everywhere have a tendency to view the way they speak their native tongue as the correct way—everybody else's dialect "murders the language!" Hence difference, in a normally homogeneous rural area, tends to be viewed not only as peculiar but also as inferior and bad.

How do children—how does anyone—react to ridicule and rejection? One way the two children described in this chapter reacted was that their behavior in the classroom also became "different."

1. Can you remember being rejected when you were a young child? How did it make you feel? How did you react? Did you keep your feelings inside or did you "act your feelings out" in some way? If you acted them out, what did you do?

2. Can you remember a time as a child when you or your peers rejected another child because he or she was different? How did you feel about it at the time? How do you feel about it today?

3. To what social class do you belong? Justify your answer by listing the specific characteristics or resources you have that you feel define your class.

4. Identify at least five of your values or behaviors that you believe to be related to your social class standing. Then interview someone from a different social class and compare your values or behaviors with theirs.

5. Take a moment to review your current situation, thinking especially about your possessions and your accomplishments. How much credit do you give yourself for your successes? What other people have been important in getting you to where you are now? How do you think answering this question might make you a better social worker?

*6. Jeffrey Redcloud's disruptive behavior in the home and classroom probably related to a variety of factors regarding who he was as a person and the environment in which he found himself. Identify as many of these factors as you can and explain how they might interrelate to produce the disturbed young man described in this chapter.

*7. After Jeffrey's court appearance, Norman Werner commented, "Justice is blind without a dollar bill." What do you think he meant?

*8. Identify a helping situation in which you were involved that included intergroup differences. How did these differences affect what happened? What did you do that now, looking back, seems to you to have been in response to the intergroup differences that existed?

---

*Questions notated with an asterisk are intended for advanced students who have had or are currently having some social work practice experience and who have made at least a tentative commitment to the profession.

CHAPTER 15

Mrs. Hosmer Isn't Home

or: Working with Families Where Problem Denial
Is a Lifestyle

Concepts Covered in This Chapter

1. Stigma
2. Value conflicts
3. A change-of-life baby
4. Mainstreaming
5. Partializing a problem in social work

Learning Objectives After reading this chapter you should be able to

1. Define *stigma* and discuss its significance for the delivery of social work services
2. List at least three values that conflict with social work values
3. Define a change-of-life baby and discuss why such babies sometimes are seen as problems by their parents
4. Define *mainstreaming* and list at least three special needs groups that can often benefit from this process
5. Define *partializing* a problem and give an example, using the Hosmer family

Brenda Hosmer was a pretty little fourth-grade girl who looked as if she had stepped right out of the pages of a mail-order catalog. Her clothes were fresh, colorful, and clean; her complexion glowed peaches and cream; and her bright blond hair shone with the finest shampoo and primping. When she smiled, she showed lovely dimples and a set of perfect white teeth. She was a daughter any parent could be proud of. She even wore tiny white earrings most of the time and kept her socks clean and her shoes shiny.

But Brenda was also flunking out of the fourth grade in Kingston. And there wasn't anything wrong with her intelligence. She was smart, and she didn't have any kind of physical disability to interfere with the functioning of her keen mind. Brenda's vision and hearing were tested within the normal range, and she didn't have any type of learning disability. She just wouldn't do her schoolwork.

It had been that way right through school, but Brenda's previous teachers had passed her anyway. She just looked too good to flunk. There just couldn't be any real problem, or so they thought. But when Brenda got to the fourth grade, she ran into Mrs. Lyons. Mrs. Lyons was a no-nonsense teacher with lots of demands, and soon she and Brenda were at war.

"She's a totally unpredictable child," wrote Mrs. Lyons in her ED referral. "One day she may act nice to the other children in the classroom, and the next day she is mean to everyone. She may be nasty to me today and nice tomorrow. She is never organized or prepared for school, and she never completes her work. She seems a very unhappy child, and I am afraid it is her unhappiness that is keeping her from progressing in school."

It wasn't long before I learned this was probably going to be another one of those evening families. Norman, who set up the schedule for the initial staffing at the school, said that both parents demanded to come to the staffing meeting and both worked during the day. They insisted on a staffing meeting at 5:00 in the afternoon, after they got out of work.

Norman said he had agreed because Mrs. Lyons had warned him this would be a difficult family to work with. They would not want it known their child was being considered for a classroom for children with emotional disturbance. They probably would not agree to an evaluation in the first place. And if they did agree and the evaluation process revealed that little Brenda would indeed meet the criteria for enrollment in special education, then it was going to be a delicate job to try to persuade the parents to agree. But Mrs. Lyons felt it would be worth a try because Brenda was getting nowhere in the regular classroom.

Mrs. Lyons had inside information about the family because she had distant relatives who were distant relatives of the Hosmers. The Hosmers were proud of their respectability in the community. They kept their house spotless and shiny inside and out, and they wanted their children to be spotless and shiny too. Any indication that things with the family were anything but perfect would be fiercely fought.

The meeting for Brenda's initial staffing was stiff indeed. Mr. Hosmer filled most of the meeting by insisting that teachers and schools in his time were much better than today and that if only his daughter had things done right for her at school, the way things were done when he was a boy, then nobody would need to be bothered by a meeting such as this one today.

Mr. Hosmer announced that he had had an important commission in the military at one time, and so he knew exactly how discipline should be maintained. He assured the staff that he maintained discipline in the home with military precision. Perhaps if Mrs. Lyons would just do things his way in the classroom, Brenda would get her work done and everything would be all right.

I could see Mrs. Lyons wanted to ask Mr. Hosmer why Brenda came to school every day without her homework done. Or at least, I thought I could see this—Mrs. Lyons's face looked so strange and so twisted. But alas, she didn't quite work up the nerve.

Instead, Mrs. Lyons cautiously described to the Hosmers the patterns of behavior that made Brenda difficult to work with in the regular classroom, avoiding the issue of what happened at home. Mrs. Lyons explained that Brenda wouldn't pay attention, interrupted constantly, called people names, refused to complete her assignments at school, and sometimes sulked and refused to do anything at all. She then politely asked Mr. Hosmer whether he had any ideas for her regarding how to make Brenda more compliant at school.

"Hell, that's your job, right, teacher?" he replied. And he looked entirely self-righteous, even pleased with himself.

Spontaneously, Norman Werner, the school psychologist, and I began to describe the ED classroom option to Mr. Hosmer in cleverly militaristic terms. Nobody besides ourselves apparently noticed we were having a little fun, but for us, it lightened the experience of that conference considerably! We explained that the ED classroom was fully confined by four solid walls (Brenda's present classroom was of the open variety) so attention could be more effectively commanded and that the ED teacher was trained in a consistent regimen that would require strict obedience and controlled change of identified target behaviors.

We explained that we didn't know at this time whether this type of game plan might meet Brenda's educational requirements, but we would like to requisition Mr. Hosmer's informed consent to investigate the merits of the situation.

Mr. Hosmer seemed flattered by all this attention and the strategic-sounding words, and he agreed to permit the ED evaluation.

I should have scheduled my social history appointment with the parents right then because I knew they both worked, but somehow I didn't think of that at the time. Maybe I was too caught up in the tension and drama of that initial meeting. But I called the Hosmers several times to make an appointment in the next couple of weeks, and I never reached anybody.

Then one day I tried calling the Hosmer home just before I left work in Kingston, somewhere around five o'clock in the afternoon. A female voice answered the telephone. Good, I thought immediately. Brenda's mother, probably.

"Mrs. Hosmer?" I asked.

"Mrs. Hosmer isn't home," the voice replied. I was to hear this reply on numerous occasions in the future.

I asked the voice whether she knew when I might be able to reach Mrs. Hosmer.

"Well, she should be home now," the voice answered. And then, very politely: "May I ask who's calling? I'll try to have her call you back."

"This is Carolyn Wells from the school," I replied briefly. I thought the voice might belong to a neighbor. The Hosmers might be trying to keep their daughter's involvement in special education a secret, so I wasn't about to reveal any more information than that.

But this voice seemed to know who I was. "Oh, from the special education program?" it asked.

"Yes," I answered without elaboration.

"Well, hello, I'm Tina, Brenda's next oldest sister!" the girl introduced herself to my surprise. "I've just dropped out of college for awhile, and I'll be living here for now. You just can't imagine how bad things are for Brenda here at home, and that's one of the reasons I'm sticking around. I hope the school can get her into special education. Mom's in favor of it, but Dad says he won't permit Brenda to be placed in some crazy special class."

"Well, that is really why I'm calling, to talk with your parents more about Brenda. Will you have your mother or your father call me?"

But Tina wasn't about to be silenced. She went on eagerly. "Dad's always cracking Brenda on the butt, and Mom and I can't stand it. He's always acting like he's still in the army."

This was interesting information, but receiving it in this way could cause problems. Family members testifying against each other in private to an outsider could create all sorts of realistic paranoia. That might result in Mr. Hosmer's refusal to permit Brenda to receive special education services.

I thanked Tina for her comments and asked her to let her parents know I'd like to meet with them. Tina was welcome to participate in the meeting, I said, if her parents would agree. Meanwhile, would she have her mother or her father call me?

They didn't, and I kept trying to reach one of them. Finally I got Tina again. Neither of the Hosmer parents was at home. As cooperative as ever, Tina agreed to set up a meeting time with her parents and call me about it herself. I let her take that responsibility.

Tina called me the next day with an appointment date and time. She wanted to talk again, and I heard a fair amount more about family stress before I was able tactfully to end the conversation.

Tina called again the next week to cancel the first appointment and reschedule. This time I called the Hosmers in the evening to try to confirm the date. Again, the phone was answered by Tina: "Mrs. Hosmer isn't home." Tina explained that her mother was at church and that she herself would be there, too, except she had returned too late from a shopping trip to go with her mother. Mr. Hosmer was home, however; he confirmed the appointment date for the social history. The appointment was in the evening, after my normal working hours. That was the only time he would consider.

There it was again. If I insisted on a meeting time that would fit into my own working hours, it was probable Mr. Hosmer would refuse to meet with me at all. Then there was virtually no chance Brenda would be able to participate in special education. If I catered to the Hosmers' schedule, on the other hand, I was inconveniencing myself and my own family.

The night of the appointment, I felt weary but not too surprised when Mr. Hosmer didn't attend the meeting he scheduled. I thought of my husband waiting home for a late supper and wondered whether my values were in the right place. But Mrs. Hosmer and Tina were present, looking anxious, and I thought that as long as we were together at last, I could at least gather Brenda's social history. I would have to attempt my public relations work with Mr. Hosmer at another time.

Mother and daughter clearly belonged to a coalition. Mr. Hosmer should have been home to defend himself, although perhaps the mother–daughter coalition was precisely why he wasn't there! The two women said they were becoming active in a local evangelical church, partly to develop enough spiritual power to defy their respective husband and father, Mr. Hosmer. Mrs. Hosmer and Tina expressed all sorts of resentment against Mr. Hosmer, and it was obvious that the veneer binding them all together in the respectable world of the intact nuclear family was thin indeed.

In the midst of all the potent feelings, I had a difficult time collecting the social history information regarding Brenda, the purpose for my visit. I was beginning to suspect the family could use the services of a family therapist. I had done that sort of work in the past, but that wasn't my role with the school special education program. I would need to channel the family pain with care, here, during my social history interview and then make an appropriate referral. I simply couldn't provide ongoing family therapy myself because of lack of time and the potential for role conflict.

In fact, I found myself doing a great deal of referring in my job as a school social worker. All kinds of problems that needed attention revealed themselves during social history interviews, and I couldn't intervene personally in many of them. I also had to do some mighty fancy footwork during interviews to enable family members to express important thoughts and feelings to me but not to open themselves up so wide they would resent my intrusion into their privacy later. Usually, I succeeded in straddling that fence pretty well, but there had been a couple of situations already in Orangetown where families later complained that I "made" them talk too much.

So I firmly kept the interview focused until I had the early developmental information for Brenda, all normal. Then I asked about Brenda's behavior at present in the home. It was at this time that the feelings broke loose.

"Brenda's behavior is absolutely awful," Tina said. "She won't study, won't do her chores, won't do anything she's told. She gets spanked all the time, and she still won't do what she's told. But it isn't her fault."

"It isn't her fault?" I repeated, leaving an opening to continue.

Mrs. Hosmer began to sob. "Mr. Hosmer never wanted Brenda," she cried. "And I didn't, either. Brenda was a mistake. All the other children were in their teens when she was born. I was tired, and I was so looking forward to some time to myself. Brenda is a cross to bear."

Mrs. Hosmer went on to describe Brenda as a cranky baby who had grown into an unpleasant and disobedient child. Brenda actually seemed to enjoy making her parents angry at her. That made sense to me because a child who cannot gain attention in positive ways will often experiment with negative.

Tina said she could get her sister to study and behave better than her mother could and that she tried hard to correct the child. Tina was afraid for Brenda at times because when her father got too angry with the little girl, he would spank her hard. The father had never really injured Brenda yet, Tina said, but spanking made the little girl more stubborn than before, and then nobody could do anything with her at all.

Mrs. Hosmer then said that perhaps things could be better with the family situation if she herself didn't have to work. She had a factory job, she said, and she hated it. But her husband insisted she earn extra income so he could continue his endless remodeling projects in and around the house.

I let the feelings run on for awhile, and then I summarized the situation for the two Hosmer women as they had described it to me. Mr. Hosmer was perceived as trying to run the family like the army, and the adult women didn't like it. They were, in fact, trying to gain spiritual renewal from a church to resist him more effectively. Brenda was a family problem, in that neither parent could control her easily, and Tina had a hard time handling Brenda too.

There was a problem, then, in the interaction between Mr. and Mrs. Hosmer themselves and between the parents and Brenda. There was some, though a lesser, problem in the relationship between the sisters. Another problem involved Mrs. Hosmer's full-time work outside the home, which she didn't like.

Their situation was, I explained, clearly one that warranted family counseling. I described the services of the Emmett County Guidance Clinic and urged the women to utilize them. Counselors at the clinic, I explained, would not try to force them to make any particular decision. Rather, the counselor's task would be to help the Hosmers individually and as a group explore and clarify their relationships and goals and help make their lives more satisfying.

I was concerned enough about the family situation that I spent a good deal of extra time with the two women that evening. When I left, I thought there was a chance they might seek the services of the clinic.

But I also knew there was a good chance they would not. First, going to the clinic would be a new and threatening step for them to take, regardless of my careful description of the services offered. Second, the evangelical church seemed to be meeting many of their emotional needs for uplift. The uplift was fine, in my opinion, but I feared the doctrine that accompanied it might not be the most useful one for solving this particular family's problems. I didn't think the church, for example, would support the drive of the family women to increase their power with respect to the male "head of household!"

A short time later, Norman completed his psychological testing with Brenda, and the ED teacher completed her classroom observations. Both felt Brenda demonstrated serious evidence of emotional disturbance. An M team date was tentatively set.

I made an appointment to meet with the Hosmers prior to the M team. Mr. Hosmer had told Norman he would not be willing to meet with the M team when Brenda's case was discussed, but he would be willing to meet with one person afterward to discuss the recommendations. I decided to meet with him before the M team date, if possible, to help satisfy any objections to a probable ED recommendation in advance.

Mr. Hosmer himself was present for my second home visit, and he was positively charming the entire evening. Tina and her father seemed much more amiable together than I would have imagined from Tina's previous bitter words. The girl seemed skilled at buttering up her father, and she was using all her considerable charms that evening to persuade Mr. Hosmer to consider special education for Brenda. I thanked my lucky stars that Tina felt so favorable toward the ED program! Mrs. Hosmer wasn't present at this family meeting but went to church instead. It really did seem to me by now that Tina was Brenda's most consistently concerned parent.

Mr. Hosmer wouldn't commit himself one way or another about permitting an ED placement, almost, it seemed, to tease Tina a little. He actually said the words I knew he must be thinking: "What would the neighbors think? Our daughter, emotionally disturbed?"

I carefully reinforced Mr. Hosmer's notions of what was right and good for American children in general. Perhaps schools did need to offer more structure, discipline, and the three "Rs," I expounded. The ED classroom today, I sighed expansively, might indeed be the only place where an American girl could get that good old-fashioned discipline and that good old-fashioned basic education. I considered humming the "Star Spangled Banner" to accompany my words but managed to suppress the impulse. Mr. Hosmer expounded and harangued about what was wrong with the schools and with teachers today, and I kept trying to tie his words into the wonderfully rigid conditions still miraculously available in the good old ED classroom.

When the M team met at school the next week, ED placement was unanimously recommended for Brenda. Neither parent attended the meeting. Most of the team members knew the father, though, and informal bets were out that we would never be able to obtain his signature.

Norman Werner and I decided to visit the Hosmer home together, bringing along the M team document, to ask for Mr. Hosmer's signature. We knew we could obtain Mrs. Hosmer's signature on the sly, but we felt that to avoid future trouble for both the school and the family, we had better approach both parents openly. We planned to make our visit a solemn occasion, during which two school professionals, the psychologist and social worker, would make themselves humbly available to answer any and all questions of the dutiful parents.

And it worked. In this case, all the extra work and care paid off. Mrs. Hosmer wasn't home, but Mr. Hosmer and Tina were both present and attentive. Mr. Hosmer played his role beautifully and asked all sorts of intelligent and dignified questions. Then, in the spirit of straight rows of desks and the three "Rs," he proudly permitted his daughter to participate in a good old-fashioned American classroom with discipline. Tina topped off the whole ceremony with a kiss.

Brenda's was a success story, as far as the school was concerned. Structured discipline and targeted behavior modification worked for her. She got rewarded for positive behavior. She completed fourth grade with better than passing grades, and she earned them. It is my own hunch that the small class size and the abundance of positive personal attention did the trick in her case. During the next year, she would be "mainstreamed" in nonacademic subjects, and probably by sixth grade she would be back in the regular classroom.

As for the Hosmer parents, they are still a proudly intact marital pair. Mrs. Hosmer told me later on the telephone that the church had worked for her, and so she hadn't needed the services of the guidance clinic. Tina was back in college.

I've been curious about all that came to pass at the Hosmer home. My hunch is that those good folk were able to stay together just because Mrs. Hosmer never did come home for very long.

DISCUSSION AND STUDY QUESTIONS

This chapter raises the interesting question of how a social worker deals with too much information. Actually, this is a good illustration of the difference between generalist and specialized practice, as well as the process called *partializing* a problem. In this vignette, the two types of practice are used together. The social worker approaches the family for a specific purpose—improving a child's school behavior. She knows that the parents have the legal authority to allow her to work with the child, although it soon becomes clear that the child's sister wields considerable influence in the family. It also becomes clear that there are a number of areas in which family dynamics appear to be harmful to family members.

In sorting out this complex situation, the social worker makes several decisions. The first is to focus only on one part of the overall problem, the aspect relating to the child's school behavior. This is an example of partializing. Then she actually avoids getting information from the girl's sister, fearing it will worsen family relationships and involve her in problem areas needing specialized expertise she cannot or is in no position to provide. These are all wise decisions because they allow her to focus her energies and to keep clear what her area and level of responsibility are to be. Although the author navigates these complexities very well, one is not always so successful in steering clear of overinvolvement.

1. What *would* the neighbors think, in your opinion, if they heard Brenda Hosmer was an "emotionally disturbed child"? Why do you think they would react that way? How do you think you would react if you heard that one of your neighbors had such a child?
2. Do you ever partialize problems in your own life? Can you think of an instance when you worked on a larger problem by taking it piece by piece? Do you find it difficult to do this? Why or why not?
*3. Why did the author channel the energies of Tina, Brenda's older sister, into helping set up an interview between the author and the parents, rather than having Tina supply the social history herself? Would you have done this? Why or why not?
*4. Give an example from your own social work practice of partializing a problem. How successful were you, and what problems did you encounter when trying to partialize?

---

*Questions notated with an asterisk are intended for advanced students who have had or are currently having some social work practice experience and who have made at least a tentative commitment to the profession.

CHAPTER 16

Henry's Calling

or: Meeting the Needs of Gay, Lesbian, and Bisexual Youth

Concepts Covered in This Chapter

1. Sexual orientation
2. Heterosexual
3. Homosexual
    a. Gay
    b. Lesbian
4. Bisexual
5. Sexually transmitted diseases
    a. AIDS
6. Discrimination
7. Support group

Learning Objectives   After reading this chapter, you should be able to

1. Define sexual orientation and discuss its significance in the lives of children and teenagers
2. Understand the difference between heterosexual, homosexual and bisexual orientation
3. Define gay and lesbian
4. Understand the importance of support groups for people with homosexual or bisexual orientation
5. Understand why it is difficult to provide education for youth, both heterosexual, homosexual, or bisexual, regarding both sexuality and sexually transmitted diseases
6. Understand the concept of discrimination
7. Understand that AIDS is a disease all people may contract, regardless of gender or sexual orientation

As I was planning the third edition of this book, I decided to include a chapter illustrating sexual orientation issues. I expected that these issues would be better recognized today than when I worked in Kingston and Orangetown. Still, I expected to have an easier time finding a case example I could write about in a more anonymous sort of setting. So I approached a friend who works as a school social worker in a large urban area, hoping to identify an interesting case. But I was told in no uncertain terms that sexual orientation is an issue too hot for social workers to handle in most schools today, even for my friend, a concerned, committed professional.

Undaunted, I continued my search. My friend referred me to a friend of her own, a social worker who happened to be of homosexual orientation, believing that this social worker could provide me the case I sought. But again I was confronted with the same alarming, though far from surprising, report. This social worker also perceived sexual orientation as too touchy an issue to deal with in the public school setting. However, she referred me to yet another social worker, Henry Walker. Henry was employed by an AIDS awareness organization, not the public schools. But part of his job involved negotiating with numerous schools, both public and private, to offer AIDS prevention programs.

Henry Walker was most accommodating and took his valuable time to talk with me in depth. He explained that he was committed to helping gay and lesbian youth (male and female youth who were homosexual, or sexually attracted to members of their own gender). However, he found it very difficult to reach them. Most schools did not provide ready access. But the AIDS prevention programs provided him access to some. Henry told me he usually offered his programs as part of a health class. He presented AIDS information to all students available because, contrary to popular belief, AIDS is not a disease affecting homosexual males only. The disease can be transmitted to both males and females, whether heterosexual or homosexual. And AIDS is spreading all too fast among teens today. But while Henry was glad to educate any youth about AIDS and other sexually transmitted diseases, he carefully presented his programs in such a way that gay or lesbian students, or those who thought they might be gay or lesbian, could feel comfortable enough to confide in him later.

Henry knew from personal experience that students who were uncertain of their sexual orientation often felt forced to hide their confusion and pain. Henry himself had suspected he was gay from his early teen years. Out of fear of being ostracized, he had refrained from disclosing his concerns to anyone, even members of his own family. The teachings of his church and parochial school made him fearful that he was a sinner against God. Henry's emotional pain as a teen was intense, and he suffered alone. As an adult, however, he became aware of organizations run by and for gay people. After a great deal of soul searching, Henry began to participate in some of these programs. He gradually learned to accept himself as he was, and eventually, even to embrace gay pride. Pride was a liberating concept for him, and Henry finally learned to like and respect himself. He now wanted to help brighten the lives of other people who might be suffering from sexual orientation issues.

Henry went to graduate school and earned his master's degree in social work. He completed his degree the year after Ronald Reagan was elected president, however, and many social programs were being slashed. Henry could not find work in his chosen field. So he kept his job as a hotel clerk on the night shift, the job that had financed his graduate education. Henry's unpaid social work career began immediately after earning his M.S.W., however. With extra time on his hands after completing graduate school, he noticed that the family next door in his central city neighborhood was struggling. The mother, a single woman of African-American descent, was trying to raise her two sons alone. The oldest boy, 14, was withdrawn and depressed. He spent most of his time at home baby-sitting the 10-year-old while the mother held down two part-time jobs.

Henry took on the role of "big brother" to the children, with their mother's gratitude and blessing. He introduced them to basketball games on the weekends. He played baseball with them in the local parks. He took the boys on trips to neighboring cities, introducing them to public museums and plays. Soon the older boy was no longer depressed, and both children blossomed.

One Saturday night, as the threesome returned from a soccer match, Henry's "little brothers" spied two cousins on the street. The boys called out and before long all four children were enjoying the comfort of Henry's ancient but roomy automobile. Thus began a tradition of group activities including Henry and several children from the inner city, mostly of ethnic minority background. Henry's original "little brothers" have grown up and taken on jobs and families of their own, but more children have taken their place. Henry says he feels more like a substitute father than a big brother now, given that he has grown older along the way.

A few years ago one of the children Henry befriended, a young teen named Tyrone Perry, asked Henry why he didn't have he a wife. Henry explained as simply as he could. Tyrone burst into tears. He said he thought he too might be gay. Henry talked with the boy gently, explaining that same-sex orientation is a fact of life for many people, difficult to cope with in today's society but nothing to be ashamed about. Before long Tyrone brought another boy to talk with Henry about sexual orientation issues, and then another. An occasional parent or older sibling came to meet Henry as well, clearly checking to make sure he was maintaining appropriate relationships with the children. Henry's articulate, commanding presence reassured them. When the social worker eventually secured his job with the AIDS awareness project, he began a formal support group for the boys. Later, he developed a leadership training program for gay youth of both sexes. Today he even runs a television program specifically geared toward gay and lesbian youth.

As part of Henry's job as a social worker with the AIDS awareness project, he was committed to introducing AIDS prevention programs into the public schools. He felt that basic information about AIDS could help prevent this devastating illness from spreading among children in general. In addition, programs such as these could introduce youth who were experiencing confusion with respect to sexual orientation to community resources such as the support group he had organized.

Henry initially met strong resistance when he approached school administrators—they were fearful of potential negative reactions from parents. For example, Henry's presentations necessarily involved discussion of specific sexual practices and safety measures for disease prevention, including use of condoms. Many parents might disapprove. Initially stymied, Henry then "cashed in" on his prior work with gay youth. He sent his business cards to school with the teens involved in his programs.

He asked the teens to tell their teachers about his availability to teach preventive health courses at no cost to the school. This strategy worked. Given a positive introduction by children the teachers knew, Henry was soon invited to present his information in health classes at several schools.

"You have to have passion for this work," Henry declares firmly. "You have to get the kids to laugh. You need to avoid the scary messages, and focus on the informational approach, using a strong dose of humor. Humor about sex can help these kids laugh about their fears and foibles, and then they'll be able to hear your message about preventing sexually transmitted diseases. One of the problems with AIDS is that it takes advantage of the poor and disadvantaged. People with money can fight the disease, or at least hold off symptoms for awhile. But poor kids from the inner city are easy game. They don't have access to adequate health care, so AIDS gets them quickly. It's my mission to even up the score if I can—to give these kids the tools they need to prevent the disease."

As Henry was considering how best to present an AIDS prevention program in a certain central city high school to which he had received an invitation, it occurred to him that he might bring along a teenager from one of his leadership groups to assist. Speaking in front of a class might provide an excellent experience for the teen and provide the students at the school with a peer to whom they could relate. Henry decided to ask Tyrone Perry, who was now 17, to assist him. Tyrone agreed reluctantly, fearing he would be embarrassed or shamed in public about his sexual orientation. Henry promised to protect the boy if necessary.

As Henry tells the story, the first part of the AIDS prevention program in which Tyrone participated went well. But during a break between sessions, Tyrone was accosted in the hallway by youths who had heard that people who were homosexual were giving a presentation in health class. Students not involved in the program tumbled down the long hallways of the school to take in a piece of the action. "Look, there are the fags!" an excited shout could be heard somewhere along a distant corridor.

"Watch out," a large young man jeered loudly right next to Tyrone, pointing at him aggressively. "That guy's a queer." The harsh words reverberated back into the room where the health class was being held. Tyrone was frightened, of course. Henry shielded the boy physically as students began calling him other nasty names. Due to Henry's large size and imposing presence, he was able to prevent any serious trouble. But Tyrone was angry and hurt by the mocking words with which he was assaulted. Henry was shaken himself.

As the second part of the program on AIDS commenced in the health class, a powerful tension could be felt throughout the room. A young man raised his hand. Before he was even called on, the youth suddenly bellowed loudly at Tyrone: "Are you really a fag?" Tyrone, furious, responded with something almost equally abrasive: "That's none of your fuckin' business." The tension in the room, already high, escalated palpably.

Henry, rarely at a loss for words, turned what could have been a nasty confrontation into an opportunity to discuss issues of discrimination. The students he and Tyrone were addressing were inner city teens, almost all of ethnic minority background (as was Tyrone himself). "What if," Henry spoke directly to the youth in question, "you were invited to give a talk in a white suburban school, and someone called you a 'nigger'? Tell me, how would you feel?"

In this way, Henry was able to focus the students' thoughts on issues of discrimination. He asked several more questions of this nature, assisting students in the room to identify times in which they themselves had experienced discrimination. Henry then explained that people of minority sexual orientation suffer from discrimination too. Students could choose to make discrimination even worse, or they could act responsibly and lessen its effects. The students understood Henry's message. The class was completed successfully, without further harassment.

And to Henry's great satisfaction, after the class was over a student came up to the social worker and the teen and asked to talk with them privately. Henry and Tyrone took the boy to dinner, and listened with empathy to his tale of confusion and pain about what he perceived as his bisexual orientation (sexual attraction to members of both genders). They helped him understand he was not alone. The youth was referred to the services of the AIDS awareness project where Henry was employed, especially to the support group for boys experiencing sexual orientation issues.

Henry thought to himself later how sad the situation really is for homosexual and bisexual youth. Young people who feel unhappy, or who experience low self-esteem or confusion related to their ethnic or racial minority background, can usually turn to their parents, friends, and even their churches for support, understanding, and coping strategies. But young people who feel unhappy, or who experience low self-esteem or confusion related to their sexual orientation often have nowhere at all to turn.

Henry felt that his personal and professional mission was to make a difference for these youth. It was clear to me that he was accomplishing his calling with skill and resourcefulness.

DISCUSSION AND STUDY QUESTIONS

People of homosexual or bisexual orientation routinely experience discrimination in this country. Even institutions that normally teach tolerance, such as many churches, may revile them as sinners. However, sexual orientation is not usually a personal choice. Human sexuality seems to fall along a continuum that includes homosexual, heterosexual, bisexual, and even asexual. Many cultures outside our own accept this continuum as natural, and do not discriminate against people who happen to fall at one end or another.

Social work as a profession recognizes that people with homosexual or bisexual orientation comprise a natural and legitimate minority who should be accorded the same rights as any other people, including the right to be treated with respect and dignity. Protection of these rights may require not only assistance under the law but education of the public and modelling of tolerance and respect by our social institutions. However, only small steps have been made in this direction today and a backlash threatens some of the gains that have been won.

1. Examine your own beliefs and attitudes about people with homosexual or bisexual orientation. How would you describe your beliefs today? How have they changed over the past few years?
2. Think about your family and friends. Are you aware of any who may have a homosexual or bisexual orientation? If so, are you aware of any complications that has caused in their lives? How well have they been accepted by others who know of their sexual orientation? How well have they accepted themselves?
3. Did your school provide any education about sexually transmitted diseases? About AIDS? About alternative sexual orientation? If so, do you think the information provided was well presented and adequate? If not, why not? If no education of this nature was offered, do you think it should have been? Why or why not?
4. If you learned that a good friend was homosexual or bisexual, how would you respond?
*5. What do you think are the reasons that people of minority sexual orientation are discriminated against? What do you think about these reasons? If you think the reasons are unjust, how do you think they might best be addressed?

---

*Questions notated with an asterisk are intended for advanced students who have had or are currently having some social work practice experience and who have made of least a tentative commitment to the profession.

PART FOUR

Policy Issues

INTRODUCTION

Probably the least understood part of social work is the relationship between practice and policy. Social workers are quick to concern themselves with specific practice skills but usually are much less eager to consider the policy aspects of their work. This is a pity because it is policy that makes practice possible and that shapes the directions it takes. Unless policy-making bodies—at the national, state, county, and community levels—enact policies that mandate social work services, services will exist only to the degree that individual charitable impulses create them. Similarly, mandated services get filtered through specific agency policies, interpretations of policy, and operating procedures.

The link between policy and practice is made very clear in this section of the book. In Chapter 17 the fact is emphasized that organizational procedures mandated by policy strongly affect whether and how services can be delivered. Chapter 18 clearly illustrates the effect that ambiguous and overlapping policies have on the practice efforts of social workers. Chapter 19 demonstrates how following procedures established by policies can protect social workers, and the close link between societal values and policy is explored in Chapter 20. The multifaceted interplay between policy and service delivery, then, is well captured by the chapters in this section.

At a number of points throughout the book, the author raises the question whether she, as a direct service provider, should be concerned with policy. She raises this question as part of her regular evaluation of her practice. At several points she realizes that her practice efforts are very much bounded by the policy within which she works, and she considers policy change as a potential role for herself. Indeed, she takes on the role at some points when she questions the competence of Mr. Murdock and seeks to have his supervisor intervene in his behavior and when she keeps pushing the county to acknowledge and fulfill their responsibilities to Spanish-speaking students.

These examples demonstrate how policy involvement can and should be part of day-to-day social work practice. Such involvements may not lead to massive policy changes, but they do improve service delivery in some way—and that is the goal of every social worker. To participate in policy at this or any other level, the social worker must be aware that he or she *can* affect it. Then there must be a commitment to exercise that ability by analyzing the policies that affect one's practice and by acting appropriately when policies impede practice and impede the self-help efforts of all client groups.

In Chapter 21, the author raises the issue of large-scale policy change as a part of day-to-day practice. In her assessment, working on a long-term basis in Emmett County would have required efforts to change policy that went beyond what she was able to accomplish in her day-to-day work. This, she recognizes, would potentially risk her job, and it is one of the reasons why she decides to move on to another job. Her analysis does help us to see that large-scale policy change entails risks and specialized expertise. Some social workers specialize in policy development, implementation, and change and are perhaps best prepared to address issues of large-scale policy changes. Nonetheless, the author makes it clear that *every* social worker can elect to enter the large-scale policy change arena, although with some risk. But most important, the author firmly asserts that some level of policy involvement is not only possible but also a responsibility of every social worker.

CHAPTER 17

Homebound

or: Policy Barriers in Providing Assistance to a
Pregnant Teenager

Concepts Covered in This Chapter

1. The differential application of laws
2. Denial of need for service
3. Reaching out to anxious clients
4. Starting where the client is
5. Self-determination as a social work practice value
6. Developing trust in a professional helping relationship

Learning Objectives   After reading this chapter you should be able to

1. List at least three reasons why laws are applied differentially to members of different groups
2. List at least three reasons why people sometimes deny their need for service
3. List at least three strategies social workers can use to put anxious clients at ease
4. Explain what is meant by starting where the client is
5. Discuss why self-determination is considered an important value in social work practice
6. List at least three strategies social workers can use to develop trust in helping relationships

A t last! An unsolicited referral from the high school guidance counselor in Orangetown. A breakthrough. A chance to prove how useful I could be. The referral involved a young girl, only fourteen, who had just told the high school guidance counselor that she might be pregnant and was planning to quit school.

Suspected pregnancy officially qualified her for referral to special education services. This was the first time I had been voluntarily consulted by a staff person other than the special education teachers. I knew that doing a good job was going to be crucial if I wanted other referrals.

I was also personally and professionally interested in Ronda, and, in fact, in the issue of teenage pregnancy itself. Young boys and girls are learning who they are at this time in their lives, and sexuality is an important part of their self-exploration.

Courses on sex education, however, had been expressly forbidden by the Orangetown school board. That sort of thing should be taught within the home, according to those good gentlemen and several vocal parents who had expressed their opinion in a special meeting on that subject the year before I came. This I had learned from the young high school gym teacher, who had been hired only last year right out of college with some shiny modern ideas. She had begun to teach a health unit in her physical education classes, including basic information on the reproductive process, and had been discovered and nearly fired as a result. She was back in Orangetown this year only because she had promised to behave and because her frantic search for a different job had proved fruitless.

I thus approached Ronda quite gingerly in our first interview. I needed to know why she thought she might be pregnant and to give her some clear information if she were mixed up on the facts of life. Yet I knew that she might take my information home, and, lo and behold, I could become a sex education teacher too. I could become the next victim of the family privacy attack, and that could set back almost irreparably my efforts to have social work become an established function at the school.

It turned out that Ronda thought she might be pregnant for good reason. She hadn't had her period for two or three months, and she had also been getting sick a lot. She had talked first to some of her girlfriends and then to the same gym teacher. The gym teacher had taken her to the guidance counselor.

I asked Ronda whether she knew how girls got pregnant. She didn't. Now it is true that people can fool me, and sometimes I discover it and sometimes I don't, so perhaps Ronda really did put on just a good show. But I don't think so. I think she had no idea how she got pregnant, although she did know it had something to do with boys. She had a boyfriend, aged fifteen.

So I drew Ronda some pictures to explain the fertilization process, and I was as gentle in my description of intercourse as I could be. She got tears in her eyes and said yes, she had done that with her boyfriend. He wanted that, and she liked to please him however she could.

We discussed options and alternatives, in case she really was pregnant. Ronda was Catholic, but she didn't want to marry her boyfriend. She herself insisted they were both too young. She was certain her parents would never permit an abortion, but if she had the baby, she thought she should keep it. She thought that was what her parents would want.

I explained to Ronda some options available through the school. She would not need to quit. Thank heavens, one genuine advance in public education is that pregnant girls are no longer forced to quit school, at least not by law in most places. Wouldn't she consider keeping up with her education? She could stay in school right up to the birth of the baby if she felt physically able, and she could come back afterward as soon as she was ready.

Ronda said she would like to stay in school, but she thought her parents wouldn't permit it. They would be too ashamed of her. When I suggested talking to her parents myself about it, she became very frightened. She was afraid they would be angry that the school knew about her pregnancy.

Later in the interview I described to Ronda another possible option to keep up with her education—homebound services. Under some circumstances a "disabled" student could receive tutoring at home. Ronda might qualify, if her parents would permit it. Ronda was indeed interested in this option. By the end of the interview, she promised to talk with her mother about her fears of pregnancy, and she would also ask her mother whether she would talk to me about ways to continue with her schooling.

Ronda told her parents the afternoon of my conference with her that she might be pregnant. Her parents were very angry at her and told her she would have to leave school immediately if it were true. She had four brothers and sisters in the school system, and the parents were not going to have these children embarrassed. However, Ronda's parents loved her, and so they did not beat her or kick her out of the house, as some parents do. I learned of the parents' reaction from Ronda in a conference at school the next day and was greatly relieved for her. However, Ronda said, her mother did not want to talk with anyone at the school. The family would take care of everything.

I was not surprised at Ronda's parents' reaction. Parents usually dislike having a child who is visibly imperfect because the imperfection casts a stigma over the entire family. They usually prefer to hide any problem, if at all possible. Out of the public sight, out of the public mind, they hope.

But that would mean loss of at least Ronda's freshman year of high school and, as I viewed it, a great increase in the likelihood that she would enter adult life as a high school dropout. Dropout status would virtually assure that Ronda would live her life at the bottom of the socioeconomic heap. As long as she lived with her parents, she would probably be economically protected, but in four short years she would be eighteen, with a three-year-old child to raise. There was not much likelihood Ronda would be kept on in the family home when she came of age because in addition to her four brothers and sisters in school, Ronda also had a brother and sister still in the toddler stage at home. That was a lot of people for one household.

As a person in the middle, I was going to have to persuade Ronda's parents to allow her to continue her education, and if homebound services were the only option they would consider, I was going to have to persuade a multidisciplinary team and the county special education administrators to authorize them. Otherwise, Ronda was likely to go the way of all too many pregnant teenagers—she would probably become another uneducated single mother, both partially supported and abused by the general public. She would have no skills to help her break out of her unenviable position.

I asked Ronda whether she would mind if I took the initiative to call her mother. She seemed not only pleased but relieved at the suggestion. On the telephone, Ronda's mother came across as very cool, very distant. She told me that her family was doing everything for Ronda that she needed and that they didn't need any assistance from the special education program. No, they were not interested in provisions to help Ronda remain in school.

"But . . ." and she paused then. There was something in that "but" that gave me cause to hope. I asked Mrs. Taylor whether Ronda had mentioned my name to her. Well, yes, Ronda had spoken of me. Well, in fact. Perhaps there might be some advantage to learn what services were available. She would talk to her husband and see whether he would allow me to visit—just to talk things over. Could I call tomorrow?

Ronda's father had given permission. And now, besides the pleasing prospect of intervening on Ronda's behalf, I had the unexpected pleasure of enjoying one of the best parts of county social work—the countryside. Ronda's home was a good 15 miles from the school, and the only way to reach it was by car.

It was a beautiful autumn, and every moment outside made all those diligent working moments inside seem like just so much foolishness and a deserved punishment for puritanical compulsiveness. Out on the road I enjoyed the wonderful burst of color provided by the blue sky, the silver horsetail clouds, and the amber cornstalks. It was the time of year when farmers were harvesting, and the feed corn is left in the fields for all sorts of periods of time, depending on the weather. The longer the ripe ears can be left to dry in the autumn fields, the less time and expense to the farmers in drying and storing them.

I was looking for a house with a turquoise garage door next to a round, red swimming pool. With a description like that, I hadn't expected to have any trouble identifying the place. But some farmer had subdivided his back 40 into 1-acre lots, and there were at least 20 awkward little multicolored, fake-sided houses sporting garages and swimming pools, and several seemed to have some combination of turquoise and red.

At last I found the right combination of colors on the right items; the address I had been seeking belonged to one of the spanking new houses. The place certainly didn't look like the site of a family problem.

I walked up the steps, curious about the people I would find within. The door was promptly opened by an attractive young woman who had clearly been watching for me. She looked about my age, and when I remembered that she had seven children and was about to have a grandchild, I suddenly felt as old as Methuselah.

Out from behind her legs peeped two toddlers. I looked beyond her into an absolutely empty living room. There was nothing at all in evidence in the form of furniture, rugs, curtains, or the like. Even our breathing at each other seemed to echo.

Mrs. Taylor's first words were apologetic. She explained that they had just bought the house, as they needed more room for the family. But they did not have enough money to afford a finished house or furniture. They were doing much of the work themselves, and the furniture would just have to come when it could.

Ah, a point of contact. As I followed Mrs. Taylor into the dining room, which was sparsely furnished with a table and chairs perched on a subfloor and framed by unfinished walls and woodwork, I laughingly made a few comments about the joys of house building. I explained that I was involved in somewhat the same thing and that our house wasn't as far along as hers. That seemed to put her much more at ease.

Mrs. Taylor and I continued to exchange pleasantries while she served me some coffee and cookies, another joy of the most fortunate kind of social work. Actually, I don't drink coffee on my own, but I never refuse it on occasions such as this. In fact, I made a point to admire her coffee pot and the matched set of cups. And I admired the toddler in her lap and the other one hanging onto my leg. I sipped my coffee slowly, allowing for natural pauses. It takes time for a nervous parent to begin to develop trust, and before that has happened, most of the information offered will be forgotten or misunderstood. I intentionally spent this time on the little nothings that help form the first bridge between strangers.

I frankly liked Mrs. Taylor and the house and the children. There was warmth here. That genuine liking, of course, facilitated the comfortable feelings that began to develop between us. Mrs. Taylor gradually told me that she had had to beg her husband to let me come. She told me that she herself had had to marry young because of her pregnancy with Ronda. She felt lucky because her young man had stood by her and was still standing by her. But she felt bad because she had never finished high school herself, and what would happen to her if something should happen to her husband? He worked as a laborer at a foundry, and it was not all that uncommon for serious accidents to happen to the workers at the plant.

When we got down to business, it became clear that Mrs. Taylor would like Ronda to continue with her schooling. I didn't have any work to do in that area. We then discussed the father of Ronda's child and his youth and the unsuitability of marriage between a fourteen-year-old and a fifteen-year-old. We also explored the religious prohibition against abortion. Without that, Mrs. Taylor stated frankly that she would have advised her daughter to go that route. But she said she felt abortion would be morally wrong. I accepted Mrs. Taylor's religion as her framework for decision making. My own framework is different, but it would have been inappropriate to impose my own value system.

I spent a long time explaining the advantage of Ronda's staying in school up to her time of delivery. But that was clearly unacceptable to Mrs. Taylor. It was just too demeaning to the family. Homebound instruction—that was a different story. Mrs. Taylor would be grateful for that, and she was sure her husband would approve.

I decided that Ronda's chances of getting through her freshman year of high school, given her parent's values and experiences, would be far greater with homebound instruction. But this service would have to be recommended by an M team consisting of the school psychologist, the guidance counselor, the high school principal, the liaison from the county special education office, and me. The evaluation process would also require a pregnancy verification and a recommendation for homebound instruction from a physician, as well as final approval by the top administrators at the county office.

A lot of details, confusing to a bewildered mother and grandmother-to-be, who had just had her interest in homebound instruction whetted only to be told that the new option might be unavailable to Ronda because she was not actually physically unable to attend school.

I explained to Mrs. Taylor that by law, the parents must be informed of the time of the M team meeting and that parents have the legal right to attend. But Mrs. Taylor did not want to come to any meeting of the M team. She was too shy, and I could not persuade her. But she was willing to take her daughter to her doctor to confirm the pregnancy and to get the doctor's recommendation for homebound instruction.

At this point, I decided we had talked about enough for one day. I made one last recommendation and referral: that Ronda, her boyfriend, and her family consider counseling together at Catholic Social Services or at the Emmett County Guidance Clinic to explore more fully what to do when the baby arrived, if Ronda was indeed pregnant.

Then I reviewed the contents of our immediate discussion with Mrs. Taylor, checked out our tentative contract concerning who was to do what, and made preparations to leave. Mrs. Taylor promised to explain everything to her husband and to get Ronda to the doctor as soon as possible.

Mrs. Taylor did take Ronda to a doctor, and Ronda left school immediately thereafter. She was indeed pregnant. I talked with Mrs. Taylor by telephone, and she explained, as before, about family embarrassment. Her husband was agreeable to homebound instruction if the county would authorize it, but he would not allow Ronda to remain in school. Mrs. Taylor said that she had left the form to verify Ronda's pregnancy with the doctor and that the doctor had promised to fill it out and send it at his earliest opportunity.

The doctor, however, did not return the form. In the meantime, I convened the M team without the form, as I wanted to get the homebound instruction to Ronda as soon as possible. The M team agreed to homebound instruction, and the high school guidance counselor, bless him, knew about an available tutor. The papers were written up and sent to the county for administrative approval, without the doctor's report.

I now felt wonderfully effective, a success. Within two or three weeks of a referral, I had carried the unwieldy evaluation process from start to finish with only one small detail missing—the medical form. Surely, the guidance counselor would be impressed and would flood me with appropriate new referrals. I felt almost heroic.

But a few days passed, and still there was no doctor's report. I began calling him. He promised to fill out the form and send it immediately. But another full week passed with no medical report. I called Mrs. Taylor to ask her to talk to the doctor. That didn't work, either. Finally, I got a genuine brainstorm. I called the office nurse. Office nurses have always seemed very efficient to me. And in two days the form arrived.

But—there was still a problem. The doctor should have checked two boxes on the form—one confirming pregnancy and one recommending homebound instruction. The doctor had checked only the box confirming pregnancy.

Would the form be acceptable to the county administration as it was? I wasn't sure. But what did the doctor know, anyhow, about Ronda's personal situation and the appropriateness of homebound instruction for her? I decided to take the medical form in person to the county office so that I could get some immediate feedback and get right back to the doctor, if necessary.

When I reached the county office, my county supervisor for Orangetown, Martin Murdock, was the only one there, except for the secretary. According to the proper decision-making hierarchy, Martin should be the one for me to consult. So I showed him Ronda's medical form and pointed out the empty box next to homebound instruction. Martin said there would be no problem. After all, he said logically, the M team had authorized the homebound instruction, and all the doctor's report would be needed for would be to verify the pregnancy. That's what I had wanted to hear, and I started to leave the county office with a contented smile on my face. But then, just as I was outside the door, Martin called out that he wasn't sure.

I went back into the office and asked him whether he knew where I could find Dr. Knight, the director of the Emmett County special education program, or Ms. Jean Fillmore, her administrative assistant, for consultation. Martin had let me down before in seeking needed information, so I wanted to do it myself in this situation. Martin seemed visibly upset that I wanted to speak with other authorities. He assured me he would take care of the matter. I decided I would be wise to let him do his job. It seemed simple enough.

That was a mistake. Mr. Murdock dropped by the classroom I shared with David Chase at least twice a week for the next two weeks, and at least twice a week I asked him whether homebound services had been authorized for Ronda. He didn't know. At least twice more each week I called him at the county offices, and he still didn't know.

Ronda was sitting home idle, and I was getting embarrassed. So I drove out to see her and her mother at home. I wanted to explain what I thought might be causing the delay, and I had some other ideas to share about services. I referred Ronda to a university extension course I had found that was geared to expectant young mothers, to a course in natural childbrith, and to the nearest Planned Parenthood agency. The referral to Planned Parenthood was made cautiously, given the religion of the Taylors, but, to my surpise, *both* mother and daughter wrote down the address and telephone number!

I also gave Ronda a packet of pamphlets about pregnancy, which I had obtained from the county nurse. The final referral I made was a repeat of the one made before: Catholic Social Services or the county guidance clinic. Ronda and her boyfriend were still uncertain of their relationship even though they both seemed to agree, along with Ronda's parents, that she should keep her child.

I have found that often it is very difficult to get troubled people to counseling, and in this case, I failed once more. That was frustrating for me. Sometimes I can get people to go by obtaining their permission to make the first appointment for them, sometimes even dialing the clinic and then putting the potential clients on the telephone, but this time I couldn't get even that far. The Taylors felt they were in agreement on the important question—what to do about the baby—and they felt the young people would be able to work out their own relationship in good time. Perhaps they were right.

By now, the high school guidance counselor was asking me regularly when he could send his tutor to work with Ronda. The tutor was ready to work, and the guidance counselor was having some difficulty accounting for the delays. I was virtually squirming with my inability to get the services moving.

Finally, one morning at the time that Mr. Murdock customarily dropped by my joint classroom for his informal supervisory session, I went over to the county office. For purposes of protocol I asked first for Mr. Murdock, but when he wasn't there, as I had expected, I asked to see Ms. Fillmore.

She was visibly impatient when I insisted on talking with her in person. But her impatience could not match mine when I learned that she had had the medical form for Ronda for two weeks and had come to the immediate determination that the form was insufficiently completed by the doctor. She said, firmly, that *of course* the doctor would have to authorize homebound instruction.

I said a few reasonably careful words about how much I would have appreciated being informed of this sooner. Ms. Fillmore responded quite sweetly that I had no cause for impatience. "Really now, Carolyn," she said with dignity, "you know we are all very busy up here, and Mr. Murdock and I are working very hard. Besides, you could have the school file truancy papers in this case and force the girl to go back to school. Then we wouldn't have to pay for homebound instruction, which is quite expensive, you know." Ms. Fillmore then actually put a hand solicitously on my shoulder.

I burned. Was it harder to work with clients or with the administration? At that time I had no question. I wished the entire Emmett County special education office would dissolve in smoke. Count to ten. Hang on. Don't blow things.

I asked Ms. Fillmore whether she was trying to tell me that the county would not approve the recommendation for homebound instruction even if I could get the doctor to put the check in the right box. She assured me that she meant no such thing. She said she would approve the recommendation for homebound instruction as soon as she had the necessary documentation.

When I left, I was cool, calm, and collected. After all, I am a professional, and professionals are cool, calm, and collected. Yes indeed, I told myself, the fact that I felt wildly hot, was sweating, couldn't speak without stuttering, and had turned deep purple in color could not possibly have been observed by anyone else.

When I got the nurse at the doctor's office on the telephone again, she told me rather icily that "these girls don't deserve instruction at home. When they do bad things, they shouldn't expect any favors." The nurse said that the schools were getting too soft on wayward girls, to say nothing of their parents.

A small light bulb turned itself on in my mind. So the nurse had filled out the form. The doctor had probably never even looked at what he was signing.

When I had let her go on a bit and felt the time was right, I asked her whether she would prefer that I try to persuade the doctor myself, in person, to sign the form and to put a check in the homebound box or whether she would prefer that I let her try again herself. I made it sound as if I knew she had done her best to get the doctor to do what was required but that it was just too difficult under the circumstances. I sympathized with her about her difficult job and let her know I was willing to help. In fact, I made it clear that I wouldn't give up easily.

The nurse finally decided that she could get the doctor to sign another form, this one authorizing homebound instruction. The nurse said she rather liked Ronda's mother, who kept having so many children herself. The poor dear, she sympathized, just had so much to contend with.

The medical form came, there was a check in both necessary boxes, and the county released its formal approval for homebound instruction. Ronda got her tutor. The whole process only took about six or eight weeks longer than it should have. Ronda and her mother were invariably gracious.

The high school guidance counselor on the whole was still speaking to me, but he didn't refer any more pregnant girls.

DISCUSSION AND STUDY QUESTIONS

Although referrals are made at many points throughout this book, this chapter is a particularly good example of the use of this practice skill. Making referrals illustrates what can be seen as a managerial function of the generalist social worker. We have discussed in earlier chapters how generalists utilize the special expertise of their social welfare colleagues when appropriate. This can be done in any number of ways. One is through consultation, already discussed. There the generalist social worker gets information from those with specialized expertise and incorporates this into his or her own practice with a client. Another method is by putting together a *team* of professionals, each of whom has specialized expertise. The team then jointly makes decisions and together provides services. The M team used in Emmett County is an example of the team approach.

A third and most commonly used form of management of social work services by generalists that builds on the expertise of others is *referrals.* A referral occurs when the social worker provides information about a useful specialized service to a client. As the author demonstrates in her practice, referrals have several parts. The first is a professional assessment of needs and a determination of specialized services available to meet those needs. The second is a careful discussion with the client that conveys there are additional services available that might be of interest. It is important at this stage to describe the services fully and explain how they might be helpful. This often entails helping the client acknowledge and work through feelings she or he might have about using such services. A third step is providing the name of the referral agency, its address and phone number, and if possible, the name of a specific person to contact. Finally, there is follow-up. Did the client actually make the contact? Is more help needed to carry out the contact? Or if the client elected not to make contact, is some other referral possible? This chapter illustrates well the utility of referrals, but the process itself must be managed sensitively.

1. The Orangetown School Board has a policy that forbids sex education in the town's public schools. The rationale is that this sort of information should be taught in the home. Without arguing the moral correctness or incorrectness of the school board's position, how is their policy likely to affect the frequency of unplanned preganancy? What other information besides sex education per se would be useful for a teenager potentially vulnerable to pregnancy? For example, what basic facts are known about the impact of pregnancy on the life of a teenager? Consider biological, social, psychological, economic, and any other factors that seem relevant.
2. What views do you hold regarding sex education and/or family life education in the schools? On what factors are your opinions based—biological, social, religious, economic, psychological, or other?

*3. The author makes a number of referrals in this case, identifying service options for Ronda Taylor and her family. The Taylors choose to follow up on only a few of them and not necessarily the ones the author felt were most important. However, the author chooses not to pressure the Taylors to follow up on her referrals. Why? Would you have handled the referral process in the same way?

*4. The author mentions two or three specific situations in this chapter in which the Taylors make choices that are different from the choices she would have preferred them to make. What are these situations? How does the social work profession guide its practitioners to conduct themselves in situations such as this? How would you have wanted to handle these situations if you had been the social worker?

---

*Questions notated with an asterisk are intended for advanced students who have had or are currently having some social work practice experience and who have made at least a tentative commitment to the profession.

CHAPTER 18

Special Education and the "Bad Apple" Classroom

or: Trying to Differentiate Children with Emotional Disturbance from Children Who "Just Need Discipline"

Concepts Covered in This Chapter

1. The relationship of private troubles and public issues
2. Nontraditional social welfare programs
3. Phobias
4. Linking similar programs provided under different auspices

Learning Objectives   After reading this chapter you should be able to

1. Describe how truancy is a problem for the truant student as well as for the community in which he or she lives
2. Identify at least three differences between the traditional special education program and the nontraditional disciplinary classroom
3. Cite at least two advantages and two disadvantages of the nontraditional disciplinary classroom (these may relate to treatment provided or organizational procedures)
4. Define a *phobia* and give an example of one without using the school phobia described in this chapter
5. List three issues faced by social workers who want to use similar programs that are provided under different auspices

Orangetown absorbed the county-administered special education programs for emotionally disturbed children with great reluctance, only because more effort would have been required by the town to keep the programs out. Court action would have been necessary to delay their implementation, and Orangetown would probably have lost a court battle, anyway, because of the new state and federal laws broadening the definition of "disability."

Emotional disturbance was a relatively new concept in public education, and many of the students previously labeled as nothing other than disruptive brats might qualify for special education services under the ED category of disability.

But Orangetown knew how to handle its badly behaved kids all by itself, and it could do so better without interference from the county, it believed. Orangetown believed that badly behaved children needed stricter control, not special services.

So when Emmett County moved to obey the new special education laws and began to plan for programs for emotionally or behaviorally disturbed children in Orangetown, Orangetown moved to set up its own version of a better program in its junior high wing: a disciplinary classroom.

Thus when I first arrived in Orangetown, there were two programs for badly behaved students just getting started in the junior high, the county ED program and the town disciplinary classroom. Naturally, everyone was confused about which students to refer where.

Junior high was where most of Orangetown's difficult students were in fact located. By the time these more difficult students should have entered high school in Orangetown, most of them had dropped out of school completely. No one had dealt with their special needs, and so they got out of school as soon as they could.

This suited the local administration quite well. They busily suspended badly behaved students, anyway, while they were still nominally enrolled. And although the very young disruptive students in elementary school might certainly be able to cause a commotion, they were still small enough in size to be physically controlled (if not educated) by their regular teachers.

Neither the Orangetown school administration nor the Emmett County special education program staff made any effort to help David Chase and me understand how the junior high program for "bad apples" (as it was affectionately called by the teachers) was to be coordinated with the special education ED program in Orangetown. At first, I thought only that Mr. Robert Marein, the teacher for the "bad apple" classroom, was David's counterpart in the junior high. I thought that David would be working with kindergarten and elementary school children who exhibited disturbed behavior and that Mr. Marein would work with the junior high students of the same category.

But David soon straightened me out. To his own dismay (because he preferred working with younger students, although he had the professional credentials to work with all grade levels), he discovered that Mr. Marein had no training at all in special education. And he learned through a telephone call to the county offices that he, David, was indeed responsible for ED evaluation and services to the junior high students.

Now, what in particular would be different about the junior high students who would be placed in Mr. Marein's classroom and those who should be referred to special education for ED evaluation? We struggled with this concept for a while, thinking that surely there must be a difference. Surely the county would not have permitted, at least without staff preparation, the introduction of a town disciplinary program for children with behavioral disturbances at the same time it was developing its own treatment-oriented program for approximately the same pool of children.

But the county did just that.

Had systematic and careful training by the county or the local school administration been offered to both regular and special education staff, we all might have learned how to make reasonable rule-of-thumb distinctions between students with emotional disturbance and "bad apples," so that referrals might have been directed toward the appropriate program. Under certain circumstances, I can concede there might be a difference in symptomatic behavior.

But in general, the behavior in question looks quite similar. I can't make the distinction myself, certainly not without a thorough evaluation by the special education staff. In a special education evaluation, the social history might reveal that the child who is a disciplinary problem in school is not emotionally disturbed by special education criteria. For example, the child who is badly behaved at school might turn out to be a veritable angel at home and in the community. Thus the ED diagnostic requirement of disturbed behavior in at least two environments would not be met. This child, according to Orangetown's educational structure, would properly be the true "bad apple." From my point of view, of course, a disciplinary classroom might still be a totally inappropriate placement for him or her. My approach instead might be "So what's wrong with the school, if this child is doing so well everywhere else?" I am obviously not a birthright advocate of a disciplinary classroom.

In the junior high, as in the elementary school, the regular classroom teachers were supposed to refer children for special education evaluation if they were having trouble controlling behavior in the classroom. They might also refer children exhibiting other unusual symptoms, for example, suspected pregnancy or extreme withdrawal (which could include repeated truancy, possibly an emotional problem labeled "school phobia").

Special education evaluations were required by law to follow certain procedures, procedures legislated for the protection of the referred student and her or his family. After a referral, (1) if the referred child's parents agreed to an evaluation, (2) if classroom observations verified evidence of emotional disturbance, (3) if a social history revealed evidence of disturbed behavior in the home or community, (4) if an M team recommended special services, (5) if the county special education administrators approved the M team recommendations, and (6) if the parents approved of the final plans in writing, *then* the referred student could receive ongoing special education services. All these careful processes took precious time.

And the junior high teachers in Orangetown rapidly learned that they could get much quicker results for themselves if they referred their troublesome students (any and all of them) to the "bad apple" classroom. A referral to Mr. Marein's classroom resulted in the immediate removal of the referred student from the regular classroom; no approval was required of parents. The only criteria required for placement of the student in the disciplinary classroom were the request of the regular teacher and the consent of Mr. Marein. And Mr. Marein and the regular classroom teacher could decide by themselves how long the student should remain in the disciplinary classroom. Some students, in fact, spent the entire year there.

Mr. Marein wanted students. More exactly, he wanted a secure job. Plenty of students in his classroom meant he had one. His energy for suppression of undesirable behavior was admirable and exuberant. He was a man you could understand fairly easily, if he was not especially easy to like.

When I first met Mr. Marein, I was particularly intrigued by his remarkable height. As I recall, his knee joints were about all I could see at my own eye level. When I raised my eyes to find his face, my first attempt located only his angular hip bones and elegant belt buckle.

Lifting my eyes to the level of his face required heroic effort. My eyes would sweep up the front of his nicely pressed ruffled shirt in a wavy fashion, as Mr. Marein's torso was unsteady. If he were walking beside me, the jolting characteristic of his gait tended to make me feel off-balance.

His face was pleasant enough to look at, once you got up there, being dark-complexioned and angular of feature, but the expression was a puzzle. Mr. Marein looked for all the world like a high school jock at the height of his success. And yet there was something else about his face too—something so sad you couldn't quite overlook it. There was a sort of pleading aspect, a pleading to be accepted as that very jock he wasn't anymore.

For Mr. Marein had been ill a long time. He had been a fearless and successful athlete in high school and had that success still written all over his basic posture and movements; nevertheless, transplanted on top of all that was a life of pain and uncertainty. Mr. Marein had been struck down in his prime with a rare nerve disease that left him partially paralyzed. He could get around, he could make most of his body work, but it cost him effort, and it was awkward. Fate had robbed him of the supple, fluid muscular control and coordination he still only knew as himself.

A brave man, he was, and I felt for him. But on the other hand, it was hard for me to like him a whole lot. For one thing, whenever I approached him for a conversation, he seemed to rise up on his tiptoes, in contrast to the more low-key tall folk who may sit down for an eye-to-eye discussion.

Moreover, Mr. Marein didn't give a hoot about "special needs," and he wasn't interested in trying to learn how to identify children who might qualify for special education services because of "emotional disturbance." He didn't have any training in working with children with behavior problems; he just knew he could handle them all. He said so frequently and clearly. And the local administration gave him just about anything he asked for.

David and I discussed the situation with Mr. Murdock, our supervisor from the county. We explained to him that we felt the simultaneous existence of two programs for junior high children with behavioral problems might lead to conflict. We wondered whether a child who might need special education services might be dumped instead into the "bad apple" room for the convenience of the regular classroom teacher.

All those regulations protecting the rights of children and their parents that had been written into the special education law were conspicuously absent from the regulations governing admission to the Orangetown disciplinary classroom. That made Mr. Marein's program much more immediately responsive to the needs of the classroom teachers than was the elaborate evaluation process of the county special education program.

Mr. Murdock absorbed our worries in one of our early morning supervisory sessions. "Well, well," said he. "Well, well. Now I wonder what might be the reason for this. Certainly the town must have had a reason for starting this program. Yes, they did. I'm sure they did. They must have had a reason. Now, let me see. I think Dr. Knight has mentioned this program to me. What did she tell me? Oh yes, now I remember. She was interested in finding out something about it. I think she wanted to know something about it. What might that have been. Hm. Hm. Now I just can't quite remember much about that—"

Mr. Murdock went on in this vein for some time. He promised to discuss the situation with Dr. Knight.

Life went on as usual after that conversation with Mr. Murdock. No word came from the county regarding the disciplinary classroom or anything else in particular. And then a minor crisis actually occurred concerning a disciplinary referral to Mr. Marein's room, a crisis that involved the special education program, in particular, me.

The referral involved a girl I had been working with. Unfortunately, the issue of choosing between a special education evaluation and a placement in the disciplinary classroom did not involve a clear pair of alternatives, for I had been unable to obtain permission for a special education evaluation by the girl's mother. I had already tried. But the episode certainly revealed to me the dangers of a disciplinary program into which students could be catapulted with no right of evaluation or review.

Gail Stewart was an eighth grader, the only offspring of divorced parents. She lived with her mother. I had become aware of her special needs through Polly Hinkle, the woman hired as a Title I tutor who actually spent her time as a surrogate mother/nurse/social worker.

A few weeks into the school year, Polly had told me about Gail and her having already missed more days of school than she had attended. The year before, Polly said, Gail had been held back because of her infrequent attendance. Polly took me in her car to Gail's home, a ramshackle house trailer in a mobile home park about 10 miles from the school. There was Gail, at midday, watching television with her mother. Both were clad in bathrobes.

Gail put on a wonderful show of illness, and Polly put on a wonderful show of what she wasn't either—a stern, authoritative school official. By the responses of Gail and her mother, Polly had clearly been there before. Gail, besides holding her stomach and rolling her eyes a bit, acted contrite. Mrs. Stewart kept quiet. I stayed in the background during this encounter.

I got to know Gail fairly well because I visited her and her mother at home a few more times when Gail was absent from school. Although Gail was clearly a little actor, she also convinced me that she was genuinely uncomfortable at school. She complained that she suffered severe stomach cramps whenever she approached the school, and she said she hated the school. She described how the teachers acted as if they didn't like her and treated her unfairly.

Gail's mother made feeble attempts to get her daughter to go to school, but it was clear to me she enjoyed Gail's presence at home. The mother worked sporadically to supplement her limited child support payments (sent irregularly by her ex-husband), but she was often home alone and lonely, and sometimes she drank a little too much. It seemed to me that Gail was trying to take care of her mother by staying home.

It also seemed to me that Gail wasn't lying when she described her physical symptoms of illness as she approached the school. I'd had those stomach pains myself when I approached Orangetown in the morning! Although aware of the problem of overidentification, I knew that school phobia is frequently associated with children trying to protect their parents (often a mother) by staying home and that it can be expressed through somatic symptoms.

I thought that perhaps I could help create for Gail a better environment at the school by referring her to special education for suspected school phobia. Perhaps she could work part time with David as a teacher and me as a counselor. The special education program had a consulting psychiatrist, also, who might become involved in the evaluation. Perhaps just the attention during an evaluation might make school a more positive place for Gail, whether she ended up with a diagnosis of school phobia or not.

But to make a long story short, this was one of the few situations in which I was unable to secure parental permission for a special education evaluation. Mrs. Stewart—who was always pleasant and warm toward me, who welcomed me into her home, fed me cookies, and talked endlessly about her dissatisfaction with her own work and her daughter's schooling—nevertheless said she would be absolutely unwilling to provide a social history for Gail. Thus she would not agree to permit a special education evaluation.

Mrs. Stewart's reluctance to sign the permission form for special education evaluation seemed related to the one area of her life she never discussed with me during my home visits—her former marriage. Whatever the reason, I was unable to change her mind.

Although the special education program directed its staff to work with special education referrals only, I knew that on occasion exceptions were made. The special education office insisted on 99 percent conformity in terms of working with special education referrals only but would look the other way for the last 1 percent. Over in Kingston I talked with Gertrude Baker and Norman Werner, social worker and psychologist respectively, about my desire to work with Gail and about my inability to secure her mother's signature for a special education evaluation. Norman suggested that I ask Mrs. Stewart's permission only to counsel Gail myself. He produced a sample permission slip that he used on occasion in similar circumstances.

Taking Norman's advice, I wrote up a special permission slip for Mrs. Stewart to sign permitting me alone to counsel Gail. That would protect me at least from the legal wrath of the mother if something should go wrong in the counseling process. Mrs. Stewart signed the new form without hesitation. Now it was up to me.

Gail began to come to school more often, and I began to counsel her regularly. Her attendance improved markedly, and she began to report some positive feelings about a few of her classes. Being in junior high, she had a homeroom teacher but also a teacher for each academic subject. Some teachers she liked fairly well; she was less enthusiastic about others. Things sounded about right for an eighth grader who had been held back.

But then one day Gail came leaping into my office, clearly just inches away from a full-blown temper tantrum. She was never coming to school again, she screamed. Nobody was going to hit her again, ever again. Nobody. Absolutely nobody. And she was never going to go into that classroom for crazies again, not ever, not even one more time.

When I could get Gail calmed down a little, she spluttered that her homeroom teacher, who also served as her mathematics teacher, had stuck her in Mr. Marein's disciplinary classroom, as punishment, during math class. Well, Gail admitted, she *had* been a little obnoxious during the first part of the class. She had insisted on doodling and making silly faces. Besides, she confessed, she had missed school again yesterday and had been late this morning. The teacher had already been annoyed with her before she fooled around during mathematics class.

But Mr. Marein's classroom was an insult, Gail fumed. So when she was sent in there, she was furious and wouldn't do the work Mr. Marein assigned. Mr. Marein took her aside and tried to make her admit she was in the wrong. She refused, she said; that was all. And then suddenly Mr. Marein had hit her in the face. After the first shock, Gail had run directly to me.

Well, there it was in raw form—the straightforward disciplinary approach to handling behavioral problems versus the treatment-oriented approach of special education. And how ironic. Even if I might be able to persuade the school to postpone placing Gail in the disciplinary classroom, I would probably still be unable to secure permission from her mother for a special education evaluation. I wondered whether all the attendance improvements that Gail had shown over the past few weeks were about to go down the drain.

It was near the end of the school day, and so I kept Gail with me until she was calm again. I walked her to the bus when the bell rang and headed back to my office to think about what to do.

Before I had come to any plan of action, Mr. Marein walked into my room. He looked very grave and tall and proud. I was positively astonished. It hadn't occurred to me that he might come to talk with me on his own. He probably knew, I thought quickly, about my counseling relationship with Gail, perhaps through the homeroom teacher.

I immediately invited him to sit down for a cup of coffee. There was method in my madness. First of all, I figured that if I *didn't* invite Mr. Marein to sit down, I would have one very stiff neck by the end of our conversation. But more important, conducting conversations informally on the tattered couch while sipping a cup of something hot, watching the steam rise slowly, and savoring the aroma often produced favorable results. People could relax and become more human in circumstances such as these.

It took Mr. Marein a long time to get it out, but by the time he did, I was feeling better about him and the whole situation. He described for me Gail's myriad, insolent facial expressions, every smirk and devil-may-care giggle I knew so well, right down to the last detail. Mr. Marein wasn't used to them. His pride couldn't handle the mockery. Something slipped inside him, and before he knew what he was doing, he hit her.

He hadn't meant to go so far, only to create a little respect. He had rarely hit a student before, he said, and never a girl. He certainly wouldn't ever hit Gail again. Now what did I think he ought to do?

I asked Mr. Marein about not accepting Gail into his program at all, about letting her have another chance to make it on her own in the regular classroom. But Mr. Marein didn't want to do that. The homeroom teacher had told him he didn't want Gail back in his room, not until she was all straightened out.

Mr. Marein wanted to prove himself. It was still early in the school year, and he had only four other students in his disciplinary room. Gail was the first girl. He wanted to increase his enrollment. Mr. Marein was adamant about that. He was willing, however, to release Gail to attend some of her regular classes if her behavior and attendance improved. He was willing to work out concrete guidelines regarding how Gail could earn her way back into most of her regular classes, in time.

That seemed like the best bargain that could be worked out under the circumstances, and so I decided to do what I could to get Gail's career in Mr. Marein's classroom off to a more positive start, since I couldn't change his decision to keep her there.

We decided that it might be wise to go together to the house trailer that afternoon to talk with Gail and her mother and explain the positive aspects of Mr. Marein's program. Perhaps in person, Mr. Marein would be able to apologize for striking Gail and would be able to secure some initial cooperation from her mother.

And I felt rather like Florence Nightingale as I rushed with the penitent Mr. Marein to visit Mrs. Stewart and her daughter. I thought a little discussion and apology could put things right.

But no one was home. It was a terrific anticlimax. All we could do was leave a note requesting Mrs. Stewart to call one of us at school the next day.

Gail didn't come back to school, Mrs. Stewart didn't call, and my own phone calls to the house trailer brought no answer for the next full week. Finally, one afternoon at school, I ran into Mr. Burr, the elementary and junior high school principal, in the hallway. I asked him whether he had a few moments to talk and then shared with him my concern that Gail would remain truant if she expected she would be kept in the "classroom for crazies," as she viewed it.

Mr. Burr grinned. "What could be better?" he mused.

"It's a real shame the girl is only fourteen," he continued seriously. "If she were sixteen, we could just forget about her. You know she'll only get pregnant and drop out anyway. Her mother's drunk most of the time, and you can be sure all she wants is Gail home to take care of her. Heck, we'll just keep her in Marein's room, and that will take care of it. Gail Stewart won't hang around here for long."

"But Mr. Burr," I gasped. "Gail is an intelligent student. Don't you think it would be a good idea to give her a chance to make it here at school?"

"What do you mean, give her a chance?" he responded. "She's got all the chance she deserves. She's had plenty of chances, and she won't make it anyway. Why bother with her? In fact, I'll bet the school board would give her permission to drop out of school this year, if we could get the mother to request it. Girls like her are more trouble than they're worth. They're all alike. All they care about is boys, booze, and babies. Why push a truancy case?"

In my naïveté and concern for Gail, I was shocked at Mr. Burr's attitude. And I tried to prove him wrong. Gail was a strong-minded girl, and with the right motivation, I thought, she would be able to develop competence in a career that could provide her some independence and pride.

I got Mr. Marein to agree to meet with Mrs. Stewart and me to discuss together Gail's educational needs and the direction Mr. Marein could provide. I finally reached Mrs. Stewart by telephone, and she agreed to an appointment. But she missed it. Next, I arranged to bring Mrs. Stewart to school. But she missed that appointment too. Finally, she just told me outright: she didn't want to have anything to do with the school. She really didn't want to meet with Mr. Marein. And she still didn't want a special education evaluation. She didn't believe that Gail was school phobic. Gail just didn't like school. And no wonder, she said, the way they treated her down there.

I was stuck. Here was a problem where the school system itself was exaggerating an original problem—poor school attendance—by an assignment to a disciplinary classroom. But the responsible parent would not let an alternative system (special education) try to intervene.

My counseling alone with Gail did not fill the gap. Although Gail did come to school haphazardly after a couple of weeks, she missed most of her appointments with me. Feeling frustrated and ineffective, I discussed this situation with her one day when she did keep an appointment.

Gail responded that she was never going to like school, particularly Mr. Marein, and I just couldn't help her. I couldn't get her out of that classroom, obviously, so seeing me was a waste of time. We talked about other reasons for counseling sessions, such as talking over ways to make the best of a difficult situation, but we just didn't seem to be reaching each other anymore. Gail couldn't accept the fact that I was willing to work along with Mr. Marein.

We agreed to terminate our sessions until Gail actively chose to come and see me. I called Mrs. Stewart and explained the decision, referring her to the Emmett County Guidance Clinic if she would like additional counseling for herself or her daughter by a different agency.

I cautioned Mrs. Stewart about the possibility of truancy proceedings by the school, knowing that I was licked now that I had resorted to a hollow threat. We had discussed the possibility of truancy proceedings by the school administration before, and the threat just hadn't seemed to make a bit of difference. Besides, I now knew the school wouldn't bother. I just hoped to scare Mrs. Stewart a little, on the off chance that it would get her to put her daughter on the bus one more morning. I offered my own services again if she should ever choose to call.

Gail continued to miss school until soon she wasn't coming at all. The school never initiated truancy proceedings. And so there was another fourteen-year-old, fe-

male, junior high school dropout wandering without direction through the population.

She was late. I had the restaurant table by the window all to myself for a good fifteen
minutes while waiting for Dr. Knight that morning. It was very cold outside, and there
was snow on the ground. When she finally arrived, she stumbled in the snow near the
doorway of the restaurant. She had to stop outside for a few moments while she
brushed herself off with anxious, jerky movements. When Dr. Knight finally came inside, she was still breathless and there was snow in her hair.

It was hard to be reserved and political in a circumstance such as this, even with
the director of the Emmett County special education program, and so, I wasn't. A mistake, again.

This breakfast meeting was planned for the purpose of discussing with Dr.
Knight my particular perceptions of the progress of the new ED program in
Orangetown. Dr. Knight had suggested the meeting, but I was more than pleased at
her invitation, as I had been planning to ask her for a private consultation myself. On
my own agenda were three items: first, the necessity for administrative clarification
concerning the relationship between the Orangetown disciplinary classroom and the
ED program for junior high students; second, the desirability of a full-time social
worker for Orangetown, since the time had already come when I couldn't accept any
more referrals for ongoing counseling; and third, the supervisory abilities of Mr. Martin
Murdock, or the lack thereof. This last item, I knew from my previous experience with
Dr. Knight, would be especially sensitive, but the problem of Martin's work performance was becoming pressing. Mr. Burr, the elementary and junior high principal in
Orangetown, had recently confided to David Chase and me that the local school administration was about to bar Mr. Murdock from participating in any more routine administrative meetings at the local school. He took up "entirely too much time talking
about nonsense," to quote Mr. Burr verbatim. Mr. Murdock was, in fact, becoming a haz-
ard to the survival of the special education program in Orangetown, in my opinion.

My morning conference with Dr. Knight began with the issue of the disciplinary
classroom, and shortly after the meeting began, I was satisfied that she understood
and accepted the need for her to intervene personally to establish a clear administrative policy of linkage between the two programs. Dr. Knight followed up on this request, in fact, only a couple of weeks later. As for the issue of a full-time social worker
for Orangetown—that was something for the future, obviously. Dr. Knight seemed
open to the idea, however.

But the issue of Martin Murdock—that was another matter entirely. Possibly, by
the time I broached that topic with Dr. Knight, toward the end of our breakfast conference, the animated conversation, the warm food, the informality of it all had stolen
too much of my caution. I do think I remember speaking carefully, however, describing only specific behaviors of Martin. But I clearly failed in my intent to raise what I
considered legitimate concern about the man's work performance. What I accomplished was to make Dr. Knight angry at me. Possibly, my previous words to Dr. Knight
at my earlier supervisory conference with her made her already displeased with me.

Perhaps, whatever I might say about Martin Murdock from that time forward, Dr. Knight would hear my words as insubordinate, insolent.

At any rate, when I left the morning meeting with Myrtle Knight, I thought that I had reached her constructively on all three of the major issues on my own agenda and that I was on good terms with her. I hadn't, and I wasn't.

Happily, Dr. Knight did visit Orangetown shortly thereafter, and she did settle the linkage problem between the disciplinary classroom and the ED program in the junior high. David Chase and I both urged her, of course, to try to persuade the Orangetown local school administration to screen all disciplinary referrals through the special education evaluation process first. We urged Dr. Knight to work out that procedure because of the case of Gail Stewart. We knew for certain that the mere precipitous placement of a disturbed child in the disciplinary classroom could be damaging.

But such an idealistic arrangement was not to be part of the real world. The very purpose of the disciplinary classroom, from the point of view of the Orangetown school administration (of course, never openly stated), was to circumvent the time-consuming evaluation process of special education. The introduction of the special education program into the local school system made it suddenly difficult for local officials simply to suspend or expel difficult children, as had been the norm in the past. Someone would be too likely, now, to refer these children to special education. That might keep them disrupting their regular classrooms for months, it was feared, while being evaluated. How much easier just to impound the little rascals in a separate room.

What Dr. Knight did arrange and approve was a process whereby any referral to the disciplinary classroom would automatically result in a referral to special education. The referral would be made by Mr. Marein, the disciplinary classroom teacher, after the child was already in his program. Since ED evaluations usually took a few months, Mr. Marein wouldn't have to worry about losing too much of his business this way. In fact, it even gradually occurred both to Mr. Marein and to David Chase that they could work together with the same children during the evaluation period, if they chose to do so.

So the linkage issue was settled, with reasonable, if not ideal, established procedures. The settlement wouldn't have helped Gail Stewart. But now, at least, the special education staff knew their rights and responsibilities with respect to children transplanted into the disciplinary classroom.

If only the issue regarding Mr. Murdock could have been settled as cleanly. It soon became apparent to me that I had been pegged as a troublemaker by my attractive and energetic boss, Dr. Knight. She warned me shortly thereafter that I had better make my peace with Mr. Murdock. I must say for Martin that he was more than willing to try to make peace. We talked about our expectations for each other, later on, in some detail. The problem was that neither of us ever measured up to what the other wanted. And I clearly had sabotaged my chance to have easy influence with the top administrators of my county program.

Eventually, Mr. Murdock was relieved of his supervisory position, and sometime after that he was fired, I learned much later via the grapevine. So I felt somewhat exonerated about my assessment of his work. But those things happened a year or more after I had left the special education program on my own.

DISCUSSION AND STUDY QUESTIONS

This chapter offers a good example both of values affecting policy decisions and of policy affecting practice. In an era of financial constraints, it makes no sense to have two programs to meet the same need. Actually, the two programs in question—the disciplinary classroom and the special education program for children with emotional disturbance—were more than just duplications. The confusion they created for school personnel, social workers, parents, and students wasted energy and resources that added to the waste inherent in the duplication. Yet Orangetown insisted on having both. Each clearly reflected different value stances regarding the causes of disruptive behavior among junior high school students. Unfortunately, only the special education program was based on empirical data and conceptual knowledge.

Regardless of the reasons for the existence of two programs, that they were mandated by policy affected the author's work. She had to clarify for herself and others the purposes of each. She had to try to minimize the negative effects of the disciplinary classroom, and, as the chapter shows, she was not always successful. She also had to struggle to operationalize the more cumbersome procedures built into the special education program. Although these procedures in fact better protected the rights of clients, they had the unintended effect of benefiting the competing program and thereby disadvantaging clients. The chapter shows, then, that values, knowledge, and policy are closely linked and that policy is a major source of *what* services are available and *how* they are provided.

1. Think about your own junior high or high school years. Did your school have a disciplinary classroom? A special education classroom? Do you think either or both would have been helpful for any students with behavioral problems that you knew personally? If your school lacked either program, how were behavioral problems handled in the school?
2. How do you go about making policy for yourself? For example, how do you decide to do certain things needed every day and in terms of longer-range objectives? To what degree do values enter into these policy decisions? How about your use of knowledge?
*3. What is the policy-making structure of the agency in which you are working (or one in which you have worked)? If it is a public agency, be sure to include policy making at the county, state, and national levels, as appropriate. Even if it is a private agency, be careful to identify whether policy is in fact influenced by fund-raising bodies like the United Way. Are clients or direct service social workers formally part of the policy-making process?
*4. Why do you think the author brought up again the subject of Mr. Murdock's work performance with Dr. Knight, even though she suspected that it would not be a popular topic? Do you think she should have done so? Under the same circumstances, what do you think you might have done to help resolve the difficulty with Mr. Murdock?

---

*Questions notated with an asterisk are intended for advanced students who have had or are currently having some social work practice experience and who have made at least a tentative commitment to the profession.

CHAPTER 19

Paperwork

or: Attending to Paperwork, Though Annoying,
Can Avert a Malpractice Suit

Concepts Covered in This Chapter

1. Psychological factors in physical illness
2. The legal basis for social welfare services
3. Maintaining professional records
4. Public image of social work
5. Legal risks faced by social workers

Learning Objectives   After reading this chapter you should be able to

1. Discuss how psychological factors can have an influence in physical illness
2. List at least three reasons why there are laws that determine what social welfare services exist and the manner in which they are provided
3. List at least three functions of the professional records that social workers maintain
4. Discuss your understanding of the public image of social work
5. List at least three ways in which the public image of social work affects the services provided by social workers
6. Discuss the legal risks faced by social workers
7. Identify at least two strategies that social workers can use to reduce their legal risks

"Oh, really? For sure?" I asked out loud. Inside I said a lot of other things, very unlady-like things.

I was at a routine pupil services meeting for the elementary school in Kingston, and my supervisor there, Dan Dwyer, had just been dicussing with me my new refer-ral from the LD teacher. Dan told me that in order to proceed with the requested counseling with the new referral, I would have to obtain parental permission in writ-ing and reconvene the original M team. Counseling would have to be officially added to the original M team recommendations, with signatures from all the members, in-cluding a parent, officially approving the addition.

Oh, lord, more paperwork. And more meetings.

Over in Orangetown, I had been counseling regularly with referrals from the LD teacher there, without a scrap of paperwork being involved. I just phoned the parents of the children referred to establish informal contact and permission.

Dan Dwyer might be a far more knowledgeable supervisor than Martin Murdock, but he surely made life difficult sometimes. Counseling little kids might be fine, but paperwork was a pain in the neck.

"Really, Carolyn," Dan articulated carefully, his sad brown eyes peering mourn-fully out of his thin, long face. "It's only for your own protection. Anything you do with a child in special education must be approved by the parents by law, you know. And nothing is legally approved unless it is listed on the M team document and the par-ents have signed it."

So if I wanted to work with Louis Lambert, I would have to persuade his mother to sign a permission form, and I would have to reconvene the M team to obtain the signatures of the other members. What a bother.

I talked with Louis's teacher again about the urgency of the referral, thinking I might just let it go. But her input convinced me to bother.

"The boy is almost too haughty," she said.

"Haughty?" I asked, somewhat astonished at her use of that particular adjective.

"Absolutely," she replied. "I know it sounds funny for a fifth grader, but Louis acts like he is just too good for this classroom. The other kids can't stand him, and I can't either, to tell the truth. Whenever he gets anything wrong in his schoolwork, he blames me or he cries. So he spends all his time in this classroom either acting like he's King Louis the Fourteenth, or else he's crying."

"I think part of the problem," the teacher continued, "is that Louis's father is on the school board. He just can't accept the fact his son has a learning disability. So he tells Louis he doesn't belong in here with the other kids."

"How on earth did you get the father's permission for an LD placement in the first place?" I asked.

"We actually didn't," the teacher replied. "Louis was flunking out of school last year, and his mother signed so he wouldn't be left back. I think Mr. Lambert just de-cided not to notice."

I decided to discuss the situation with Mrs. Lambert, Louis's mother. I called her and scheduled a visit. Before I had a chance to meet with her, however, Mr. Dwyer, my painstaking supervisor, brought me a special M team amendment form. He went out of his way to explain that he had learned that the procedure to amend an M team rec-ommendation could be done more simply than he had informed me at our prior meeting. I could just obtain the mother's signature on the amendment form, if she were willing to sign. Then I could take the signed form to the other members of the original M team individually for their signatures. In that way, I could avoid the necessity of calling a meeting, difficult because of the variety of schedules that would have to be coordinated.

I thanked Dan Dwyer sincerely for his information and briefly reflected on the difference between my Kingston supervisor from the county office and the one with whom I dealt in Orangetown. Mr. Dwyer actually knew the rules and regulations of the special education program and would tell me about them. He would check up on his own instructions to make sure he was correct. He would let me know promptly if he thought he had misinformed me. Mr. Dwyer was a professional.

So with a mixture of gratitude and stubborn grumbling, I arrived at Mrs. Lambert's house, M team ammendment form in hand.

Mrs. Lambert was a pleasant sort of woman. She had a wan little smile and a tired air about her, but she was cordial and responsive. I introduced myself as the social worker with the school special education program, and she seemed almost impressed. She talked about her son with concern. When I mentioned to Mrs. Lambert about the crying at school, she told me that Louis cried frequently at home too. Sometimes he cried over his homework, and sometimes he cried in fear of his father's wrath when he couldn't do his homework.

During this visit, I asked Mrs. Lambert whether she might be interested in the services of the Emmett County Guidance Clinic for possible family counseling. I explained that families frequently had trouble adjusting to the stresses surrounding learning disabilities in children, and I explained that the Emmett County clinic was familiar with the public school program. Counselors there might be able to work with Mr. Lambert's feelings about the learning problem as well as with Louis himself.

"Oh, no," Mrs. Lambert exclaimed, a little too hastily. "Everything is just fine here at home, and if you want to work with Louis at school, that's all right too."

Before I left, I wrote "counseling with school social worker" on the M team amendment form for Louis, and Mrs. Lambert signed quite casually.

In a short time, I obtained the rest of the signatures required from the other members of the original M team, and I was legally set to begin my work with little Louis.

Louis really was little for his age too—wiry, but very small. That made his strutting about in the LD classroom a particularly ineffective means for him to try to build his self-esteem. The boy was a social outcast, and he knew it. The other children saw him as "stuck up" and a "poor sport," according to his teacher.

When I took Louis aside and began to work with him, I began in my usual way. I showed him the cozy, private counseling room available in that school and let him delve freely into the pile of toys and games stashed there to help facilitate communication with children. Louis chose the checkers game.

I had a sense that Louis would need to win a game or two before we could get into anything serious, so I let him. At first, the boy wouldn't talk at all, but gradually, he opened up a little.

But not much. As we played checkers, Louis would alternately crow with triumph or cry with anger as he jumped or I jumped a checker. He was humorless and without mercy in his winning streaks and sulky when he was losing. He wasn't much fun to play with, in fact. It was hard to carry on any sort of conversation with him during a game because he got so totally lost in his need to win. I tried to interest Louis in noncompetitive play after a while, such as drawing, painting, or modeling clay. But he couldn't be diverted.

Finally, curiously, after a few sessions like this, I creamed him—not slowly, after a tight game, but right from the start of a match. Louis's tears flowed copiously, and he seemed absolutely irreconcilable. However, the experience seemed to jolt him into a need to talk. Gradually, Louis said he studied so hard he had headaches all the time, but it didn't do him a bit of good. Crying made his headaches worse, and he couldn't stop himself from crying, either.

When we parted that day, I thought we'd made a breakthrough and learned how to talk to each other. But such was not the case. Louis continued to play checkers desperately to win; if things didn't go as he hoped, he usually sulked. If I attempted to introduce a noncompetitive game, he yawned and doodled. Asking him about his doodles brought silence. We didn't seem to be developing any easy rapport. In fact, we seemed to be going in circles. Gradually, however, I noticed a string of consistent feedback: Louis always said he had a headache.

One day the headache talk seemed to leap at me in a stronger way than usual. I pursued this line of discussion further.

"How much of the regular school day would you guess you have a headache, Louis?"

"I don't have one every day when I get up in the morning, but I usually do. And then whether I have a headache or not when I get up, I always get one on the way to school. It gets worse all day."

"Every day, Louis, or almost every day?"

"Every day. I get a headache every single day."

"How do you feel after school?"

"Oh, it isn't much better. I want to play baseball or something with the other kids, but they won't let me. Sometimes I get so mad my head hurts and my hat gets so heavy I take it off."

"How about once you get home?"

"Oh, I get a headache at home all the time too. I can't ever do my homework right, and my father gets mad and tells me I never do anything right. And then Mom gets upset and she tries to help me, but I think she's really mad at me too. My head always hurts at night at home when I try to do my homework. Nothing ever helps. But then Mom will let me go to bed early."

"How well do you sleep at night, Louis?"

"How well do I sleep at night? What do you mean, how well do I sleep? How should I know? When I'm asleep, I'm asleep!"

"I mean, is it easy for you to fall asleep, or is it hard?"

"Oh, real easy. I like to go to sleep. I can sleep all day if people will let me. Lots of Saturdays I never even get out of bed."

"Does your head hurt on Saturday?"

"Not when I'm asleep."

"How about when you get up on Saturday?"

"Oh, when I first get up I'll feel all right. Then Dad will yell at me or something, and I'll get the headache back again. It'll get worse all day just like it always does."

Well, maybe Louis was exaggerating. But if he wasn't, he needed some intensive evaluation and intervention, more than I was able to give at school, I thought. I suspected those headaches were caused by tension and the sleeping was a means of coping with depression. However, there could also be something physically wrong with the boy. A fifth grader shouldn't be having all those headaches or craving sleep so much.

I took this case to Norman Werner, the psychologist with whom I usually worked in Kingston, for consultation. In reviewing the limited facts we had on hand, we agreed that a referral to the psychiatrist at the Emmett County Guidance Clinic would be the most appropriate course of action to take at this time. The psychiatrist at the clinic would have the medical knowledge to investigate further physical causes of the headaches, including making appropriate referrals to specialists if he thought that was necessary, and he could work in conjunction with a social worker in providing family therapy, which, we hoped, could help the Lamberts deal with each other in less stressful ways.

When I called Mrs. Lambert for a second visit, I was worried. I remembered she had brushed off my tentative referral to the guidance clinic at the last appointment, and I also remembered that Louis's teacher had told me the father had had difficulty accepting even a learning disability in his son. How would Mr. Lambert react to the information that the school social worker thought Louis should be referred for psychiatric and medical evaluation, along with family counseling?

But when I got to the Lambert home, the interview with Mrs. Lambert seemed to go smoothly enough. Louis's mother seemed to understand the reasons for my referral, and she wrote down the address and telephone number of the clinic. She noted the names of the psychiatrist and the social worker I recommended, in particular. She seemed worried about her husband's reaction to the referral, but not unduly so. We agreed I would terminate my own counseling with Louis over the next few weeks.

A couple of weeks later, I made a follow-up phone call to Mrs. Lambert to see whether she had contacted the guidance clinic as planned. The week before, I had talked with Louis about bringing our own visits to a close shortly, and he had seemed to think that was a fine idea. I had tried to work through with him any sense of rejection or disappointment, but humbling as it was, there didn't seem to be any problem in that area. My original sense that Louis and I had never developed real rapport was apparently correct. I planned to see the boy only one or two times more at school and wanted to make sure that the alternative plans were under way.

But Mrs. Lambert told me she had not called the clinic and was not planning to do so. Her husband refused to let her, she explained. Mr. Lambert didn't believe anybody in his family could possibly need to talk to a psychiatrist or a social worker.

Mrs. Lambert's actual words brought a message of finality, but her tone sounded tentative. That gave me an opening to try again. I asked her whether she thought it might be useful for me to meet with her husband and her together to discuss the reasons for the referral. She thought it might. So I scheduled an evening appointment at their home, the only time Mrs. Lambert thought her husband would be willing to see me, after his regular work hours when no one would know.

There it was again, the double bind. I didn't like night work because it kept me away from my own home, to say nothing of the fact that I received no compensatory time or pay for the work. I would be expected at school at 7:45 the next morning as usual. Night work was, in fact, a charitable donation on my part, evidence of my bleeding heart. And I knew bleeding hearts were likely to get themselves into trouble. To put more energy into problem solving than a client is willing to invest is usually a poor omen for achieving anything worthwhile.

The people I worked with at night were usually those people who didn't care enough to make the necessary arrangements in their own work schedules to see me during my working hours. And they were, of course, the hardest ones to deal with. Sometimes they caused me positive grief, so that I would resolve never to attempt an act of charity again. I would go home at night, that place I would much rather be, to sip cocoa with my husband and friends in front of my safe, warm fire.

That resolve usually worked pretty well for me when my primary clients were adults. But when the client was a child—there I often felt I had to go the extra mile. Since children are legally dependent on their parents, it was the parents I especially had to reach to secure the services I thought were needed for the child. And parents who don't want their children to have problems (and that category, of course, includes most parents) sometimes have a very hard time recognizing the evidence. It takes skill, patience, flexibility, and time on the part of the social worker to enable those parents to take a careful look.

Feeling both noble and tired in advance, I scheduled the night appointment to meet with Louis's father. But before I had a chance to perform my charitable act, I received another call from Mrs. Lambert. Her voice sounded strained. She had taken Louis to the family physician, she said, and so there was no need to meet with her and her husband at home. The family physician had assured her that Louis's headaches were not normal for a boy his age, and he had referred the child to a neurologist for a detailed physical workup.

Mrs. Lambert seemed to want to say no more, but I had a hunch a neurologist was not going to be the answer for Louis. The family would want the problem to be entirely physical, of course, because that would explain the headaches in a manner that was socially acceptable. Physical illness would not embarrass the family; the Lamberts might even get sympathy from the neighbors. Psychological or emotional disturbance, on the other hand, would be difficult to explain and might bring whispers and pointed fingers. The neighbors might say there was something wrong with the parents too.

But the onset of Louis's headaches, at least as the boy described them to me, seemed to occur after he had had a frustrating experience with his homework or after a parent had scolded him. Therefore, I suspected a psychogenic factor in his pain. So I asked Mrs. Lambert whether I could call her again in a few weeks, after the appointment with the neurologist, to see how things were going. She said that would be fine.

A few days later, Mrs. Lambert apparently called me again, but I was not in Kingston at the time. Norman Werner took the call and left me a message. The neurologist for the Lamberts wanted Louis's school records. Norman, always organized, wrote in his note that he had already sent Mrs. Lambert the release of information forms, so that we could forward the records to the physician.

When I got Norman's note, I took Louis's special education file out of the locked cabinet, intending to select the materials to send to the neurologist right away. But I received a crisis call from Orangetown that day. I shoved the Lambert records into an obscure drawer in my desk in the Kingston pupil services office and left in haste.

So it happened that Louis's file was not accessible to anybody else in Kingston on the day his parents stormed the pupil services office, demanding to see it.

And they did just that. Shortly after I left for Orangetown, Louis's parents apparently roared into my shared Kingston office, demanding to see both myself and their son's file. When they couldn't do either, the couple allegedly became outraged and absolutely terrorized everybody in the office. They accused the staff of being a pack of liars trying to protect that scoundrel social worker.

Now, I didn't know Mr. Lambert personally, so I could imagine him as a fiery man of monstrous proportions, as vividly described by the office staff. But to try to envision poor Mrs. Lambert—pale, tired, but cordial Mrs. Lambert—in the role of monstress simply stretched my imagination beyond limits. I really couldn't believe the tale I heard.

But, according to Norman's version of the story, embellished luridly by the secretary and the school nurse, the Lamberts furiously demanded to be shown exactly what information was going to be sent to the neurologist. They wanted to make sure there were no records included that had been written by that busybody social worker. In fact, they spewed, under no circumstances would Ms. Wells have been allowed to talk to their son if they had ever known she was a social worker. Mrs. Lambert had been deliberately misled by the nefarious Ms. Wells who had misrepresented her credentials and passed herself off as a respectable psychologist. The Lamberts intended to sue Ms. Wells, in fact, now that their son had been permanently damaged by exposure to her meddling ways.

Norman was genuinely afraid for me. The Lamberts had the money and the social competence to carry through with a legal suit. Norman hadn't been able to find Louis's file that day, of course, to see what Mrs. Lambert had agreed to in writing. The parents called poor Norman personally a liar on the day of their visit and several other things, or so I was told, accusing him of hiding the file to protect his incompetent colleague, me.

I returned to Kingston the next morning to get all this exciting news and wondered and learned. I learned firsthand why files should be left in their appropriate place; I made Norman a well-deserved apology. But I also learned about the lengths an ordinary person will go for self-preservation. For Mrs. Lambert had known all along I was a social worker, of that I was positive. And she was basically a nice lady; she meant well.

But her husband was hysterically prejudiced against the social work profession, as are many typical, bootstraps-type Americans. When, in the process of explaining my referral to the guidance clinic to her husband, Mrs. Lambert had had to explain to him who I was, Mr. Lambert had apparently blown up at her in violent anger. He had scared her so much she denied she knew I was a social worker. Mrs. Lambert apparently came up with the story that the first time I had visited her, I had told her I was a psychologist. Only just recently had Mrs. Lambert learned the terrible truth regarding my unspeakable profession.

This fixation with my profession, be it space lady or Sunday school teacher, performed the function of blocking the need for the Lamberts to face the fact that their son might have a serious problem that could relate to the Lamberts themselves. If the Lamberts could rest certain that social workers in general were incompetent, then either I must be wrong in my assessment that Louis had an emotion-related problem, or else if Louis did have an emotional problem, then I personally must have caused it.

I had been afraid of the family's reaction to the referral to the guidance clinic, and here it was, a bit more exaggerated than I had originally feared.

When I called Mrs. Lambert on the telephone, I had another surprise in store for me. I suppose I expected an apology when I spoke with her in person, some explanation in private between the two of us that she had acted out of immediate duress. Hadn't we developed a pleasant personal relationship between ourselves? But she acted like a different person. She was impolite, unfriendly, accusing. She spoke with a voice that was as cold as ice, and she threatened to sue me for misrepresenting my credentials, just as though she believed her own tale!

To say the least, I was astounded. I have been lied to before and not known about it, I'm sure. I've also been lied to and known it, but in circumstances where the person lying to me didn't know I knew it. I have much more rarely been lied to when both liar and I knew we both knew. And little Mrs. Lambert? What was going on to make her act in this way?

Reminding Mrs. Lambert gently that I had informed her of my profession didn't have the least effect, and I decided that accusing her of lying could only make her feel more defensive. So I invited her and her husband to come in and see the files, as they had requested. I gave her an opportunity to talk about her feelings a little further, but I couldn't reach her.

And to tell the truth, a sneaky part of me started to look forward to the Lamberts' visit. I wanted to see how each of them would handle themselves and each other when they saw the big, clear, signed form permitting counseling of Louis Lambert by the school social worker, me.

Worse than that, Lord forbid, I've always had a little bit of the moralist in me. I felt wronged by the Lamberts, used, so to speak. I didn't feel I deserved so cruel a treatment, such a nice person as myself. I didn't feel I could wring an ounce of contrition from Mr. Lambert, as I had no prior relationship with him, but I expected I could tingle Mrs. Lambert with just a little pang of guilt. Shouldn't she squirm just a little for her dishonest behavior?

The Lamberts stalked quite haughtily into the pupil services office in Kingston on the day of their appointment, forming a stiff, gruesome twosome. I greeted both most politely, but the sneaky part of me held Mrs. Lambert's eyes in a deep, searching gaze. She didn't look away. She gazed back coolly and steadily. Heavens, the woman had a core of steel.

She introduced her husband cordially, and I greeted him politely but looked her in the eye again. Pure innocence must have radiated from my face. She glared back balefully this time. The subtle lift of my eyebrow brought a new, abstract uplift of the nose on the part of Mrs. Lambert.

By now, I wasn't enjoying the game anymore at all. I could tell there weren't going to be any tears of contrition. All the fun was creeping away. The Lamberts were there to play their roles of wronged parents to the bitter end. Oh well, let's get on with it. At least there was still the signed addendum form to display, and besides, it would protect me legally.

I murmured a few pleasantries, called Norman in as bodyguard, and sat us all down at a small conference table in a private room. I began the conference by explaining that I understood an apparent misunderstanding had occurred concerning my involvement and professional role with little Louis. I asked whether the parents would like me to review my work with Louis further with them.

"Not at all," Mr. Lambert stated flatly. "We intend to review the records, clean them up of any reference to our son's being seen by a social worker, and take this outrage to court. You, Ms. Wells, will be held personally responsible for misrepresenting your credentials." He spoke with the confident, articulate tones of a man accustomed to authority and action.

Suddenly I felt tired and mean and unprofessional in my need to make poor Mrs. Lambert suffer for her lies. I had thought I understood the problem intellectually before, of course, but now, suddenly I felt the Lamberts' plight in my guts. Mr. Lambert had a tough image to maintain, to make it in the world he lived in. He expected his wilting wife to keep the family image polished and shiny. The family couldn't afford a deeply troubled son with a learning disability.

But the play had to continue. I was still curious about how the Lamberts would react to the signed M team addendum, prominently displayed near the top of Louis's file. I had made a photocopy of that form and put it in a separate drawer prior to the meeting. I had done that just in case they should tear up the original. I was getting crafty in my old age.

Mr. Lambert saw the M team addendum form first. When Mrs. Lambert saw his studied look and looked down to see the form herself, she tried to cover her signature in an offhand way with another piece of paper. But her husband grabbed the addendum form out from under her hand, stared at it, and then glared tensely at his wife. The words "school social worker" seemed to vibrate on the page.

Words came to a ragged halt. For a long moment, Mr. Lambert looked as if he might tear the form to shreds. He didn't. He just looked at his wife in an ugly way, and her facial features went still. "I didn't know," she said blandly. "I didn't know I signed a paper like that."

She didn't apologize; she didn't lose her composure.

What happened next was somewhat anticlimactic. Actually, Norman and I had worked out a little scheme in advance. We had expected that the Lamberts would need to remove something permanently from Louis's file, to save face, so we had arranged the needed prop in advance. We had put a paragraph describing the social worker's reasons for referring Louis for psychiatric evaluation into the file.

Norman's report, including identical information, was also in the file, but we didn't expect the parents would read that. First of all, Norman's report was fairly technical and lengthy, recording a number of test scores, and second, Norman was a psychologist, and the Lamberts' excuse for challenging my own report was that I was not a psychologist. Through the psychologist's report, the neurologist would receive all the information relevant to suspected emotional components of Louis's headaches.

Our hunches were only partly right. The Lamberts did demand removal of my report and acted satisfied when we complied. But they also read Norman's report, every word. They remained silent. They didn't demand removal of that report nor removal of the form signed by Mrs. Lambert permitting my work with Louis. Perhaps they knew they couldn't legally insist on those things.

The conference didn't last much longer. The Lamberts left quietly. I was awfully glad I'd done my paperwork. I knew I owed that precaution only to my county supervisor, Dan Dwyer, whom I later thanked. I've been just a little more religious about my paperwork since then, but not entirely, not entirely.

Because I'd done my paperwork in the Lambert case, I wouldn't have to face a lawsuit. I would be okay. As for little Louis and his blustering dad and his cool-running mom, that, unfortunately, wasn't likely to be the case. I didn't really think any one of them was going to be okay. I didn't feel very good about that, but I did know the family knew where they could go for help.

DISCUSSION AND STUDY QUESTIONS

Although the need to follow agency procedures was discussed earlier, this chapter is a good illustration of a number of reasons why practice is enhanced by doing so. Having files processed in orderly ways makes them available when needed by professional staff persons authorized to use them. Having set procedures to follow in getting permission from clients to provide services protects both the social worker and the agency. Having a hierarchical supervisory structure gives social workers a formally defined support system to use when confronted by a formal challenge from a client (the social worker would also have more informal support systems, of course). Although the author correctly laments the amount of time and energy social workers spend doing paperwork, this activity, when carefully designed, has an important place in professional practice. Naturally, useless paperwork, which serves no useful function in terms of service delivery, is to be avoided.

1. Why do you think the author thought it would be easier for the Lamberts to accept physical disease in their son rather than psychological or emotional disturbance? Do you think she was right? Would you feel as the Lamberts did if confronted with a similar problem with one of your children?
2. What kind of paperwork do you least like doing—perhaps filling out dorm applications or job applications? Do you feel these procedures are necessary? Try to be as specific as you can in explaining why or why not.

*3. The author reflects that to put more energy into problem solving for a client than the client himself or herself is willing to invest is usually a poor omen for accomplishing anything worthwhile. Based on your experience, what do you think about this idea as a general guideline for practice? Why would working with children as primary clients complicate this approach?

*4. The author mentions in this chapter that she took Louis's record from the special education files and left it in her own desk drawer when she was out of the office. Why was this an inadvisable act? How did her hasty action inconvenience her colleagues in Kingston? Why do most offices have regulations regarding the removal of files and rules regarding where they must be kept when not in use?

---

*Questions notated with an asterisk are intended for advanced students who have had or are currently having some social work practice experience and who have made at least a tentative commitment to the profession.

CHAPTER 20

Talking to Mr. and Mrs. Responsible Taxpayer

or: Arguing Various Pro's and Con's of Voluntary Private Charity Versus Tax-Supported Public Welfare Programs

Concepts Covered in This Chapter

1. The voluntary charitable approach to social welfare
2. The public institutional approach to social welfare
3. Individual responsibility for helping
4. Social responsibility for social problems
5. Regulating social welfare programs for social accountability
6. Individual values and their effect on social welfare
7. The social worker's role in advocating social welfare services

Learning Objectives   After reading this chapter you should be able to

1. Define voluntary charity and describe its role in social welfare
2. Define public institutionalized social welfare and describe its role
3. Discuss the reasons for having both voluntary and public components in the social welfare system of the United States
4. List three reasons why individuals have a responsibility to help others
5. List three reasons why society has a responsibility to help its members
6. Discuss your views on who you feel you have a responsibility to help
7. List at least three reasons why social welfare programs should be regulated
8. List at least three ways that individual values affect social welfare
9. Discuss your view of the social worker's role in advocating social welfare

P roblem situations such as that of Robert Casey, the little Kingston boy who needed glasses, a sheltering home life, and someone or something to see to it that he (and his several brothers and sisters) got to school, did not just take place in my professional life and keep themselves neatly filed there in my desk drawer at the school. The problems begged for solution, and so the thinking went on in off-hours, seeking solution at best or a place to pin blame at worst.

Whose fault was the situation of that eight-year-old boy? His own, because he wouldn't go to school on his own? His mother's, for not sending him? His father's, for not being around to help out? Mine, for not being able to motivate the family to do something? Society's, for not being more responsive to Robert's special needs, for not providing, for example, an active protective services agency to intervene forcefully to make Robert go to school while he was still too young to understand his own best interests?

Why didn't society intervene at least to supply Robert's glasses with regular public funds just because he needed them or to repair his already rotting teeth? Clearly, his parents weren't going to do that for him; and was it Robert's fault that his parents were poor, uneducated themselves, and had been convicted of welfare fraud?

Why was society so reluctant to provide the means for mandatory intervention in a blatant, if nonmalicious, neglectful situation? Whose fault? Whose fault? Why?

These thoughts about Robert Casey and children like him continued to work themselves around in my head throughout the school year and right into my summer vacation.

And there I was, the blissful vacationer, standing on the edge of a log pier that jutted out into a lovely lake, surrounded by green hills, blue sky, and sun. I was on an island and had arrived the night before by motorboat.

I was surrounded by wonderful, enthusiastic people who had taken my husband, Dale, and me in at a moment's notice. The amazing part of it all was that the people who had taken us in in such grand style hadn't seen us for more than five years. Yet the gulf of time that divided us was gone at first glance.

Dale and I hadn't really known quite what we were getting into. We knew our friends had undergone a fundamentalist religious conversion and had settled in at some kind of wilderness mission. We were curious about their lives and wanted to see how they were—that was all. The mission was an earthly heaven. Anyone would have to be refreshed there, and we most assuredly were. But what I did not expect to do in that glistening mission on the sunny island was to continue my musings about private troubles versus public issues. But that's just what I did, over the several days we spent in that people-made paradise.

Dale and I paid for our bed and board in spirit, attending (so as not to cause our friends embarrassment or to be considered ungrateful) several rousing singing meetings and testimonials about the power of God in our lives. But what interested me most and what started the serious conversations with our friends was the number of persons among the saved at the mission who had suffered tragedy in their lives. Everybody there had survived some awful trauma (including the trauma of intense loneliness), after which each had turned to the Almighty.

For them it had worked. Everybody at the mission was living in comradeship on that glorious island, praising not only the Lord but each other. People were working together, appreciating each other, helping each other about, abounding with good cheer and good will. That good cheer and good will were graciously extended to include Dale and me. Courtesy abounded in that we were spared any heavy attempts at conversion, although it was clear that people directed hopeful vibes in our direction and looked to us for a sign of dawning faith.

The mission had a couple of philanthropic projects under way, which, of course, intersected with my interest in social work. I had just completed my year's stint in Orangetown and Kingston, and I had all sorts of thoughts and ideas running through my head regarding social services for the needy.

Our friends helped to run a dental clinic for natives, lumberjacks, and miners in the area. There had also been a large hospital at the mission, the mainstay of the mission ministry for 50 years. But the hospital had just been closed, replaced by a modern, secular facility on the nearby mainland. This potential catastrophe for the little religious community had been characteristically interpreted as a sign from God. The whole mission was cheerfully casting about for His meaning.

The latest interpretation was that a large home for needy children and spiritually suffering families should be established on the island. Because of their own personal tragedies, people at the mission were interested in helping these kinds of people. The former hospital, a comfortable and rambling old building, could provide plenty of space for dorms and classrooms. The place could become, in secular terms, a live-in family service agency, offering total milieu therapy.

Being of a practical bent, I asked my friends how the mission might finance the project. The former hospital had generated its own income via patient fees and volunteer services by doctors who rotated their visits to the mission monthly. A number of medical doctors of religious bent had spent their annual vacations at the mission serving free of charge.

Perhaps a rotating, volunteer staff could be worked out for a live-in family service agency, but I doubted it. Rotating staff would introduce more chaos into the lives of disturbed children and families. I expected that an ongoing income would be needed to maintain a stable staff. Would the mission consider becoming a licensed group home or other licensed child-care facility so that it could become eligible for public funding?

My innocent question catapulted a response of wonderfully fiery proportions. In fact, the man who brought his fist down on the table in front of me with such force looked like a Norse sun god, with his glinting blue eyes and flaming red-blond hair and beard.

Bret, the husband of the woman we had primarily come to see, had been an English sailor before his religious conversion. He had previously assured me that his language was considerably altered from its former heathen vernacular. His discourse now rang with righteous respectability, power, and that delightful British accent.

"To accept money stolen through taxation would be sin indeed!"

Now, there are certain taxes that I, myself, with my own belief system, consider near extortion. War taxes, or taxes supporting our so called defense budget.

I wondered whether this was what Bret was getting at.

But no. Militaristic self-defense was basic to survival, in his belief system. War taxes were not his problem.

"No government has the right," Bret expounded further, "to take money away from me and give it to another person."

Ah. The transfer payment problem.

"But, Bret," I argued, "what about the helpless kids and the disturbed families you are considering taking in at this mission? Most of them won't have the money to pay for the services you want to offer them. Don't you think it's okay to tax the general population to provide income and services for people who can't survive without them, for one reason or another?"

"No," Bret replied. "And besides, as soon as you have protective laws and services, you have regulations. Regulations make you do what you don't want to do. For example, this mission might not be able to teach the children what we want to teach about the power of God."

It seemed to me that the incredible faith in the ever-present guiding hand of the Almighty abiding at this mission could work on disturbed children and families in two ways. One, it could provide an energy level that could indeed create miracles and heal starving souls. But, on the other hand, it could also stifle the freedom of the individual sinner by refusing to sanction other ways of perceiving the world.

The secular world of government might indeed intervene in the affairs and teachings of the mission, if it were paying for services offered here; and, of course, in my own heathen opinion, it might intervene for the right reasons. And that would totally change the wonderful energy charge of the place, which would be to do the wrong thing for the right reasons. The place would dry up.

It really was quite complicated.

"So," continued Bret, "we want to avoid the help, meaning the regulations, of the government. God will provide. If we decide God is asking us to serve needy children and families, we will find the way to do it."

"Okay, Bret," I said, "but what about taxation to provide for the general public good? You know that lots of families have children they just can't provide for. Take kids born by accident to single teenagers. It happens, you know. And sometimes their families throw them out. Doesn't society need to step in to give those teenage mothers and their babies a chance? And doesn't society have a right to tax itself to provide the needed resources?"

"No," Bret said. "Life isn't fair. We don't know all the reasons why, but we know life isn't fair. Sometimes misfortune brings a person into the hands of God. That is what misfortune is for. Of course, misfortune brings others to the Devil, but that is the eternal test for the soul."

"No," Bret continued grandly. "Life is not fair. To try to make it fair doesn't justify taxation. No one has the right to tell me that I *have* to help someone else or go to jail. It is up to the God in me to want to help others, and I do. But I want the right to help when God moves me, and only when *He* moves me. Is that not the meaning of freedom?"

Good grief, he had an argument.

But I thought about little Robert Casey. I had an argument too. What chance had little Robert or others like him to develop mind, body, or soul, for that matter, to a responsible level?

"My God, Bret," I sputtered. "Little kids don't even have the chance to become fully human if they are born into the wrong families. Their brain cells may not even get the chance to develop if they don't get proper nutrition to start with. They may be permanently brain-damaged before they have time to save themselves. Isn't there a responsibility for society to help each child at least to develop a healthy body?"

"No," said Bret. "I personally have nothing to do with the birth of the kind of children you are talking about. It is not my responsibility to take care of them. Later on, if one of these children comes to me and asks for help in the name of God, I will help him. But that is my choice. Nobody, not you or the government or anybody else, has the right to *order* me to take money out of my pocket to provide for somebody else's child."

"But, Bret, listen to me. If neglected children drop out of school, they can't learn a legitimate way to support themselves. They may learn to steal and to hate other people and themselves as well. Doesn't that kind of thing just help perpetuate unhappiness for all of us?"

"Perhaps," Bret said, "but stealing is their responsibility, not mine. And every sinner can still repent."

Robert Casey, neglected child probably growing into an uneducated, inadequate, and frustrated young man. Private trouble or public issue? Sinner or victim of societal neglect?

I reflected back to a conversation with a neighbor, Rita Dorsey, an energetic, inquisitive, and capable middle-aged woman. She chose, after bringing up three fine children of her own, to work as a teacher's aide in a special education classroom.

"They're nuts in that special education program," she announced to me one day when Dale and I were visiting. This struck close to home because we both worked for the same county administration and sometimes I thought the same thing. But for different reasons.

"They're always looking for money to make these programs bigger, and they keep telling us it won't cost anything, that the federal government will pay for it. Well, anybody can see through that. It's our money that gets taken and sent to Washington, as well as our money that gets taken and given to the local school district."

"Why," she continued, "look at how much of our money goes to taxes as it is. As we get older, I'm getting afraid we won't be able to keep our homes. Then what would we do? Where would we go? We can't afford any more taxes. It's programs like special education that keep trying to expand, and they just have to stop. We can't afford them."

I guess I was surprised to hear Rita oppose the very program that provided her a job. I probed a little more. The problem and the fear were immediate and practical: that expanding public programs would create taxation so heavy middle-class people would lose their homes.

A realistic and sobering fear at the time, made more pressing by inflation and its inevitable push of average people's incomes into higher tax brackets. Moreover, average people's homes were also being assessed at inflated values, taxing marginal people out of their proud status as homeowners.

It seemed to me that the historic public game was again at work—pitting the marginal against the poor, the poor against the poorer. In my view, most of the inflation and the onerous tax bites were being stimulated by something quite other than social programs—by, in fact, the much larger consumer of the income tax dollar, the legendary "military-industrial complex." All those dollars producing weapons that at best were stockpiled or used for nothing, providing empty currency that drove up prices, siphoning off scarce resources to fuel only big bangs and death to the enemy—with God on our side.

But Rita thought that at least the defense budget offered her something—security or something like that. That tax money wasn't just pilfered on the "no-goods" who kept having more "no-good" children.

"Why," Rita continued, "just last week Mrs. Igley's daughter had an illegitimate child. She's sixteen, and she's only doing it for the money."

"Well," I commented, "a mother and child on welfare hardly live in luxury. I think they get around $450 a month in this state, and I'd sure have a hard time living on that. Wouldn't you?"

"Maybe it's not much money for us older gals," Rita said, "but for some of these young teenagers that money looks pretty good. It's more than they ever had before. It gets them out from under their mothers. And the next thing you know, I'll have the Igley baby in my special education class. You can bet on it."

"None of the Igleys know a thing about raising kids," she continued. "I've seen them at home. That baby will be retarded or emotionally disturbed by the time it's old enough for school. We shouldn't have to provide public programs so idiots like the Igleys can have more disturbed kids."

"Maybe that's so," I said, "but once a baby's born, do you really think the public ought to refuse it basic support or special services if it does become disabled? In fact, wouldn't it be better to provide a more responsive early childhood program than we do now, so a specialist could work with the Igley girl at home, right this minute? Maybe that might prevent the disturbance you're worrying about from happening?"

"That girl's too far gone, anyway," Rita responded. "She should never have had that baby. And the problem is, she's the kind that will have more of them. This baby won't be her last. You just wait and see. The next one will have a different father too. She's like that."

"What were her parents like?" I asked.

"Stupid, just plain stupid and no-good," insisted Rita. "It's no wonder the girl turned out like she has."

"Then what about special services to people in their own homes to help kids born in disadvantaged families to have a chance to develop normally? To try to stop the cycle of disadvantaged kids having more disadvantaged kids?"

I thought I was becoming veritably silver-tongued, marvelously eloquent and persuasive.

"Well," Rita stopped me beautifully. "The real fact is none of them should have those kids in the first place."

I parried back. "How about licensing parenting, then," I said. "If some people really shouldn't have kids, do you think society has a right to try to regulate birth?" I was interested in Rita's answer, particularly as she is Catholic.

But Rita didn't answer that one. By then, something on the television set had caught her eye.

And then, there's Uncle Joe. Uncle Joe invariably provides me with a battle of wits. Uncle Joe might admit that there really are poor unfortunate people out there.

But he says, "I myself can spend my money so much better my own way, without the government taking it away from me first."

"Why," he says, "the government spends millions on people I can't even see. Most of the money gets wasted. But when I spend my money on dear old Mrs. Gibson down the street, I know where my money is going."

Uncle Joe has a point. And I admire him because he puts his money where his mouth is. He really does give help, both time and money, where he sees a need, if he thinks the need real and the person deserving.

The problem is, Uncle Joe doesn't know all the old Mrs. Gibsons who need help. And if he did, he doesn't have the means to help them all. It's as simple as that.

And Uncle Joe doesn't know all the needy and deserving disadvantaged children like Chad Rothberg, the Orangetown boy with spina bifida, or Gunda Schwartz, the homely foster child who felt like Cinderella before the fairy godmother came. Uncle Joe lives in too nice a neighborhood. Moreover, I doubt whether he'd consider a needy child like Robert Casey deserving, if he did know him. Robert just wouldn't be presentable enough for Uncle Joe to understand, and he certainly wouldn't seem deserving, not a young punk who wouldn't even bother to go to school.

As with almost everybody who likes the charity approach to public welfare, Uncle Joe wants to help the people he sees and knows, and his own reward is gratitude. There's nothing wrong with that. But Uncle Joe and others with his point of view don't have to see or cope with the people who don't get help but need it desperately.

That's the difference between the nebulous, struggling concept of public welfare as an institution and, say, charity. It's a difference between aid to "the stranger" and aid to nice, old Mrs. Gibson, who did our laundry all these years. It's not part of the average person's psyche to get all hepped up about aid to the stranger.

Religion can do it sometimes. A religious approach can make the stranger part of the affective community by some kind of gifted energy transfer. But the stranger, now "brother" or "sister," has to buy into a required belief system. There are strings attached.

It took me a long while to figure out why my tear-jerking approach ("Oh, but listen to the misfortunes of this poor helpless child") or my scientific statistical approach ("But a welfare family has only an average of two kids too") or my threatening approach ("You must help this individual or she or he will turn to crime") all seemed to fail to reach people.

I think I have the basic reason figured out now, and I've learned to live with it. It's so very simple. I won't accept it though. Rather, I won't accept it intellectually. In fact, the reason is part of myself too, part of the basic fiber of my own being. I'm in large part just like everybody else in my world because that's my greater American cultural heritage.

The reason I'm referring to is the cultural concept of survival of the fittest, the ingrained notion that all life must be competition. If only the fittest individuals can survive, as our society teaches, then the affairs of ourselves and our immediate family and children must come first. These are the persons we know best and care about most. And they also just happen to be the ones we most need to ensure our own survival. Resources are limited, we all know that, and we must take what we can for ourselves.

We have inherited, as well, a cultural concept of fairness. That can give us a certain motivation to help the helpless. But not enough. For why help the disadvantaged if that might give them the ability to compete successfully with us or our children? Then, good heavens, they might beat their way ahead of us, and we might fall down instead, me and mine, and be trampled on ourselves by the rest of the herd.

They, those unfortunate others, are not really a part of our lives. We don't know them. They aren't ours. They come from origins we don't like. Some come through sin, in lifelong punishment. They aren't part of us. They aren't part of us unless we know them and they find a place in our hearts.

There's also that other intriguing facet on the gem of life: Not one human being has ever made it alone. Not one. Ever. What would happen if we were to recognize fully this fact, as a society? As a world?

DISCUSSION AND STUDY QUESTIONS

The fragility of social work as a part of society's organized response to human need is emphasized in this chapter. There can be no social work as we know it without a societal mandate. Yet that mandate is subject to reconsideration at any time—it is basic to a democracy that this should be so. And there are certainly any number of value systems that would argue for the reduction—if not the outright elimination—of social work as a societal *responsibility* (it might be allowed to remain as a charitable *option*). Unfortunately, many social work services are not very visible and, hence, are overlooked by the very people who benefit from them. Social workers in hospitals who help people adjust to illness and plan for the time when they are released are often overlooked in a setting most people think of as medical, for example.

The reality, however, is that the institutional structure of social welfare, of which social work is a critical part, benefits everyone. There are direct benefits, such as Social Security payments and tax exemptions. There are also indirect benefits, such as social legislation to protect consumers and to prevent harmful pollution. Still, many people insist on thinking that everyone can "make it" if only she or he tries hard enough, forgetting about little boys with no sphincter muscles, single women raising families and caring for aged parents, persons from different cultures struggling to understand who they are and what is expected of them, and "upstanding citizens" who are so insecure they psychologically destroy their children and their spouses.

It will never be easy for social work as a profession to fight for the disadvantaged and the oppressed. It has been hard in the past, and it will continue to be in the future. Yet social workers know that not everyone can grow and survive on his or her own. Indeed, as the author points out, no one can. Some are better able than others because they possess various resources, but we all need and depend on each other. Social work is part of society's recognition of this fact. So every social worker continues to struggle for the societal mandate, knowing the very survival of the society is at stake. The struggle is sometimes a quiet one, in informal discussions with friends and neighbors. Sometimes it is a loud struggle, with picket lines and media coverage. But it is an endless struggle to which every social worker is committed.

1. Has anyone ever made fun of you for taking a social work course or considering social work as a career? How did you respond to these taunts?
2. Do you sometimes worry that social work may remove incentives from people and create dependency? What evidence do you have to lead you to worry about this? Have you sought and found any evidence to the contrary?
3. The author suggests that historically the marginal have been pitted against the poor in a struggle for survival. Can you think of specific examples of historical and contemporary legislation that might support this point of view?
4. Can you imagine another view of human survival besides that of endless competition and survival of the fittest? If so, what? In thinking about this question, try to define for yourself what is meant by the term *fittest* in this context and in this society today.
*5. How do people react when you tell them you are studying to be a social worker? Do they have an accurate understanding of what social workers do? How do you attempt to respond to the issues they raise?

---

*Questions notated with an asterisk are intended for advanced students who have had or are currently having some social work practice experience and who have made at least a tentative commitment to the profession.

CHAPTER 21

Juggling Decisions: Evaluating and Terminating

or: Deciding Whether or Not to Keep One's Job

Concepts Covered in This Chapter

1. The decision-making process involved in changing jobs
2. Processes of termination with clients, colleagues, and agencies of employment
3. Potential roles in orienting one's replacement on a job

Learning Objectives   After reading this chapter you should be able to

1. Identify at least three factors to be considered in deciding whether to take a different job
2. Describe why choosing a job can require substantial time
3. Identify why conscious terminating processes should be undertaken with clients
4. Understand why terminating processes with colleagues can be different from terminating processes with clients
5. Discuss ways in which one can help a new staff member's transition into one's former position

Sometime in early spring of the year in which I was working in Emmett County, I received a letter from the new chairperson of my former department at the university. The letter was straightforward, asking me whether I planned to return to the university the next year. If not, the department needed to know, to begin recruitment processes to find someone else.

I had been expecting the letter. I didn't know how I was going to respond when it came. Social work practice is different from teaching about social work practice. There are important areas of overlap, of course; both roles involve working with people, for example, and require an ability to adapt to the unexpected. But I preferred daily practice. The children and the parents I worked with kept me growing, and the ongoing contact I had with other professionals in the special education program was stimulating, at times heartwarming. The whole experience with the special education team felt so very alive, the cooperative effort so productive and real, despite the frustrations involved.

On the other hand, I wasn't getting along so very well with the Emmett County administration. If I were to stay with the special education program for any length of time, I knew I would have to become thoroughly involved in reorganizing it. That would be the only way I could begin to do the kind of job I wanted to do at the direct service level. But just because I *was* on the direct service level, I had very limited power to create any needed organizational change by virtue of my own position. I'd have to start investing serious efforts in developing grass roots-style coalitions as pressure groups for change.

But if I wanted to do organizational types of work, I could do that at the university. I was already involved in program development there. And although I wasn't in a position at the university, either, to do just the sort of work I wanted to do, I still had a good deal more freedom there. I had already been able to develop a social work major for undergraduates, from the bottom up. The amount of professional time and energy I had invested in that project left me with an undeniable personal involvement in the success of the program as well. The new major still needed its professional accreditation, and that would involve further curriculum development and a variety of related tasks that were new to me and that would present an interesting challenge.

If I were to return to my university job, then, I would be able both to teach and to continue program development in a setting where I had considerable freedom to develop and exercise my own ideas. But the freedom had a price. I had to work there virtually by myself. That was a major reason I had left.

My dilemma remained unresolved for a few weeks. I considered personal satisfactions with each position. They were different but weighed about the same. I considered my perception of the social value of each position. They weighed about the same. I stooped to consider the mundane influence of salary. The public school position paid a little more but not enough to tip the balance.

Finally, I decided to set some conditions on my return to the university. I thought that if they were met, I would probably return to a more favorable climate. Most important, I would gain regular assistance with social work teaching, freeing some of my time for program development and administrative tasks. And I would have someone to talk with who spoke my own language. If my conditions weren't met, I expected I would do better to work things out with Emmett County.

A few more weeks of uncertainty passed. Then the university, almost to my surprise, met my conditions. And with mixed feelings, to be sure, I signed the contract to return. Then began the painful process of termination with my ongoing clients in Orangetown and Kingston. In addition to the students I was counseling individually, I was meeting with two separate groups of students by then. One of the groups was formally organized and has been described briefly in an earlier chapter; I helped coordinate it with the help of several other staff members in Orangetown. The other group was my own personal responsibility. This group developed spontaneously one day when a student client brought a couple of friends to one of our regular weekly appointments. From then on, we met as an informal group, a lively bunch filled with energy and laughter. We talked a lot about sex and drugs, and I suppose I was lucky because I never did get run out of town for it.

The idea of bringing these sometimes tense but often warm and humor-filled groups and individual relationships to a close was hard for me to accept, and I think that was so for many of the children concerned as well. But painful as it was, I began the process of termination a couple of months prior to the end of the school year. Of course, school years have natural and expected ending points, so that helped. I wanted to avoid, as much as possible, any sense of surprise or rejection on the part of the children.

Termination processes with colleagues were occasionally painful as well. The many crises weathered throughout the year had brought some of us close, even though we usually saw each other only at work. In the case of David Chase, I never really terminated, although I gradually lost touch with Constance after these two fine professionals divorced.

Yes, I did know I would miss the little daily challenges of direct social work practice. And I most certainly have. Or have I?

I called my replacement in Orangetown early the next school year, a young woman right out of graduate school. Her name was Olga Dobbs. I went over to Orangetown to meet her. I wanted to help Olga get started, for her own sake, and I wanted to maintain continuity in social work services in the schools for the sake of the children. I felt responsible to help give the person assigned to Orangetown a better start than I had.

On the day of my visit, Olga chose to meet with me alone, outside the school. She climbed into my car with a grim expression on her face. As soon as the door was closed and we were headed safely down the highway toward a café in a neighboring town, she began to speak rapidly.

"Good grief," she exclaimed in obvious confusion and pain. "Nobody seems to want me to do any work in that place! Nobody will give me anything to do! I don't even have a regular desk in that dumb classroom they have the nerve to call an office, and that David Chase keeps glaring at me like there's something wrong with me! It feels like there are all these secrets everybody knows about at that school, everybody except me!"

I spent the best part of an afternoon orienting Olga to the peculiarities of Orangetown as best I knew how, including the hidden treasures as well as the obvious problems. Then I invited her and her husband, along with David and Constance Chase, to my house for a long evening dinner. I suspected that creating a working relationship between Olga and David would be crucial to Olga's mental health during the coming year—and perhaps to David's as well.

On the evening of the dinner, I went out of my way to create a cozy atmosphere. I had a cheerful flame crackling in the fireplace and an aromatic dinner roasting in the oven when everyone arrived. My husband, chuckling over the whole affair, lent his own peculiar brand of warmth and blessing to the occasion.

But from the start, I found myself observing the two intended colleagues-to-be with some alarm. David, that handsome, clean-cut character out of the Ivy League, and Olga, that articulate, energetic young M.S.W. graduate, seemed to be circling each other warily, searching out the weak spots. As they sparred and parried their way out the door that evening, good wine not withstanding, I had the strange sensation I'd seen it all before somewhere—

DISCUSSION AND STUDY QUESTIONS

1. How did the author use the evaluation process to help her make the decision whether to stay or leave the Emmett County special education program? What were the factors she apparently weighed most heavily in making the decision? Would you have made the same decision, under the circumstances? Why or why not?

2. Why do you think the author felt she would have to become involved in reorganizing the special education program in Emmett County in order to do acceptable direct service social work practice with the program? What kinds of changes do you think she would have wanted to make? Why? Do you think she would have been able to do so, had she stayed? Consider the information you have been given about the authority structure in Emmett County, including both positions of authority and personality factors of the occupants of those positions.

*3. When a direct service-level social worker decides to get involved in efforts to change the structure and the policy of the agency of employment, what ethical considerations must be kept in mind? What tactical options are potentially available?

*4. The author mentions that she made conscious efforts to terminate her relationships with students and staff in Emmett County. She reports that the process was difficult for her and that, in fact, she did not terminate her relationship with the Chases. Why do you suppose she didn't just decide to continue her relationships with the other staff and students as well, so that she would have been able to avoid the termination process? Or why didn't she just leave at the end of the school year without telling anyone she wouldn't be back?

---

*Questions notated with an asterisk are intended for advanced students who have had or are currently having some social work practice experience and who have made at least a tentative commitment to the profession.

PART FIVE

Values, Social Justice Issues, and Populations at Risk

INTRODUCTION

This section of the book, entirely new for the third edition, focuses on case materials which illustrate aspects of curriculum content recently required in baccalaureate social work education by the Council on Social Work Education (CSWE): values, social justice issues, and populations at risk. Alarming trends in social policy, from the national level down through the state and local levels, have tended to disempower poor people significantly by reducing their options. These trends are counter to social work values and have clear social justice implications. The CSWE appears determined that social work students fully understand the implications of contemporary social policy. Thus the new curriculum requirements.

Major populations at risk in this nation include women, children, the elderly, ethnic and racial minorities, gays and lesbians, and people with disabilities. Being "at risk" means that these populations do not get to play on a level playing field. They may work as hard or harder than other populations and still not attain the same standard of living, on the average. Not getting a fair shake is counter to the concept of social justice.

The first chapter in this section examines social work values and shows how they promote social justice, rather than undermine it as current social policy threatens to do. The chapter revisits several cases presented earlier in the book to indicate how, sadly, current social policy provides even fewer resources for problem solving than were available nearly two decades ago.

This section also illustrates why generalist social work skills must be fully utilized in today's social and political climate. The need for work with organizations and communities as a whole has never been greater, to help stretch scarce resources and direct them to where they are needed most. Problem prevention becomes a major focus. An entire chapter, Chapter 23, is devoted to describing macro-level social work practice in a contemporary urban setting designed to prevent problems and teach leadership skills to inner city youth. Other chapters illustrate the predicaments of various members of populations at risk. For example, the struggles of an elderly couple to provide care for younger family members at great cost to themselves are described, as well as the struggles of a courageous school-age mother to care for her baby and graduate from high school. Assistance that would have been available to the teen mother before welfare "reform" laws took hold is gone.

Like Part Four, Part Five illustrates the need for social workers to become involved in advancing social policies that promote social justice. Policy making is value-driven. Hopefully, the values of the social work profession will prevail some day, so that the legitimate interests of populations at risk will again receive priority on the national agenda.

CHAPTER 22

Values and Social Justice Issues

or: How Values Shape Social and Economic Policy Decisions

Concepts Covered in This Chapter

1. The importance of values in shaping social and economic policy
2. Social justice
3. Human diversity issues
4. Populations at risk
5. Entitlement programs compared to charity
6. The social work code of ethics
7. "Survival of the fittest" compared to "interdependence"

Learning Objectives   After reading this chapter you should be able to

1. Define values and ethics
2. Give four specific examples of how values have shaped social and economic policy
3. Define social justice
4. Provide three examples of diverse human populations
5. Discuss what factors contribute to various populations being at risk today
6. Identify at least seven populations at risk in America
7. Understand the difference between entitlement programs and charity
8. Compare and contrast the concepts of "survival of the fittest" and "interdependence"
9. Understand the purpose of the social work code of ethics

Many years have passed since the original edition of this book was written, and more than a few since the second. However, a familiar saying kept coming to mind as I worked on the third edition: "the more things change, the more they stay the same." For while I would like to report that the community resources badly needed to help resolve the cases described in this book are available today, instead, cost containment, not service, is increasingly the call (and law) of our land. Resources for social welfare concerns are scarcer than ever.

For example, consider the Tabler case described in Chapter 6, the chapter titled "Another Welfare Mother." Mrs. Tabler was for all intents and purposes the sole parent of her four children aged 2–8. She had been abandoned by her husband after the birth of her youngest child. Like many mothers, she wanted to raise her children herself until they were ready to go to school. To do so, she thought her only option was to live with her parents. She moved in with them. However, the situation turned out to be extremely stressful. Mrs. Tabler's parents viewed her and her little family as a "cross to bear." This was understandable, of course, as the parents were not well off financially themselves. Mrs. Tabler's eight-year-old daughter, Maria, began to misbehave, probably in response to tension in the home.

As the school social worker consulted in this case, I was able to refer Mrs. Tabler to the county's AFDC program (Aid to Families with Dependent Children, a program mandated and partially funded by the federal government through the Social Security Act). AFDC provided the family with a small income, enabling new choices. Mrs. Tabler could consider finding another place to live for herself and her children. Given new options, the family's overall stress level decreased and little Maria's behavior returned to normal, even though Mrs. Tabler decided to remain with her parents once her father had a stroke and needed her care.

Today, due to welfare "reform," AFDC would not be an option for Mrs. Tabler. The program no longer exists as an entitlement under the Social Security Act. (An entitlement program is one in which people are legally entitled to aid if eligibility requirements are met.) In the mid-nineties, responsibility for helping poor children and families was largely shifted to the states by Congress and the Clinton administration. In Mrs. Tabler's state, raising one's children in one's own home simply is not recognized as "work." Instead, the state requires poor mothers to find paid employment when their youngest child is only 12 weeks old. The state retains the option (but not the legal requirement) to provide work for people who cannot find jobs. All jobs provided by the state pay less than minimum wage, however—not nearly enough to bring Mrs. Tabler's family of five even close to the poverty level. And if Mrs. Tabler were lucky enough to find a job on her own, her salary would very probably still be insufficient to bring her family even close to the poverty level. That is because, due to social policy decisions made by Congress, the minimum wage has not kept pace with inflation for decades. In addition, women face discrimination in the job market and the wages they are paid are lower than men's, on the average.

Mrs. Tabler's state today also retains the option, but not the legal requirement, to assist with day-care expenses. The amount provided covers only about half the cost of care at a certified day-care center, however. The young mother would have to pay for the remainder of her child care expenses out of her own pocket, or find a non-certified source of care, cheaper but not as reliable. Mrs. Tabler and her children would be destitute today under the policy her state has developed. Moreover, by having to work outside the home, the young woman would no longer be available to care for her disabled father, further stressing her extended family—a situation echoed in thousands of homes around the nation. Women do most of the caretaking for family members who are ill, but since they are not paid, what they do is not recognized as "work" any more than child rearing.

If I were a social work practitioner today, how could I assist a family like the Tablers? I would have few resources at my disposal. Even food stamps have been made unavailable unless a parent works outside the home at least half-time. In our nation currently, cutting costs is considered more important than lifting families out of poverty or helping mothers care for their own children. I might have suggested that Mrs. Tabler get legal help to try to win child support from her husband. But her rural area has no legal services for poor people. Mrs. Tabler would probably have been unable to afford to hire a regular lawyer. But even if she somehow managed to do so, and even if her suit were successful, the majority of fathers in this country simply do not pay child support, even with a court order. Most likely, the young mother would have continued to exist as she had before, a burden on her parents, with no other place to turn. She was lucky she *had* parents who would take her in, even if they did regard her as an unwanted burden.

Interestingly enough, the very year that Mrs. Tabler's state ended "welfare as we know it," theoretically to cut costs, the same state legislature passed a new tax levy on the public to finance a huge, high-tech sports stadium. The old stadium was quite serviceable, but the powers that be apparently wanted something more prestigious. The legislators kept quiet about the importance of cutting costs in this instance. This example is given in order to prompt the reader to think about what values might have driven the different decisions in the two situations (values are preferred beliefs; they cannot be proven), and how these values might relate to the gender of the people who made them. In addition, one might consider who the beneficiaries of the new state tax levy would be, as compared to who those who lost assistance under welfare reform.

Consider the Rudolph Gonzales case, described in Chapter 13. This fourth-grade boy of Hispanic descent was unable to read. His spoken English was poor, and his school work was basically at the first-grade level. The boy frequently exploded in frustration, often at himself. He was eventually placed in a classroom for children with emotional disturbance, but much of his problem was cultural: the Anglo world around him was foreign and frightening to him. The Kingston pupil services staff, especially Norman Werner, expended a great deal of effort to obtain bilingual consultation and services for Rudolph. The primary reason services were so difficult to obtain even at that time was lack of funding. As Mr. Sorensen, the school principal, reminded me in my meeting with him to try to obtain a Spanish-speaking classroom aide or bilingual psychological evaluation, money was tight.

Today, the situation for bilingual children in Kingston (and Orangetown) is no different, even though many more such children in need live in the area. Bilingual services remain nonexistent. Moreover, nationwide, a movement has been afoot for several years to outlaw bilingual education altogether. To be sure, the values driving the "English only" movement are probably less related to cost-containment than a powerful desire to avoid diversity and change.

Factors that complicated the Jeffrey Redcloud case described in Chapter 14 remain basically the same today as they were almost a decade ago. Jeffrey, a Native American child adopted by a white family, suffered from schizophrenia and attention deficit disorder. Of junior high school age, Jeffrey was a large, physically powerful child. Unfortunately, he frequently assaulted his adoptive mother. When this compassionate woman finally was persuaded to file charges in court by the Kingston pupil services team, the judge simply released the boy to his mother with a lecture. Norman Werner explained that the county had only one group home where the boy could have been temporarily placed, and this home was full at the time. "Justice is blind," he said ruefully, "unless you have a dollar bill." Jeffrey subsequently attacked his mother so seriously that he had to be committed to the state mental hospital.

No new facilities exist in Emmett County today to meet the needs of children like Jeffrey Redcloud and their families. Group homes and public mental health services are simply considered too costly to create and maintain. However, when children fall through the cracks and end up hospitalized or in jail, as happened with Jeffrey Redcloud, the cost becomes much larger and may continue for a lifetime. Who determines what costs are worth paying? For whom? And are there costs we should consider besides monetary costs?

Over the past few years, the values expressed by various people in Chapter 20, "Talking to Mr. and Mrs. Responsible Taxpayer," have become increasingly dominant in American society. For example, the man quoted from the wilderness mission, Bret, insisted that taxation to help others was immoral. Bret believed in helping people, but only on a voluntary basis as a Christian charity (act of kindness) to people who had no legal right to such assistance. Rita Dorsey, my neighbor, believed that a local teenage girl had an illegitimate child only for the money, and would have more for the same reason. My good Uncle Joe didn't want his tax money used to help people he didn't know. He suspected most government aid was wasted. Obviously, Bret, Rita, Uncle Joe, and many citizens like them, wanted to end welfare entitlement programs like AFDC. Their values have prevailed and steer social policy today, despite the growing needs of people such as those described in this book.

"The more things change, the more they stay the same." Unless we are considering sports stadiums, it seems that cost-containment remains the major consideration in the development of public social welfare policy and programs today—only more so. Public policy increasingly reflects beliefs and attitudes similar to those expressed by Bret, Rita, and Uncle Joe so many years ago, that taxation to help the needy is unacceptable.

Not everyone agrees that current social policy trends are good ones, however. What about social workers? A strong indication of the position of the profession is provided by its code of ethics, recently revised by the National Association of Social Workers (NASW). Professional codes of ethics in general identify behaviors that are prescribed by the profession's values. The revised social work code includes strong statements that social workers should promote social justice, or the condition in which every person has fair access to the resources required to maintain a decent standard of living. Principle 6 of the code, "Social Workers' Ethical Responsibilities to the Broader Society," provision 6.01 states:

> Social workers should promote the general welfare of society, from local to global levels, and the development of people, their communities, and their environments.

Social workers should advocate for living conditions conducive to the fulfillment of basic human needs and should promote social, economic, political, and cultural values and institutions that are compatible with the realization of social justice.

Provision 6.04 states in part:

Social workers should engage in social and political action that seeks to ensure that all people have equal access to the resources, employment, services, and opportunities they require to meet their basic human needs and to develop fully.

Clearly, the National Association of Social Workers promotes social justice, and to this end strongly supports the development of social programs that can help people meet basic human needs.

What guidance does the Council on Social Work Education (CSWE) provide, the body that accredits social work education programs at both baccalaureate and masters levels? The Council has recently revised its curriculum policy statement. The five curriculum areas previously required have been maintained: social work practice skills, social welfare policy and services, human behavior in the social environment, research, and field instruction. Four entirely new ones have been added, however: human diversity, values and ethics, social justice issues, and populations at risk.

The four new CSWE-required curriculum areas all reflect concern with current national trends in social welfare policy. Several value statements identified in the new CSWE Curriculum Policy Statement make this concern explicit. For example, sections B6. 3. 3, B6. 3. 4, and B6. 3. 5 state:

Social workers are committed to assisting client systems to obtaining needed resources.

Social workers strive to make social institutions more humane and responsive to human needs.

Social workers demonstrate respect for and acceptance of the unique characteristics of diverse populations.

Clearly, the Council on Social Work Education promotes social policy that is humane and responsive to the needs of diverse populations. The CSWE specifically identifies several "populations at risk," populations that, due to oppression and discrimination, do not get a chance to perform on a level playing field. They are statistically more likely to remain mired in poverty no matter how hard they work or how hard they try to get an education. These populations include people of color, women, children, the elderly, the physically or mentally disabled, and gays and lesbians. Under the CSWE curriculum policy required today, every accredited social work program must teach its students about populations at risk.

To help students understand social justice issues related to populations at risk, the Curriculum Policy Statement asserts in section B6.5:

Programs of social work education must provide an understanding of the dynamics and consequences of social and economic injustice, including all forms of human oppression.

As professional social workers know all too well, the gap between rich and poor in the United States has been widening steadily in recent years. The children of America have become the poorest children in the western industrialized world, and suffer increasing neglect and abuse. These are predictable results of unwise and unjust social and economic policies that favor the interests of the rich and disempower the poor. Yet policies such as these are popular and continue to be enacted in this country every day. The loss of entitlement to AFDC by the poor is only one, albeit major, example.

How is such a situation possible in a nation that only a few decades ago enthusiastically embraced a "war on poverty"? My best understanding remains similar to what I wrote years ago in the chapter titled "Mr. and Mrs. Responsible Taxpayer." We Americans isolate the poor. It's still "us" versus "them" (sometimes even if we have *been* one of "them"). And in a country that believes deeply in the concept of "survival of the fittest," all life tends to be viewed as one fearful, competitive scramble. Helping somebody else just might help one of THEM get ahead of ME, so better to go on toiling fearfully alone.

But none of us can, none of us ever could, none of us ever will make it truly on our own. We are all, quite factually, interdependent. Survival of the fittest is but a well-worn myth; survival of the best-cared-for-by-others may better fit the facts among humans. Who can deny that each and every human being born into the world requires many years of care from other humans to survive? Who can deny that every so-called independent adult requires ongoing cooperation from others to continue to survive?

This second question may cause us to stop and think, we are so accustomed to believing we make it on our own as adults. But why aren't we all mowed down in traffic, for example, or poisoned by a polluted water supply? In general, people cooperate— most drive on the side of the road determined by social agreement, for example, and many work to create laws that will prevent total environmental degradation. If care and cooperation were not provided throughout one's lifetime, nary a one of us would be alive today.

Can we substitute a humble recognition of human interdependence for the myth of deadly competition and survival of the fittest? Can a recognition of the fundamental place of cooperation already essential in our lives lead to a shift in consciousness and with it a change in public policy?

The direction that American social welfare policy has taken in recent years has not been in the direction of affirming and embracing social interdependence and cooperation. It has thus not been welcomed by the social work profession as a whole. Social work, given its values and ethics, might now perhaps be considered a profession out of step with the times. I write the previous statement proudly. The values and ethics of our profession call for social policies that support and empower all populations, including those at risk. It does not demand that each individual make it on his or her own, while ignoring the fact that those who make it well usually come from advantaged backgrounds. I, for one, feel honored to be a member of a profession that dares teach against the current tide.

DISCUSSION AND STUDY QUESTIONS

In recent years, the national debate surrounding welfare reform has tended to enshrine the "work ethic." It has blamed "welfare mothers" for their own poverty because many don't have jobs outside the home. At the same time, entitlement programs such as Aid to Families with Dependent Children have been attacked as making welfare mothers "psychologically dependent." If one were to believe the media, entitlement programs were ended in large part to help poor women. Welfare "reform" was only a kind of "tough love" to help poor mothers overcome their pitiful psychological dependency. "Believe me, this hurts me more that it does you," one can almost hear the members of Congress, overwhelmingly male, moaning as they raise their studded belts.

If only things were so simple. Women have born the brunt of work performed in families—child rearing, housekeeping, cooking, care of the sick, etc.—as unpaid laborers for centuries. Their efforts being unpaid, women's work has rarely been recognized as exactly that—work. At the same time, women have faced discrimination and low wages in the job market outside the family. The high cost of child care outside the home, low wages for women, and lack of health insurance on the job (whereas it was provided through Medicaid if a mother remained on AFDC), have kept many mothers at home, not "psychological dependency."

When AFDC was an entitlement, every dollar a mother earned was subtracted from her grant. Once her pay equalled her grant, her entitlement was lost, and with it health insurance through Medicaid for herself and her children. Many mothers understandably decided to work at home, where salary was never an issue. But now poor women have no choice except to enter the paid work force. Child care, health care, job discrimination, and wage equity issues have not been addressed in any realistic way. What will happen now? American children are already the poorest in the western industrialized world, and their fates hang on the fates of their mothers, who are themselves a population at risk facing discrimination in the work force. Our nation may be engaging in a tragic experiment with its head in the sand.

1. How is the concept of "entitlement" different from that of "charity"?
2. How do you think values might affect social policy decisions? For example, if the representatives of Mrs. Tabler's state legislature had been mostly female rather than male, do you think their values might have led to a different decision regarding whether to invest tax monies in supporting poor families versus building a new sports stadium? Why or why not? Where do you think the money would better be spent? Why? How do you think your own values guide your decision?
*3. What reasons can you give from this chapter to support the argument that a program such as Aid to Families with Dependent Children should be an entitlement? How might the concept of social justice support such an idea?
*4. Does the author believe that "survival of the fittest" is a valid description of way the human beings are actually able to survive in the real world? Why or why not? What do you think? Why?

---

*Questions notated with an asterisk are intended for advanced students who have had or are currently having some social work practice experience and who have made at least a tentative commitment to the profession.

CHAPTER 23

Macro-Level Practice at a Central City Middle School

by Dr. Janice M. Staral

or: Working Toward Empowerment of Inner City Youth and Families

Concepts Covered in This Chapter

1. Understanding macro-level practice
2. Identifying community stakeholders and the value of networking and collaborating with these stakeholders
3. The importance of asking questions regarding needs and visions
4. Developing a shared vision
5. Differentiating "top-down" decision making from inclusive decision making
6. Valuing the needs and assets of a community and of specific cultural groups
7. Understanding the social work value of working for social justice
8. Introducing the concept of empowerment

Learning Objectives   After reading this chapter you should be able to

1. Explain what is meant by macro-level practice
2. Understand the various components that are necessary in working toward social justice
3. Give examples of projects that would build capacity and support empowerment
4. Discuss strategies that would insure inclusive decision making
5. List the barriers that oppressed groups often face and how these barriers can be reduced
6. Give examples of how networking and collaboration can be beneficial to both social work and client

The practice of social work never gets boring because we have to have the skills to help our clients by using individual, group, family, organizational, and community change methods. The latter methods are also called macro-level practice, where planned change or intervention is directed at larger systems, including social service agencies, the political system, and the resources within the client's community.

Macro-level practice skills are essential to the generalist social worker and are equally important in both rural and urban settings. In this case, I (Dr. Janice Staral) wanted to learn more about school social work in an urban setting. My social work colleagues referred me to Sara Cooper, a social worker who had worked in schools for the past 10 years. Currently, she was working at a central city middle school.

When I first met Ms. Cooper, I knew I was meeting someone special. She is a petite woman in her early forties, with short brown hair, casually dressed in slacks and a comfortable sweater. Almost as quickly as I noted her physical appearance, I felt her positive, focused, high energy spirit. I knew early in the interview that this was someone who acted on social work values, including the mandate to work for social justice.

Initially, I wanted to learn how school social work had changed since she began her work ten years ago. She told me that in the early 1990s, the school social worker's role was fairly standard across the various schools, but during the last five years the social work role has been changing. She explained that school principals have been given more discretion in spending and managing their budgets. Many school principals, as a result of this new discretion, have decided to hire a full-time social worker for their specific school building. Ms. Cooper no longer had to drive to two additional schools, but now could focus her time completely on one middle school.

She explained that the schools were being charged as the primary institution to resolve societal problems, even though these problems were the result of complex forces. She said the school is expected to meet the learning needs of all the children, regardless of their physical or mental health status. Also, schools were no longer isolated from their immediate neighborhoods, but were turning to their communities for assistance. Ms. Cooper responded to these changes by assimilating a macro approach into her work.

This macro approach requires new ways of looking at the surrounding school community and requires asking many questions. Ms. Cooper immediately fired off a series of them: What are the specific needs of this community, the children, the parents? What are the strengths of the parents and the children? Clients have felt needs, but they also have strengths and resilience that need to be tapped. What are the resources available in the community? What agencies and institutions are located within the community? How do we go about making the connections among these various assets and resources?

Ms. Cooper explained one way to make these connections was through the process of networking and collaboration with key stakeholders (all who feel they are partners in a common venture) within her middle school community. She named many of the stakeholders, including the parents, the children, the teachers, the school administration and staff, a mental health facility, a hospital, a two-year technical college, and a private university. She mentioned that every school setting would have different stakeholders, but the importance would be in identifying the specific ones in each setting.

Once the stakeholders were identified, it would be important to find ways to network, both inside and outside the school setting. Ms. Cooper began networking because she needed help with one of her students who had serious mental health issues, making it difficult for the student to learn. She and the school psychologist met with the head of the child psychiatry department at the nearby mental health facility to discuss this student's needs.

This initial request for help with one child generated several meetings over a two-year period. The discussion centered on how to help the teachers work with the various students who struggled with emotional disturbances that stymied the students' ability to learn. This networking was a painstaking, ongoing process. Ms. Cooper continued to remind me that during the group discussions, they had "no map." They had to continually raise questions. How could the schools meet the learning needs of the children? How could this mental health facility meet the mental health needs of this community? What did they have to offer each other? What were the constraints?

These discussions led to developing a "vision," a plan or a conceptual map of shared directions or goals. Ms. Cooper, the school psychologist, and the psychiatrist wanted to develop a "safety net"—a network where the walls of the school extended across the community, one that would support not only the students and their families, but also the teachers, the staff, and the administrators. Their vision involved the need to blur the lines between the school and the community. Help would come from the most appropriate resource through a collaborative process. There would be less concern regarding ownership or boundaries. Effort would be directed toward the professional, group, or agency which could best resolve whatever problem was under consideration. The social workers and others would need to develop an appreciation of flexibility and tolerance toward diverse opinions.

Ms. Cooper emphasized the difficulty of this process and the social justice concerns that confronted her as she participated in many meetings. The stakeholders at these meetings were in key power positions, an important part of any collaboration. However, they were white, middle- to upper-income adults. It was a "top-down approach." A social justice stance would demand that all people have a voice in developing the school's "vision." She was clear that future planning needed to include the voices of the families in the community. These families were generally low-income, African-American, and headed by single mothers. Their input was essential and yet missing.

Ms. Cooper noted these social justice concerns and identified some of the methods they were utilizing to confront these concerns. For example, a social worker from the county's Family Preservation and Family Support Project would be meeting with their group to teach the group to use a "community learning model." According to Ms. Cooper, this model was not new to social work, but was new in terms of bringing diverse groups of people together to work on common problems.

She also identified the school's parent center as a resource for resolving these social justice issues. Two parents, who were African-American and from the community, were hired as coordinators for the center to support parents in identifying needs and in developing strategies to confront concerns. Parents would have a means of entering into the ongoing discussions.

The students themselves also needed a vehicle in which they could voice opinions: a special place to meet, discuss, and recreate. Ms. Cooper collaborated with the school psychologist, the gym teacher, and the speech pathologist to establish a teen center for these purposes.

The teen center, open every Wednesday afternoon from 2:40 to 4:30 P.M., is within the school building and has been operating for two years. Volunteers, including eight teachers from the school and college students from the nearby university, assist, serving as role models, providing tutoring and one-on-one attention, and participating in games or activities. The university students gain valuable experience through the center and the teens benefit by having this networking opportunity with each other and with outside resources.

The main premise of the teen center is "not to do anything for the teens that they can do for themselves." Considered a "school-to-work" program, the teens are learning the business skills of setting up the center, ordering and selling food, completing inventory, and planning activities. With the profits made from the food sales, the teen center has become self-supporting. The process being carried out through the center is called capacity building because the teens are developing new skills and a sense of autonomy.

The teen center supports school discipline and rewards positive behavior. Anywhere from 40 to 100 teens attend the center on a given Wednesday, but the teens have to attain an "honors level one" in order to attend. To obtain honors level one status, the students have to maintain positive behavior on a daily basis. Students lose level one status for one cycle if they are involved in any disruptive behavior, such as fighting with classmates, swearing, or being disrespectful toward a teacher.

Level one status is awarded on a 14-day cycle for most teens. Students in the exceptional education program, who may have more difficulty with controlling their disruptive behavior, have to achieve positive behavior on a 7-day basis. The program is structured to make it possible for all students to be able to obtain level one status. If students lose their privileges, they can regain them at the next 7- or 14-day cycle. The teen center, another example of a macro approach, has contributed to a decrease in discipline problems at the school.

Ms. Cooper also thinks that the teen center could provide a gateway to other ventures, such as providing a way to work with the various cultures represented at the school. She mentions that the school is predominantly African-American, but the student body also includes a small percentage of Hispanic, Caucasian, and Asian students. She questions whether an international student from the university or someone from the community could be involved. This person could affirm cultural diversity by teaching the students culturally specific games. Students would be able to join in these games and gain a perspective on another culture in an enjoyable way. Perhaps various cultural clubs could be formed which could highlight the gifts of each culture.

She wonders, "Maybe we could find someone who already has an understanding of the needs and culture of the various groups, rather than the social worker doing it?" The questions begin again: "How do we meet the needs of the few and of the many? What can we put together? Maybe a student could do this? We would need to network, link, and hear what the teens need." Ms. Cooper reminds me that developing a vision begins with asking questions.

Ms. Cooper also envisions the teen center as a structure that can lead to further capacity building and empowerment. The teen center, in combination with utilizing the last hour of classroom time, could be a place where the students gain additional skills. Some of this has already been accomplished by Ms. Cooper's networking with the community technical school which has provided training for hair care and styling at the center. She hopes to network with the Red Cross in order to get a baby-sitting program at the center, one that would include learning cardio-pulmonary resuscitation (CPR) and first aid training. Ms. Cooper hopes this program would also incorporate her goal of having all the students and teachers trained in CPR and first aid.

The training for these programs is expensive. Ms. Cooper hopes to devise a way that a parent, student, or teacher could learn these skills and then pass them on to the students. In this way, the training costs would be reduced and the training could be done at the teen center.

Although the teen center is making a profit from selling food, the other components that Ms. Cooper wants to include will need additional funding. Again, Ms. Cooper has turned to networking. She and the school psychologist will soon be meeting with a stakeholder, an expert on writing grants. Ms. Cooper plans to learn grant-writing skills from this expert.

Ms. Cooper admits that working at the macro level in social work is not easy. It is exciting, but also hectic; it takes planning and juggling. At the same time, micro-level school social work tasks continue. There are, for example, the daily pressures of making referrals to the District Attorney's office when students are perpetually absent, and responding to the teachers when they request help regarding a specific student. Ms. Cooper realizes she is judged by the principal and others by how responsive she is to their requests.

Ms. Cooper explains that although the work is demanding, many of the methods she uses are necessary to work toward social justice. Being involved in social justice is an active process which includes recognizing that every person should have a voice in decision making, "leveling the playing field" by making services accessible and effective, and giving students second chances to meet "honors level one." It supports developing capacity so students and parents develop additional skills in order to take control over their lives. In this situation, both the concepts of empowerment and social justice meet.

Ms. Cooper faces many challenges in her work, but she knows her efforts are worth the cost when a teen approaches her and says, "I almost lost 'level one' today. I wanted to tell someone off, but I was cool and I just didn't say anything."

DISCUSSION AND STUDY QUESTIONS

A commitment to social justice is a part of social work's historical tradition. There are few, if any, other professions that make social justice a central commitment for its practitioners. This commitment is stated as one of the ethical principles in the recently revised social work code as: "Social workers challenge social injustice." A further elaboration of this code adds: "Social workers pursue social change, particularly with and on behalf of vulnerable and oppressed individuals and groups of people." This chapter illustrates one method of pursuing social justice and the need to develop structures in order that all voices can be heard.

1. Have you noticed social injustice in your personal or educational experience? Explain.
2. Explain empowerment. What actions or activities can you pursue to support empowerment?
*3. How might you challenge social injustice at your field placement or other settings?
*4. How can networking or collaboration benefit you as a social work student?

---

*Questions notated with an asterisk are intended for advanced students who have had or are currently having some social work practice experience and who have made at least a tentative commitment to the profession.

CHAPTER 24

Great-Grandparents' Dilemma

or: The Struggles of Elderly People to Meet the Needs of Younger Family Members When Public Resources Have Been Slashed

Concepts Covered in This Chapter

1. Elderly relatives as caretakers of last resort for family members
2. Substance abuse
   a. Alcohol abuse
   b. Other drug abuse
3. Inpatient and outpatient treatment
4. Legal custody
5. Foster care

Learning Objectives   After reading this chapter you should be able to

1. Discuss potential affects of substance abuse on parenting behavior
2. Identify stresses imposed on extended family members, especially elderly relatives, to meet the needs of younger people experiencing problems
3. Define legal custody
4. Discuss foster care as an option for children experiencing family problems

The following case from Kingston is a composite, meaning that it combines events and circumstances from more than one actual case situation to protect the privacy of any individuals involved. But the truth of the story is real enough, in that circumstances such as these are not uncommon today.

Mary Perkins was seven years old and in the second grade when her school work began to deteriorate. Until then Mary had been a better-than-average pupil, a delight to her teachers. She had a cheerful smile that revealed lovely dimples, and her reddish brown hair hovered in natural waves about her pudgy face. Her good manners made her a favorite. Mary was the kind of child who liked to help her teachers. She could frequently be seen wiping desks and picking up crumpled papers after school.

When Mary's second-grade teacher, Linda Shea, first noticed a change in the child's behavior, she noticed not a difference in school work per se but in classroom conduct. Always a help, now Mary became almost too helpful, and the "helpfulness" was accompanied by physical clinging. The little girl seemed to be asking for attention in this way, more than the teacher could give with her classroom of 35 children. Annoyed, Linda Shea found herself pushing Mary away, and then feeling bad about it. Still, Linda didn't think much about Mary's behavior until the little girl began failing her spelling and math quizzes. Then the teacher realized something must be wrong. But what?

Linda Shea referred the child to Jim Gottwald, the school social worker in Kingston today. "This isn't a special education referral, Jim," she said firmly. "This child is one of my better pupils, and she's usually very well-behaved. But over the past couple of months she's become terribly clingy, a real nuisance. Lately Mary's started failing her quizzes, even the easy ones. Something must be wrong at home. I wonder if you would have time to check it out."

Time was a limited commodity for Jim Gottwald as well as for Mary's teacher, Linda. Jim served as both guidance counselor and social worker in Kingston, a prodigious dual job description for one person. But he was the appropriate referral source for the teacher, whose job description was limited to work in the classroom. As soon as possible, Jim obtained Mary Perkins' file from the school's main office. He noticed that only a mother's name and address were listed for the little girl; nothing was listed for a father. Jim telephoned the mother, Susan Perkins. No one answered. He tried for several days without success.

Finally, Jim went back to talk with Linda Shea. "I'm not having any luck contacting Mary's mother," he said. "Have you found out anything new since you made the referral, Linda? Maybe the family's moved and that's why Mary's having problems?"

"Mary hasn't said anything about moving," Linda responded. "But she's still acting awfully clingy, and she's still failing her quizzes. She seems to talk mostly about her great-grandparents, come to think of it. I think they take care of her after school. Maybe you could try to talk to them."

"GREAT grandparents?"

"That's what she calls them, Jim, 'Great Gramma and Great Grampa.' Let me see what I can find out."

"Do you want me to talk to Mary myself?" Jim asked. "Would there be a convenient time I could take her out of class?"

"Let's not do that yet, Jim," the teacher replied. "The kids all know that when you take somebody out of class, something's wrong! I'll see what I can find out from Mary myself. Meanwhile, see if you can't reach her mother somehow."

When Jim tried telephoning Mary's mother, Susan Perkins, again, he heard a discouraging message delivered by a lilting mechanical voice: "the NUMber you have reached has been DISconnected." The mechanical voice gave no forwarding information, and a live telephone operator had no further information either. Jim was temporarily stuck. He began composing a letter to send to the address listed in the school files. Linda Shea, however, had better luck. She sent a note home with the little girl the following day, addressed to "Mary's mother or caretaker." The note asked the person responsible for Mary's care to please telephone. An elderly woman responded almost immediately.

Thus it was Linda Shea who first talked with Mary Perkins' great-grandmother, Edith Robertson. A quavery voice explained hesitantly that Mary's mother was "temporarily incapacitated" and that Mary herself was now living with Edith Robertson and her husband, Harvey. Mrs. Robertson didn't seem to want to say anything more than that. Linda then explained that she was concerned about Mary's behavior at school, and asked if Jim Gottwald could meet with the Robertsons. Mrs. Robertson agreed, and provided a telephone number to give to Jim.

Jim called the Robertson home a day or two later and was able to make an appointment almost immediately. When he arrived at the Robertson home, he was greeted by two pleasant, silver-haired adults in their mid-seventies. Both were able-bodied, but Edith Robertson had a frail look about her. She used a cane and her shoulders were stooped. Her face was deeply lined, the skin papery and pale. Harvey looked more vigorous and robust. Edith greeted Jim with a cordial smile, but Harvey, while he shook Jim's hand in the socially prescribed manner, maintained a somber expression. "This is really none of my business," he began immediately after introductions. "Mary is *her* great-grandchild." He jutted his chin toward his wife. "Not mine."

Edith Robertson spoke in a hesitant, apologetic tone. "The poor child is suffering from a mistake I made years ago. I married the first time much too young." She stopped then, looking sad. "Seems like a person's mistakes keep coming back to haunt them."

"Not just them but their spouses," Henry grumbled. "That kid is taking up space in *our* house right now and *I* have to put up with her."

Jim felt a tension between husband and wife. He remained silent, however, waiting for what might come next.

"Now Harvey," Edith sighed. "Mary's just a child. She doesn't mean any harm."

"Well—I suppose you're right about that." Harvey's tone sounded a bit more benign.

"Oh my goodness!" Edith said suddenly, remembering her duties as hostess. "We haven't even offered poor Mr. Gottwald a place to sit!" And with that, she motioned Jim toward a comfortable recliner. She set a steaming cup of coffee on a small table beside it.

"Thank you," Jim said, accepting both chair and coffee gratefully. "But please call me Jim. Would you prefer that I call you Mr. and Mrs. Robertson, or Edith and Harvey?"

"Edith and Harvey are fine," the woman responded.

"Thank you," said Jim with a smile. "Now tell me more, Edith—you were saying something about Mary being part of a mistake coming back to haunt you."

"You may as well tell Jim the whole story, Edith," Harvey muttered.

The elderly woman sighed. "Well," she began again, "I had a daughter named Ellen when I was very young. I was married, but I'm ashamed to say that marriage was the "shot gun" sort. When Ellen was only five, her father, Kenneth, deserted us. Kenneth never paid a penny in child support."

"How difficult for you," responded Jim.

"Those were hard times," Edith continued, "But I was fortunate to find a good secretarial job, and I was able to raise Ellen on my own, before I met Harvey. My mother baby-sat for me when Ellen was young."

"I imagine that was a real help," Jim reflected.

"It was a lifesaver," Edith responded in a heartfelt tone. "For both Ellen and me, really."

"And then?" Jim encouraged Edith to go on.

"Well—I guess that's about it. Ellen grew up and married a local boy named Tom Perkins. It was a good match and they were very happy together. Tom and Ellen had a daughter named Susan. A few years after that, I met Harvey. Harvey and I were married when Susan was nine or ten. We had some happy years back then." Edith smiled softly. She glanced over at Harvey, who returned her smile for the first time during the interview.

Edith continued. "But poor Tom Perkins was killed in a car accident. Ellen was nearly forty years old at the time. Between Tom's terrible death and something like a mid-life crisis, Ellen fell apart. She decided to move to California to find a new life! Susan was seventeen. She didn't want to leave her high school friends and go so far away. So Harvey and I offered to let Susan stay with us until she graduated."

"I wasn't any too thrilled about it," Harvey interjected dryly. "You can be sure about that. I raised two children in my first marriage—that was enough."

"But Harvey, what else could we do?"

"Well, there really *wasn't* anything else we could do," the man replied, shaking his head. "So we agreed to take Susan in. But I sure wasn't happy about it. After all, 'been there, done that.'" His tone sounded tired as he looked over at Jim.

"I can relate to that," Jim responded. "It's tough enough to raise children the first time round!"

"Damned right it is," Harvey agreed. "And Susan stayed with us for over a year. You know how that girl thanked us? She got pregnant by a local punk who had no interest in marrying her! At that point I insisted she move out and take responsibility for her own actions."

"It was a terrible time for me," said Edith. "I called my daughter, Ellen, in California hoping she would come home, but she had bought a house out there and was working two jobs to pay for it. She felt she couldn't leave. Ellen was willing to have Susan go stay with her but Susan refused."

"It really wasn't such a terrible time," Harvey broke in firmly. "Susan had to grow up. Her boyfriend denied paternity and left the state. Susan went on welfare while the baby, Mary, was small, and then she found a job. She managed pretty well on her own for a while."

"Well, almost on her own," Edith said. "I baby-sat for Mary just like my mother did for Ellen. Susan could never have afforded day-care on the pay she was getting."

"Had you retired from your secretarial job by then?" asked Jim.

"Yes, so I had the time to baby-sit. The problem was, I wasn't so young any more. I got tired easily. Taking care of a toddler when I was nearly seventy was much harder than I expected. But after a couple years, Mary went off to school. Things were a lot easier for me after that."

"And then," Harvey said in a disgusted tone, "Susan got involved with this guy of hers. I think she hoped he would 'rescue' her at first. She was having a hard time making ends meet, even with Edith baby-sitting free for her. Susan got the idea this fellow might marry her and take care of her and the kid."

"Well," said Jim thoughtfully, "a lot of young women hope to marry a man for that same reason."

"Maybe so," Harvey said with a wry smile. "but I sure hope they choose better than Susan did. Susan's young man has a serious alcohol problem—I suspect he uses other drugs too. Susan has an alcohol problem now also; she drinks most of the time, from what I can tell. She began arriving at work late so often she got herself fired. She couldn't pay her rent and was evicted from her apartment. She moved in with her boyfriend a few weeks ago."

"What about Mary?" asked Jim.

"Mary stayed with us. But sometimes Susan comes over here drunk and makes a scene when we won't let the child go with her like that." Harvey sounded more worried than angry now.

"You want to be sure the child is safe, Harvey, even if she's a problem for you." It was a statement rather than a question, but Jim wanted to make sure.

"That's right, Jim. Mary's a heck of a lot of work for a pair of old folks us, but I care about what happens to the child, even if she isn't my own flesh and blood."

"So you see," said Edith, "Mary is a cross to bear. Harvey and I can't abandon her now that Susan's drinking so much and living with that shameful young man. But we're tired, and the strain is hurting our marriage."

"That's for sure," said Harvey.

"I'm sure this is very hard for both of you," said Jim. "But what about Susan? Doesn't she want to have Mary with her when she *isn't* drinking?"

"Jim, every time Susan has come over here since she's been living with that guy, she's been under the influence of something or other," said Harvey angrily. "Alcohol or whatever. We don't dare let Mary go with her."

Jim shook his head. "Does Mary see her mother when she's drunk, or using other drugs? Does she witness angry scenes?"

"We tell Mary to go to her bedroom and close the door when Susan comes over here acting funny," Edith replied. "But our house is small, as you can see. I'm sure the child hears almost everything."

"Are you two in any danger personally? Does Susan threaten you or get physically aggressive when she's drunk or high?" Jim was alarmed for the old couple.

"Not if I'm here," Harvey chuckled, "and that's almost all the time. I'm a lot bigger than Susan. And so far, thank God, she hasn't brought the boyfriend."

"That *is* fortunate," Jim replied soberly. "Are you worried about what might happen if she did, though?"

"Of course we're worried," Harvey replied. "But what can we do?"

"You must call the police immediately if you are threatened, do you understand?" said Jim in an urgent tone. "You must call the police if you are threatened either by the boyfriend *or* your granddaughter. Don't wait."

"Well, we hate to get anyone in trouble, especially our Susan," said Edith anxiously.

"Of course. But Mary needs you, and to have either of you two hurt would take away the child's only stability and security. Can you understand that?"

"Well—yes, I suppose," Edith replied.

"Call the police right away if you think there's going to be any trouble," said Jim, "and if you do need to call the police, you should consider taking out a restraining order."

"What's a restraining order?" asked Harvey.

"It's an order from the court that legally requires a particular person to stay away from you and your home. It can be obtained if there is reasonable evidence of danger," replied Jim.

"How would we go about getting one?" asked Harvey.

"There's a special office where you apply down at the court house. We can talk about that procedure if the need arises," said Jim. "If you two have any trouble, will you let me know right away?"

"Yes, we'll do that," Harvey responded.

"Meantime," continued Jim, "I guess it's not surprising that Mary's doing so poorly at school, under the circumstances. Do you mind if I explain to the teacher what's going on?"

"Of course not. Anything the teacher can do to help will be much appreciated," said Edith.

"Ms. Shea will do her best to help Mary, I know," said Jim. "She's very good with children. Of course, she has a large classroom so that what she can do is limited."

"We'll be grateful for any help she can give," Edith repeated.

"And what about you two?" Jim asked. "How can I be helpful to you?"

"I'm afraid there isn't much you can do for us, Jim," said Harvey. "We have a pretty big problem here but I'm afraid we're stuck with it."

Edith spoke up then, to Jim's surprise. "We're not getting any younger, Harvey. We have to admit that. We may not be able to care for Mary much longer. What then? Jim, have you any ideas?"

"I've been wondering what alternatives there might be for Mary if the two of you couldn't keep her," said Jim. "Have you any ideas yourself?"

"Well," said Edith, "we know there are foster homes, but we don't know much about them. I'd hate to send poor Mary to a foster home, anyway. She's such a sensitive child. No matter what we said, she'd wonder what she did wrong so that we sent her away."

"I'd hate to send Mary to a foster home either," admitted Harvey, "but you're right, we aren't getting any younger, Edith. We may have to. If the time comes, Jim, how would a person go about it?"

Jim explained that the Emmett County Guidance Clinic was the local public agency responsible for foster home recruitment, licensing, and placement. He explained that foster homes were in short supply, however, and that a court order would be required to transfer custody of Mary to the county so that she could legally be placed away from her mother.

"Susan sure wouldn't like that," commented Harvey.

"Of course not," said Jim, "I can't think of a mother who would. But sometimes necessity makes us do things we don't want to do. The court can order foster placement even when the mother disagrees, if there's strong evidence of need."

Jim then suggested a different option, however. What about trying to get Susan into a substance abuse treatment program? The young mother's habit was apparently recent in origin, so recovery was a realistic hope. But if Susan could be persuaded to enter treatment, did she have any health insurance?

Sadly, Harvey and Edith shook their heads. Susan had lost her health insurance with her job, they explained. Little Mary had no health insurance now either, since that had been provided through her mother's policy. Taking Mary to the pediatrician for check-ups was becoming a serious drain on the resources of the great-grandparents, in fact.

Jim shook his head. This was indeed a family situation that could be described as "multi-problem," and he knew of few public resources to assist. Public welfare programs across the nation, including Aid to Families with Dependent Children and alcohol and drug treatment programs for the indigent, had been slashed.

Jim did have some ideas, though. He wanted to check them out.

"You know, Harvey and Edith," he said, "I think we've done enough for today. We've identified what's upsetting Mary and I can talk with her teacher about ideas to help her. But I want to check into some other possible resources for you. Would you be willing to get together again in a couple weeks?"

"Of course!" said Edith.

"Sure," said Harvey.

"Meantime, I think it would be helpful for you to have a source of inexpensive baby-sitting so that you two can get a break sometimes. How about checking with your church, or your neighbors, or maybe the Scouts or a local 4-H club?" Jim suggested.

"So far we've managed okay on our own, but I must admit we're awfully tired," Edith sighed. "I haven't thought of asking at our church. I'll talk to the minister this week. Maybe he'll have some ideas."

"Good," said Jim. "Now, I need to talk with your granddaughter, Susan. Is that okay with you?"

"Of course. Maybe you'll get a better idea what's going on with Susan than we can," said Edith.

"Have you a telephone number for her at the boyfriend's place, or an address?" asked Jim.

"Yes—wait a minute and I'll get them for you," said Edith.

Leaning on her cane, the elderly woman walked slowly off to another room, returning with her granddaughter's phone number and street address. "Good luck! I hope she'll talk with you, Jim," Edith said.

"Thanks, Edith," Jim replied. "It's time for me to be going now. I'll be back in two weeks."

"Thank you for your interest, Jim," Edith and Harvey chorused. "Good-bye for now."

Jim Gottwald had several ideas he wanted to check out. Was Susan aware that she had a substance abuse problem? Was she aware that her boyfriend did? Even those who suffer severe and multiple addictions frequently deny they have a problem, and refuse treatment even when it is available.

However, perhaps Susan Perkins *did* realize she had a problem, and that was why she had left her daughter with her grandparents, Mary's great-grandparents. If so, would Susan be willing to undergo treatment? How would she finance it? There was no longer any public aid for inpatient care in her state, and outpatient programs had long waiting lists. Susan had no private health insurance. Could Jim help Susan find any options?

If, by some miracle, substance abuse treatment could be found and financed for Susan, there was still the problem of the relationship with the boyfriend. Clearly, the young mother needed counseling, possibly couples counseling. Emmett County Guidance Clinic offered this service for a sliding fee, but Susan had no income at all. And there was a long waiting list.

But what if Susan refused treatment altogether, or if treatment were simply unavailable without money to pay for it, and the mother's problems continued unabated? Jim felt that his first goal must be to protect Mary. After all, Mary was a small child, a legal minor, and could not protect herself. To this end, Jim planned to check out options and procedures for licensing Mary's great-grandparents as foster parents. Foster parent status would relieve some of the financial strain for Edith and Harvey, since a small stipend was paid to foster parents by the county. And as a foster child, Mary would qualify for health insurance through Medicaid.

Foster placement, however, would require a court order. Legal custody, or the right to decide where the child should live, would have to be transferred to the county. How would Susan respond? Would she challenge a change of custody in court? Would the threat of losing her daughter push Susan back into more responsible behavior as a parent? Or might she give up and simply disappear from the scene? Many possibilities lay in the future. Much careful investigating and planning lay ahead for Jim Gottwald.

DISCUSSION AND STUDY QUESTIONS

Elderly relatives have provided social welfare services for their families from time immemorial. Was it Robert Frost who said something like: "Family is the place where, if you have to go there, they have to take you in?" Today's families are complex enough that only half of a couple may be biologically related to the people they are asked to care for, increasing the likelihood of confusion and resentment. But elderly relatives may be the only resource available at a time when entitlement to public assistance programs like AFDC has been eliminated and younger people, for whatever reason, are unable to carry on alone.

It usually isn't easy for the elderly to open their homes to needy younger relatives. Often older people have spent years of their lives raising families of their own and have been anticipating a time of well-deserved rest and relaxation. Being saddled with family responsibilities again can come as an unwelcome shock. No wonder an innocent child can come to be viewed as a "cross to bear." Who is looking out for the interests of the elderly themselves, whose energy and resources are frequently meager?

1. Have you known of a situation in which an elderly person or couple has been asked to take in younger family members in need? If so, how did the situation work out?
2. Think of the older people you know. What kinds of needs do they have? How well are these needs being met? What needs are apparently not being met?
*3. Why was the social worker, Jim Gottwald, interested in pursuing licensed foster home status for the Robertsons? Do you think this was a good idea? Why or why not?
*4. What do you suppose are the reasons why substance abuse treatment programs for the poor have been slashed in recent years? Think of factors besides cost-containment.

---

*Questions notated with an asterisk are intended for advanced students who have had or are currently having some social work practice experience and who have made at least a tentative commitment to the profession.

CHAPTER 25

Karen and Kevin Riley

or: The Struggles of a Teenage Mother, Ineligible for AFDC Under Welfare "Reform," to Care for Her Baby and Still Finish High School

Concepts Covered in This Chapter

1. Common components of current welfare law
   a. Workfare
   b. Learnfare
2. Establishing eligibility for public aid
   a. Status of a legal minor
   b. Status of an emancipated minor
3. Students at risk

Learning Objectives   After reading this chapter you should be able to

1. Understand several difficulties in obtaining public aid today
2. Discuss evidence that low-wage work has eclipsed education and training as a major public policy objective for poor people
3. Describe problems caused by workfare and learnfare policies from the point of view of people subject to them
4. Identify at least four programs designed to assist poor parents, and discuss complications regarding eligibility for school-age parents
5. Discuss possible sources of medical care for poor parents and understand current eligibility problems for school-age parents
6. Describe creative strategies that school-age parents are inventing to try to achieve their high school diplomas
7. Describe the role of unpaid work in assisting school-age parents to earn their diplomas

A s part of my job at the university, I set up an appointment with a dynamic young social worker, Joyce Valdez, to explain the duties of field instructor with our undergraduate social work program. Joyce was the kind of practitioner I especially liked to recruit as a field instructor, because she was an alumna who had been an excellent student in our program. With a few years of professional experience behind her, Joyce was now willing and able to take on a student. Like most social work field instructors, she offered her valuable services free of charge because of her sincere commitment to the profession.

Joyce worked in an urban "alternative" high school, so it occurred to me she might be of assistance in another way. I wondered if she might be willing to describe for me how high school students were being affected by recent changes in social welfare policy at both the national and state levels. The termination of AFDC, Aid to Families with Dependent Children, while enacted nationwide (see Chapter 22), had been accompanied by especially extensive changes in our state policy as well.

Joyce was more than willing to assist, for, as it turned out, many of her students were deeply affected by the changes in social welfare policy. Nationally, AFDC had been eliminated as an entitlement under the Social Security Act. States were allowed the option of providing aid to needy families, but for a maximum of five years. Our state limited aid to two consecutive years, and five years total in a person's lifetime. To receive aid, needy parents had to work as soon as their youngest child was 12 weeks of age. Many of Joyce's students at Urban Alternative High School, as the school was named, were members of families receiving AFDC, and vulnerable to losing their benefits. A significant number were parents themselves.

Under the new welfare regulations in our state, students in post-secondary education programs were now required to participate in "workfare." This meant they had to go to work full-time if they wanted to keep any AFDC benefits. If possible, they found regular jobs. Failing that, they had to participate in work programs provided by the state. State programs paid less than minimum wage, so they were very unattractive. However, working parents who met the state means test (income eligibility requirements) qualified for a limited day-care subsidy for their children and Medicaid for two years. This aid was crucial for many, so large numbers of young student parents dropped out of college or technical school to go to work. At first, it seemed as if high school-age parents would also lose their benefits unless they went to work. But fortunately, after much political battling, high school-age parents were allowed to keep their benefits if making satisfactory progress toward their diploma.

The alternative high school where Joyce Valdez worked had been established to assist "at risk" students. The definition of "at risk" used by the school included chronic truancy and behavioral problems. Many of the students enrolled at Urban Alternative had been expelled from other institutions for these reasons. Another criterion the school used for "at risk" was pregnancy. Ninety of the 230 students enrolled at Urban Alternative were school-age parents. Joyce Valdez not only described for me the impact of new social welfare policy on school-age parents but also introduced me to one of them, Karen Riley, 16, and her infant son, Kevin. Karen was doing her best to earn enough credits to graduate from high school while trying to provide responsible, loving care for Kevin, then eight months old.

Joyce and Karen met with me together in the school social work office. Karen was feeding little Kevin as she spoke with me, her baby gurgling contentedly as he sucked upon his bottle. Mother and son mirrored a marvelous bonding. Two sets of shining blue eyes beamed at each other frequently, and smiles were simultaneous. Karen's golden hair was only slightly darker than her son's pale, baby-fine locks, and both had the soft, smooth skin of youth. Their complexions were rosy and fair.

Karen explained proudly that she breastfed Kevin whenever she could. The milk the child was drinking from the bottle was her own. Urban Alternative High School provided a breast-pumping room where students who were nursing mothers could collect and store their milk. School social workers provided parenting classes, and also gave skills-training sessions at home for home-bound mothers. Unfortunately, however, Urban Alternative could not provide day-care facilities for its students' children. Karen said she wanted very much to bring Kevin with her to school every day, but she could not. Today she had brought her baby only for my benefit, at Joyce Valdez' request.

Joyce explained that Urban Alternative's administrators had investigated carefully the possibility of developing a day-care center for its students. Staff knew that an on-site day-care center was badly needed. Several school-age parents had recently been forced to quit because of lack of child care. But the school did not have the resources to open a day-care center. Liability issues made the cost prohibitive for the struggling, low-budget organization.

Karen Riley smiled sadly at the infant she was cradling in her arms. "Kevin's such a good baby," she said. "I feel so bad leaving him behind every day. But I don't blame Urban Alternative High School. I understand that the school can't afford to run a day-care center. But it sure is hard when I can't find a baby-sitter, or when Kevin gets sick."

"What do you usually do with Kevin during the school day?" I asked.

"Most of the time," Karen replied, "my sister takes care of him while I'm at school. She's married and has a baby too. She's lucky because she has a husband who has a pretty good job. But she has to work part-time to help make ends meet. When my sister's busy, sometimes my boyfriend's mother will baby-sit for Kevin. I'm always looking for a baby-sitter, it seems. I have to work as well as go to school. That's because I can't get any help from AFDC."

Joyce spoke up to explain. "Karen's a legal minor, you see. She's under 18. AFDC refused her application for aid because they have to use her *father's* income to determine eligibility now, not hers. Karen's father has a full-time job and he earns too much money for Karen to qualify. But he and his second wife have two young kids of their own. They don't really have anything left over for Karen and the baby."

"That's right," Karen said. "My mother died when I was eight. My father got married again when I was eleven, about five years ago. My half-brother and half-sister are only two and four years old. My father and stepmother didn't want me to stay with them after I had my baby—they said the house was too small."

"Where did you go after you had your baby, Karen?"

"My sister took us in, the one who helps with baby-sitting."

"Do your father and stepmother help with baby-sitting too sometimes?"

"Hardly ever! Mostly I help *them!* My stepmother works first shift, and my father works third, so they're pretty busy all the time."

"Do you have to pay your sister or your boyfriend's mother for Kevin's care, Karen?"

"No, I'm very lucky about that. I do pay rent, though—not much, but it's a lot for me to earn right now. And I need money for diapers, laundry, food, clothes, doctor's bills, all that stuff."

"How about the baby's father? Does he help out?"

Karen let out a long sigh. "My boyfriend, Jerry, never wanted our baby. He wanted me to have an abortion instead. I've hardly seen Jerry since I got pregnant, and we only talk on the phone every once in a while. Sometimes he picks Kevin up after school and takes him over to his mother's to baby-sit."

"You said that Jerry wanted you to get an abortion, Karen. Did you ever consider that option?" I asked gently.

"Of course I did," the young woman replied, "but I knew it wasn't for me. Besides, someday Jerry might grow up and want to settle down."

"Do you hope to marry Jerry someday, Karen?"

"Oh yes! I love him!" the girl responded fervently. Then her expression grew sad. "But he isn't ready yet."

"How old is Jerry, Karen?"

"He's sixteen, like me," Karen replied. "I met him at my last school, before I came to Urban Alternative. Jerry dropped out of school a couple months ago, though. He's living with his father across town. His parents are divorced. Luckily, Jerry's mother lives right around the corner from me and my sister. She's been wonderful—she baby-sits when she can. She works too, though, so she can't help out all that often."

"How many hours do you work yourself, Karen?"

"I work a *lot*," the girl replied. "I work after school Monday through Thursday from 4:30 in the afternoon to 8:30 at night. I have to take the bus, so I don't get home until 9:30. On Fridays, when school gets out at 11:00 in the morning, I work from 11:30 to 5:00 in the afternoon as a data processor. On Saturday, I work from 9:00 in the morning till 1:00 in the afternoon as a telemarketer."

"Good heavens, Karen," I said, "with all your part-time employment plus school, when do you have time to see your baby?"

Karen's face fell. "I don't get to see Kevin nearly as much as I'd like to," she said with a sigh. "But I have to earn money. Even though my sister baby-sits for free right now, there's so much else I have to pay for."

Joyce Valdez spoke up. "Karen really is very lucky to have a sister and a boyfriend's mother who will baby-sit for her so that she can finish high school. I've had a number of students who have had to drop out this year because of the new welfare policies. There aren't enough women available at home any more to provide free care for the children."

"What's causing the problem?" I asked.

Joyce responded thoughtfully. "There's more than a single factor involved. For one thing, relatives who provided free child care before have to report for job training or take paying work now. For another, even students who qualify for a child-care stipend through AFDC have a hard time. The stipend is too small to pay for regular day-care, and there are long waiting lists at the centers anyway, with all the AFDC mothers having to work."

"So several of your students have actually had to drop out of high school, Joyce?"

"We've lost at least a dozen this year from Urban Alternative High School alone because of lack of resources for child-care," Joyce replied. "And several other students have been cut off AFDC and forced out of school because they couldn't meet 'learnfare' regulations."

"Learnfare has forced some of your students out of school? I thought the program was instigated to motivate students to stay *in* school." (I was playing a bit of the conscious simpleton here, as I already had heard about this problem, but I wanted to hear what Joyce would say.)

"The program has backfired for many of our students. Under state regulations, students can't exceed a certain number of absences and still continue to receive their AFDC benefits. Without AFDC benefits, they can't afford to stay in school. So they have to drop out to go to work."

"Well—why don't your students just make sure they attend school regularly, then?"

"They're parents as well as students. When their babies get sick, they have to stay home to take care of them. Urban Alternative excuses the absences of teens whose babies are ill, and believe me, we check to make sure the illnesses are real. But learnfare sanctions anyway. We've had several student parents have to drop out this year because they lost their AFDC benefits due to sanctions, even though most absences were excused by the school."

"Are both teen mothers and teen fathers affected the same way, Joyce?"

"In most cases, it's the teen moms who suffer. The fathers usually don't take responsibility, either for child care or for helping out financially."

"Karen," I asked the young mother at my side, "does your boyfriend, Jerry, ever help you out financially with the baby?"

"No. Well, Jerry gives me money for diapers sometimes. That's about it."

"That must be pretty hard for you, Karen," said I. "Under the circumstances, with your having to work so much and having the baby to care for, have you ever considered giving up on school?"

Karen looked over at Joyce then, and, to my surprise, both young women burst out laughing.

I was astonished! "Did I say something funny?" I asked.

Karen stopped laughing, but still smiled broadly. "Tell her, Joyce," she commanded.

Joyce, shaking her head, said, "You don't know how funny that sounded to us, Carolyn. Karen *hasn't* considered dropping out of Urban Alternative; she's absolutely determined to graduate if she possibly can. That's because she had to work so hard to get *in*. She was kicked out of her last school."

"Kicked out?" I asked, surprised. "What happened, Karen?"

Karen looked embarrassed. "I had a girlfriend who got jumped on by somebody. I know now that I should have tried to get a teacher to help, but instead I tried to help my friend myself, and I got pulled into the fight. All three of us were expelled."

"Oh dear," I said. "Expelled for good, or just for a period of time?"

"Expelled for good. They told me I couldn't go back. I was only a freshman, so I was pretty scared."

"How did you hear about Urban Alternative High School?"

"The social worker at the school where I got kicked out. She called me into her office the day I had to leave. She asked me if I wanted to continue my education and I told her I did. She gave me the name and phone number of this school and encouraged me to apply."

"Had you met that social worker before, Karen?"

"No, I hadn't. But she told me she hated to see kids lose out on an education and wanted me to know there might be another chance."

"And so here you are."

"Yes. But I had to have an admissions interview with the dean of students first, and take a terribly hard test. And the dean asked me about a dozen times why I wanted to finish high school. I really had to convince her she should let me in."

"What made you want to come here, Karen?"

"Well, I knew I needed a high school diploma if I was going to get anywhere in life. And, also, people treated me like an adult here, like I was important."

"I'll bet that felt good."

"It did feel good. It was really different, and I liked it. But then, just after I started coming here, I realized I might be pregnant. I felt awful and told Joyce. She had the public health nurse give me a test. I *was* pregnant."

"How did you feel when you learned you were pregnant?"

"Terrible. My boyfriend didn't want the baby and he just stopped coming around. My parents were furious. As I said before, though, I didn't feel right having an abortion."

"How do your parents feel about your baby now, Karen?"

"Well, once Kevin was born they got nicer to me again, like I hoped they would. They love the baby now. But I live with my sister because it's better that way. Two little kids are about all my father and stepmother can cope with, working full-time like they do."

"How about your boyfriend, Jerry? Is he happy about the baby now, Karen?"

"Well, Jerry likes Kevin all right, but he doesn't seem to want to see us very much."

"And Jerry's not helping financially, you said."

"No, and it's funny, because he didn't even want me to *apply* for welfare."

"You said earlier that you couldn't get on AFDC because you're still a minor and your father earns too much money, Karen."

"That's right. But I did *apply* for welfare even though Jerry didn't want me to. That was because I didn't have any money and my father said he couldn't help me. But the welfare people said they couldn't help me either."

"What did you do about the cost of prenatal care, and the hospital bills for Kevin's birth?"

"My father's health insurance paid my medical bills until I had the baby," Karen replied, "but it didn't cover the birth or any medical bills after that. I couldn't get Medicaid because my father's income was too high."

"So once you were in labor with Kevin, you were on your own," I said.

"That's right," Karen replied. "I have some huge hospital bills from Kevin's birth that I can't pay, and some emergency room bills that I haven't even seen yet. I'm afraid how high they will be. Kevin had a high fever on Sunday a couple weeks ago, and I got so scared I took him in. I owe Kevin's regular pediatrician about $400, too. He's treated Kevin for an ear infection and given him his shots."

"Owing so much money must feel scary," I reflected, thinking how many hours it would take a teenager to earn enough money just to pay the pediatrician's back bills, to say nothing of Kevin's hospital bills, or any future medical care for the baby.

Joyce spoke up. "Luckily, I've been able to find some resources for Karen and Kevin," she said. "I recently referred them to a program called 'Healthy Start.' It provides medical assistance for infants up to three years old. Healthy Start turned Karen down at first because of her father's income, but I sent her back with rent receipts from her sister's place to prove she is really on her own. She's been accepted on the waiting list. The program is strapped for resources, though, and the waiting list is about three months long."

"It's still a relief to know I'll have a medical card soon, at least for awhile," Karen said. "That will keep me from running up any more huge hospital bills for a couple years anyway."

"And you'll have some help with food from WIC," Joyce prompted. (WIC is an acronym for the federal program, Women, Infants, and Children).

"Yes, Karen responded. "Joyce sent me to the program called WIC, too. They accepted Kevin and me—we get some milk, vegetables, tuna fish, and cereal, and a little money to buy a few other things at the store."

"Have you thought of applying for food stamps, Karen?" I asked, unconsciously slipping into the social work role of identifying potential resources.

"I tried," the girl replied, "but they said my father earns too much."

Joyce interjected then:"Unfortunately, it's not just the teen moms like Karen, whose parents earn too much to qualify for AFDC and food stamps, who go without assistance nowadays. Some of my students' parents who *do* qualify for aid just keep it for themselves. They don't pass it on to the teens and their babies, who are at their mercy now."

"What a problem," I responded. "Do any of these teens try to become 'emancipated minors' through the courts, so that they can receive aid in their own names? Do you think that might that be an option for Karen, in fact? She's really on her own, for all intents and purposes."

"We've talked about that," Joyce responded. "But unfortunately, when the state bureaucrats changed the AFDC policies, they anticipated that a lot of teen parents might try to become emancipated minors. So they've made it almost impossible. Legal Aid, the organization that represents people who are poor, won't even answer telephone calls any more about that procedure."

"Whew," I murmured. "things sure sound tough for teenage parents nowadays."

"That's for sure," said Karen.

"Now that you have a baby to care for, Karen, and things are so hard for you, are you still so determined to finish high school?" I asked the young mother again.

"You bet I am," Karen replied. "When I first got pregnant, I was afraid I would have to drop out of high school. But Joyce told me I could still get my diploma if I was willing to work hard."

"And Karen *was* willing to work hard," Joyce interjected proudly. "Urban Alternative provided lesson plans for her to study at home for six weeks after Kevin was born. Karen did all of her assignments and more. She kept right on working hard when she came back to school. She's about to complete 15 of the 21 credits she needs to graduate. She'll finish her degree by Christmas next year."

"That's great, Karen!" I exclaimed, genuinely impressed. "Where did you get the motivation to earn your diploma so quickly?"

"As I said before, I knew I'd never get anywhere without a high school diploma. But I also want to go to college. The company my father works for helps pay tuition for employees who take college courses. I'm hoping to get a job there after I graduate. If I do, I'll take college courses part-time."

"What do you think you want to study, Karen?"

"Computers," the young woman replied immediately. "I learned enough about them here at Urban Alternative High School to get my part-time job as a data processor on Friday afternoons. I'd like to learn more."

"Good for you, Karen," I said. "I hope you can follow that dream. Now be sure to check with local colleges and universities for opportunities for scholarships and financial assistance. You never know what you might find." I started to slip into my social work role again.

Joyce caught my eye and grinned. I caught the cue. This was Joyce's role, not mine, and she was doing it well. I grinned back at my former student, proud that I had something to do with her professional development.

"But Joyce knows that, Karen," I hastened to add, "so be sure to ask her where she thinks your opportunities might be greatest."

"I sure will!" Karen responded.

"Very good. Well, it's time for me to go now. Thanks a lot, both of you!" I rose to my feet. I gave the young mother, her tiny son, and my former student, now a full-fledged professional, each a warm hug. I wished them all well, and then walked out into a beautiful spring afternoon, welcoming the sunlight. I felt deeply moved and humbled by the courage and determination of one struggling but undefeated sixteen-year-old girl. I felt ashamed of the nation and state that made her job so difficult.

DISCUSSION AND STUDY QUESTIONS

"Workfare" is a term used to describe social policies which require poor people to work in order to receive financial assistance. "Learnfare" is a term that refers to the practice of requiring children who receive AFDC to maintain good school attendance. There are other types of programs related to welfare designed to modify behavior in a so-called positive direction as well. For example, "wedfare," or "bridefare," provides benefits for single mothers who apply for AFDC who agree to marry; some states have penalties for those who don't.

Behavior modification programs, or programs designed to change people's behavior, can work only if the people thus targeted for control *can* modify their behavior. This chapter indicates some of the problems from the point of view of real people involved. School-age parents, for example, often cannot maintain good attendance if they are to meet their responsibilities as parents. They cannot work full-time, either, if they are to earn their high school diplomas, their best key to a better future. They probably *should* not work even part-time given their developmental need to study and their parental need to bond with their children. Many single parents might like to marry, but simply do not have the option, as was the situation with Karen Riley in this chapter.

Despite punitively designed behavior modification programs such as those discussed above, fortunately there are other social programs designed genuinely to help people live better lives. Two are mentioned in the chapter above, and deserve celebration: one is Healthy Start, the other WIC, or Women, Infants, and Children. Protecting positive national programs such as these from the endless budget-cutting process remains an enormous challenge.

1. Examine your own attitudes toward teenage parents. Do you think they should be assisted in their important task of child rearing, or punished for unwisely taking on such a project so young? What are your reasons? Which approach do you think has the best chance of leading to a better future for our society as a whole? Why?
2. Describe the difficulties of being a legal minor when attempting to enroll in public aid programs. What is an "emancipated minor" and why do you believe such a status was established in the first place? Why is it difficult to achieve this status today?
*3. Sociologists identify what they call "manifest" consequences, or those obviously intended from a particular action or policy, and "latent" consequences, or those not intended or expected. What do you think the manifest consequences of "workfare" and "learnfare" probably were? What are some latent consequences identified in this chapter?
*4. If you could design an enlightened program to deal with teenage pregnancy, what components would you especially want to include? What are your reasons?

---

*Questions notated with an asterisk are intended for advanced students who have had or are currently having some social work practice experience and who have made at least a tentative commitment to the profession.

PART SIX

Epilogue

CHAPTER 26

Epilogue

or: Carrying on in Difficult Times; Looking Toward
the Future

Concepts Covered in This Chapter

1. Self-care strategies
   a. Managing unsupportive work environments
   b. Managing work overloads
2. Factors affecting decision making about social welfare resources
   a. National social policy priorities
   b. Local social policy priorities
   c. Organizational priorities
   d. Interpersonal factors
3. The impact of policy on service delivery
4. Employee assistance programs
5. Full inclusion movement

Learning Objectives   By the end of this chapter you should be able to

1. List at least three strategies for managing work environments that do not seem supportive
2. Explain how personal preferences and family obligations can influence one's response to work overloads
3. List what you understand to be current national and local policy priorities
4. Describe similarities and differences between the national and local social policy priorities you list and the needs of families and communities of which you are aware
5. List at least three ways that social policy affects service delivery
6. Describe the function of an employee assistance program
7. Define full inclusion

A
s I waited for Norman Werner in the main office of the Kingston Middle School where he now served as school psychologist, I felt a strong sense of anticipation. I hadn't seen Norman, nor his colleague, Jim Gottwald, the school social worker, for several years. Soon a tall, bearded man with a familiar warm smile bounded toward me, hand outstretched. Only the distinguished gray scattered throughout Norman's thick dark hair made me think of time's unwanted passing. The psychologist led me into his office briskly, apologizing for being a few minutes late. "I'm always behind now, Carolyn," the big man explained. "I'm serious—just take a look at this office."

As I entered Norman's office, my mind flashed back to the neatly organized desk he had always kept in the big open room shared by the pupil services team back when special education was run by Emmett County. But the county had relinquished responsibility for special education to the various townships many years before. Kingston provided Norman with a private office including a big teacher's desk, a small table, a few chairs, file cabinets, and what would seem to be a reasonable amount of room under most circumstances. But two large computers ate up most of the space on Norman's desk and table, and stacks of papers were heaped precariously on every horizontal surface.

Norman waved at the paper stacks expansively. "If I hit one of these piles by mistake, it gives way like a glacier," he joked. "Nothing happens at first, and then slowly, slowly, the whole thing melts onto the floor."

"Norman, I remember you used to keep such a neat desk in the old pupil services office!" I gasped.

"Yes, and I prefer to keep a neat desk," the man responded grimly, "but there's no time for it any more. I'm my own secretary now. Do you see those two computers?"

"Of course," I nodded.

"They were supposed to be time-savers. This one (he pointed to the machine on his desk) is hooked up directly to central office. It saves *central office* a lot of time, that's for sure. But I have to type all my own reports now. The dictation we used to do was much faster."

"How about the number of reports you have to write now, Norman. Is it any less?"

"I have more reports to write now than ever," the psychologist replied. "I'm still serving as case manager for all the special education referrals. I've had to schedule 28 M teams this month alone, and I have to write all the final reports. Besides that, I'm expected to serve all the children in this school, not just those referred to special education."

"How do you do it, Norman? You used to put in several nights of unpaid overtime every week when we talked a few years back. Do you work late every night now?"

Norman's sudden joyful smile came as a complete surprise, given the somber information he was providing me. He looked up and vigorously pointed toward the wall beside and above him. I followed his gaze to a large photograph. An attractive young woman and a little girl dressed in cheerful colors beamed happily down into the room.

"Ah ha!" said I. "So you're no longer the most eligible bachelor in Kingston, Norman!"

"That's right," the man responded with a grin. "My wife, Sandra, and I have been married for about five years now. We have a little girl, as you can see. Her name is

Jenny; she's almost two years old. We have a baby on the way. So I don't work nights any more if I can help it. Actually, I can't work nights any more. Sandra is a nurse. She works evening shift so that we can take turns baby-sitting."

"You sound like a very busy couple."

"We are, so I've had to cut out most of my overtime hours after school. But you can see what happens." He gestured expansively at his enormous piles. "Maybe I could get my work done if I put in 24 hours a day here, but, to tell the truth, I'm not sure."

At that point there was a knock on Norman's door. Jim Gottwald entered, the school social worker, a man as fair-haired and trim as his colleague was dark and muscular. I had asked Jim to be present at the interview. He had been hired after I left my position in Kingston, but I remembered him well from consulting about case examples for the second edition of this book. I was delighted to see him again.

"Norman's been talking about overtime work, Jim," I greeted the social worker. "I remember you and I talked about that a few years ago. You said that you had to put your family first. How do you feel now?"

Jim let out a long sigh, shaking his head. "Norman and I have reversed positions about overtime work in some ways," he said. "My children are older now, so they don't need baby-sitting so much. My office was beginning to look like Norman's." He swept his arm to indicate the clutter. "So I began putting in evening hours from time to time to finish my paperwork. It's a frustrating business, because the school doesn't acknowledge extra hours and doesn't pay for them."

"Do you get any compensatory time for extra work—time off in exchange for unpaid overtime?"

"I suppose I could take time off occasionally," Jim replied, "but there's just too much to do here. The paperwork required for special education is horrendous."

"It's not just special education paperwork that's horrendous," Norman cut in. "If a child is evaluated for special education and doesn't qualify, there are other laws now that we have to consider. There's a law about discrimination in the workplace, for example. Some provisions may apply to children as well as staff here. I chair a committee to implement the law at this school. The position is very time-consuming and generates a lot of paperwork. It broadens the administrative base of the school, to tell the truth, but doesn't give me any special title or extra pay."

"Sometimes I'm afraid Norman is going to lose himself entirely in administrative work," Jim mused out loud.

"I am too, to tell the truth," Norman affirmed.

"How about you, Jim? Are you doing a lot of administrative work now too?"

"Not any more," the social worker replied. "I used to be case manager for all the kids referred for emotional disturbance. I organized their M teams and wrote up their reports. That saved Norman a lot of time and I was good at it. But our job descriptions were changed without any input from us a few years ago. Norman was made case manager for all the special education referrals, and I was told to be guidance counselor as well as social worker. I have more 'hands-on' work now, and that suits me, but Norman's been left with the bulk of the administrative work."

Norman spoke up with a rueful smile. "When I began this job as school psychologist, I could work with kids who needed counseling at least once, sometimes twice a week. Now I'm lucky if I can see them once every two or three weeks. And I believe that's the work I *should* be doing, not sitting at my desk typing reports."

"How frustrating for you, Norman," I replied. "Do you have adequate places to refer these kids if you don't have time to work with them yourself?"

"I send some of them to Jim when he has time to take them. But since Jim is guidance counselor now as well as social worker, he has mini-courses to prepare and teach—sessions on self-esteem, conflict resolution, drug and alcohol issues, that sort of thing. So Jim hasn't much time to counsel individual kids either. I refer out to Emmett County Guidance Clinic, but the workers there don't have much time for voluntary referrals from the school."

"That's because the county social workers are overwhelmed with mandatory referrals from the courts," Jim explained for Norman. "The county workers have to investigate child abuse and neglect reports, and do court-ordered assessments for custody disputes. That's about all they have time for."

"Sounds like things haven't changed a whole lot since I worked here," I reflected sadly. "I remember the county workers rarely had time to work with referrals from the school. Back then, though, protective service investigations were hard to come by, and there was no follow-through on cases that clearly needed intervention. Has that changed?"

"Yes," Jim replied, "fortunately, protective services is functional now. A new director has made a big difference. But understaffing is still a problem. There are many more children and families in trouble now than there were back then."

"Are there places to refer kids for help besides Emmett County Guidance Clinic and the private agency that was operating when I worked here?" I asked.

"There's a church-related clinic in a neighboring town that will accept clients for a sliding fee," Jim replied, "but even the lowest fee is too high for many of our families. There's a new private agency in a neighboring town, too, but it's full fee and no one can afford it without insurance. Distance is a problem, too."

"I don't suppose there are any more group homes or hospitals for seriously disturbed kids."

"No. There's still only one group home for adolescents in the county, and none for younger children. The nearest hospital is over 50 miles away."

Norman spoke up: "You'd think after all these years more services would be provided for the children. Everybody gives lip service that kids come first, but nobody's willing to put up the dollars."

"In fact, it seems harder than ever to find resources for children," Jim reflected. "There are a couple of new private clinics in neighboring towns, as we just explained, but they certainly don't meet the needs of many of our kids."

"Jim and I often feel overwhelmed," Norman admitted seriously. "The schools are being expected to solve all society's problems today, without the means to do the job. Parents demand a lot and then threaten to sue us if we don't come through with what they want."

"Most parents have to work if they want to make ends meet," Jim explained. "So if their kids are having trouble, they want us to fix them here at school. They don't have time."

"The relationship with parents is often adversarial, and that's a real problem," said Norman.

"I have to spend a good deal of time just making sure my records and reports are worded carefully," Jim agreed. "That's because they could end up in court if a parent got mad for some reason."

"Every special education referral has to be assessed very carefully," Norman continued. "I make kids fight to get into the program. First, I believe that regular education is the best place for children if they can succeed. But second, I have to be careful about initiating a special education evaluation because most parents don't want to be told their kid has a problem."

"How do you make kids 'fight to get in' to special education, Norman?" I asked.

"I head a committee that screens every referral to decide if a formal evaluation is necessary. Jim serves on that committee, and so does the referring teacher. But parents still get mad at us. Some are angry if we so much as suggest a special education evaluation for their child. Others get angry if we don't determine that their child has exactly the special needs they think they do."

"We actually had a family leave the district last year because their child was referred for evaluation," said Jim. "Before they left, though, the parents demanded a dossier on every member of the special education staff."

"Whew," said I. "Sounds very uncomfortable, to say the least."

"I don't fully understand why the relationship with parents is so difficult nowadays," said Norman. "If I need help with my plumbing at home, I'll call a plumber. I'll respect his advice, and I'll take it. But after my 20 years of experience working with children here, many parents still don't respect my advice, much less take it."

"Of course, sometimes parents are right," interjected Jim. "I don't mean that parents shouldn't listen to *you,* Norman! But we know the schools don't always provide children and families with appropriate services. The problem is usually money."

"For example?" I asked.

Norman responded. "Jim's got a point. I think we have a chicken and egg problem here. The media often accuse the schools of unbalancing the municipal budget. People get mad, and then the schools don't get the money they need. Because the schools are strapped for resources, they can't provide legitimate services parents want. That makes parents disrespect the schools even more."

"Can you give me a specific example?" I persisted.

"Just last week," Norman said, "one of our parents asked the special education director to provide an aide for her child. This parent wanted her little girl, who has a cognitive disability, to be mainstreamed in the regular classroom, with assistance of an aide. My boss refused. I thought he made the wrong decision, so I talked with him about it privately later. My boss said he felt he had no choice. If he established the precedent of a classroom aide for one child, others might want one too, and the school system just doesn't have the money."

"I see," I replied. "Yet I'm surprised, Norman. The full inclusion movement has swept many parts of the country, as I'm sure you and Jim are aware. Hasn't it arrived in Kingston yet?" (Full inclusion advocates that children with special needs receive all their education in a regular classroom. Aides may be necessary to assist).

"Kingston doesn't practice full inclusion yet, and probably never will, the way things are going," Norman replied. "Budgets are constantly being cut, rather than increased to meet the needs we have. The special education director is determined to keep costs down. Otherwise he's afraid of what might happen politically. The program could get cut entirely."

"Resources are so scarce that Norman and I have been changing the way we work," Jim interjected. "Last year we applied for three different grants. We knew we couldn't meet the needs of the children individually, so we decided to reach out to the community as a whole instead. We hoped we might be able to prevent some problems."

"What kinds of grants did you apply for?"

"We applied for two grants to try to reduce drug and alcohol problems, and one to develop a class in parenting skills."

"That's great!" I said. "Sounds very pro-active. Did you receive the grants?"

"We did! We implemented two of them, one to combat alcohol abuse and the other to develop the parenting class. We got the kids involved in the alcohol education grant. We had a contest and the kids developed posters that we scattered around the school and in local shopping centers. They were great. We even had billboards and radio spots."

"Nice work!" I said.

"Yes," said Norman, "Jim and I felt very good about that. But you know, we just didn't have enough time to implement the grant we got for drug abuse prevention. We actually had to return the money."

"What a shame," I said, "but I understand you two can't do everything at once."

"Yes. If only we had more staff to help us. But that's a pipe dream."

"How about the parenting class? Did you and Jim manage to get one started?"

"Yes, we did."

"How did it go?"

"Unfortunately, attendance was disappointing. We sent out notices to all the parents and solicited coupons for free food at a local fast-food restaurant to reward parents who came. But we got a very small turnout. Our biggest class had fifteen parents and the smallest only two."

"What do you suppose was the problem?"

"We wish we knew for sure." This time it was Jim who spoke. "We think it has to do with the general disrespect people have nowadays for professionals who are associated with education or government or who come from a mental health approach."

"It may be, too, that people don't respect the schools because we don't turn out the kind of product they want," Norman added. "Society has given schools a mandate to correct all its problems, but we just can't do it alone. A friend of mine helped me frame the problem."

"What did your friend say, Norman?"

"My friend's an engineer," Norman replied. "He said that in industry, if you are expected to manufacture a motor, you can specify exactly what raw material you want. You can reject anything that doesn't meet exact specifications. You can treat and temper the raw material the way you want to meet exacting standards before assembling it to make your motor. Well, the schools are expected to develop a standard product too. But they can't select their raw material. They have a 'zero reject' policy. They have to take whatever comes—tin, copper, glass, platinum, you name it—and use it to develop the product. It just doesn't make for standard results. It's like expecting to make marathon runners out of kids who come without legs."

"The problem, then, or the beauty of it all really, is that kids do not come alike. They aren't little cogs in a machine."

"That's right," said Jim, "and we certainly don't want to manufacture cogs at school, anyway. We want to develop individuals who can think for themselves."

"So there's your silver lining," said Norman, settling back in his chair with a grin. "No matter how discouraged I may feel sometimes, I know there are staff at school who care a lot. They put in effort and time way above what they're paid for, and they suffer plenty of anxiety and stress trying to figure out: 'Are we doing this the right way? Are we doing this the right way for Jimmy, our one and only Jimmy?'"

"Thank goodness for that," I responded. "What do you foresee in the future, Norman?"

"Things will probably continue to get worse for a while. Then they'll go the other way; they'll have to. People will have to realize they've got to invest more in the children at some point." Norman's expression was sober.

As I left Norman Werner and Jim Gottwald in Kingston that afternoon, I couldn't help remembering my labors of many years before, with people such as Mrs. Casey, the Hosmers, the Holcolms, the Lamberts, and many others. Things didn't sound so very different to me now, except that the old problems I remembered seemed even more serious now. I wondered what I would learn about the situation in Orangetown during my visit there.

When I arrived in Orangetown, David Chase, still teacher for children with emotional disturbance in the elementary and middle schools, was absent due to illness. Constance Chase wasn't available for me to talk with either, as she and David had separated years before and Constance no longer worked in Orangetown. Thomas Monroe, the social worker, was busy talking with a student. So the first person I actually encountered when I returned to Orangetown was none other than Mrs. Green, the friendly and energetic secretary I remembered so well! After a few minutes of reminiscing, Mrs. Green introduced me to the current school psychologist. This tall, impressive-looking man shook my hand politely but immediately excused himself, obviously disinterested.

"Does your school psychologist serve as case manager for special education now?" I asked the knowledgeable Mrs. Green. "No," she replied. "The psychologist is still officially head of pupil services, like Lou Bachus was when you worked here, Carolyn, but the position is only half time now and all he does is testing. I'm the person who schedules the M team meetings for the pupil services team, just like I always did. The teachers act as case managers for the kids they refer."

"The more things change, the more they stay the same," I reflected aloud.

Mrs. Green smiled. "Yes," she said. "I suppose that's true in some ways. But the school's a lot bigger now. We have a couple hundred more children since our new wing was built."

"A bigger school, yet only a half-time psychologist."

"That's right," Mrs. Green said, "but we have a full-time social worker now, Thomas Monroe."

"Is it helpful having a full-time social worker on staff?" I asked.

"Oh yes," Mrs. Green responded. "We need every minute Thomas can give us. He's doing a terrific job. Let's see—I think Thomas is free now—the student he was talking to has just left. Would you like to meet him?"

"I sure would," I replied, and soon I was being introduced to the impressive young man described in Chapter 10. I noticed with some envy that Thomas had a private office, complete with computer, telephone, and even an answering machine! How different from the shared classroom I occupied with David Chase when the two of us were new to Orangetown! But Thomas was clearly working just as hard as, or even harder than, I was back then. His challenges were different but perhaps even more formidable.

David Chase and I were unable to meet together until after school was released for the summer, due to tight schedules on both our parts. We met at a restaurant near Orangetown. We had a fine lunch and then, the day being warm and sunny, walked outside to talk on a wooden bench under a big maple tree. David was the same energetic, forceful personality I remembered, full of ideas and interesting stories.

As I talked with this now highly experienced teacher, I realized that, over the years, the Orangetown schools had moved ahead of Kingston's in some ways. Orangetown now employed a full-time social worker, for example. Thomas Monroe, unlike Jim Gottwald, could concentrate his full efforts on social work issues because guidance counselors were also employed in the schools he served. Orangetown had phased out its "disciplinary classroom" by this time and invested additional resources in special education. The little community had, in fact, embraced many aspects of the full inclusion movement, whereas the movement apparently hadn't gained a toehold in Kingston. It was largely David's persistence and hard work that made the difference with respect to full inclusion.

"I'm trusted to work with kids the way I see best now," David told me with pride. "I decide every aspect of a child's schooling when there's an emotional disturbance involved. I'm seen in Orangetown now as senior staff, and as a consultant for all children with emotional problems, not just kids in special education."

David explained that for a time, he had phased out his special education classroom entirely and had worked out of a small office as a consultant to regular education teachers. But that arrangement had lasted only a year. There was no place to send the children who were acting out, except to the principal's office! The principal, understandably, wasn't very happy about that. So David reestablished his own classroom again, where children could be sent for behavioral problems whether in special education or not. However, today David does most of his work in the regular classroom.

"I develop a special curriculum for each and every child who has an emotional or behavioral problem. A lot of time for start-up work was required in the beginning. I had to develop every curriculum from scratch. But now I can adapt curricula that are fairly well developed to fit particular children. And I've learned which teachers can work with what kinds of children. I match them carefully."

"Do you need to do a lot of negotiating with the teachers, David?"

"Yes. I have to introduce parallel education in the regular classroom, and not every teacher wants to be involved. I have to persuade people that one size doesn't fit all—one curriculum can't meet the needs of all children. It takes skill and time to persuade teachers and parents alike that covering a whole curriculum isn't the most important goal, anyway. Not every child can master the academics. I think it's more important to help every child learn how to be a *person* first. It's like helping a square peg fit in a round hole."

"You're accomplishing all this without aides for the kids in the regular classroom, David?"

"Some kids up in the high school have aides; there's a different teacher for kids with emotional disturbance up there. But I've been able to manage in the elementary and middle schools without them. Sometimes I just monitor a child's behavior in the regular classroom. Sometimes I work directly with the child in the regular classroom. Sometimes I work with the child in my own classroom. But if I do that and then I remainstream the kid again, I supervise closely at first."

"How is your system working?"

"Very well. I'm pleased with the results. Each child in special education gets a report card now for what we call an 'adaptive program.' The children are doing fine according to their teachers' own assessments."

"It sounds like your work has been very successful, David, even though you've had to create your own methods as you went along. I'm impressed!"

"Well, it hasn't been easy, that's for sure."

"I'm sure it's been a real challenge! Now, tell me about relationships between parents and the Orangetown school system. Are they going any better nowadays than when I used to work here?"

David snorted. "Frankly, no. Parents want discipline for everybody's kids but their own. There's a real willingness to go to court now if the school tries to clamp down on misbehavior, so the administration is afraid to do anything. Kids are astute—they know what they can get away with. The county DA won't prosecute truancy, for example, because it's not politically advantageous. Some kids are truant all the time and fail academically. They still get promoted."

"What about the kids who are disruptive?"

"They get sent to my room most of the time. But sometimes they get so disruptive the administration has to call the police. Kids can be charged with disorderly conduct now. They get tickets. The parents have to pay, and the kids have to do community service. That helps with the more blatant problems like fighting, swearing, and harassing the teachers. But school administrators are still reluctant to call the police."

"Why is that, David?"

"They don't want to get taken to court by the parents. I'm union representative at the school, so I get a lot of complaints from teachers who don't feel protected. I confront administration, reminding them that teachers have a constitutional right not to be attacked. That works, sometimes."

"Sounds as if there's tension between the teachers and administration."

"There certainly is tension. Administration hates to go to the school board to get resources for teachers. So the union often gets called in for grievances. When I work on grievances as union rep, I have to document everything in fours. Letters have to be sent to the school administration, the teachers involved, the parents of any children involved, and the union itself."

"What's an example of a typical grievance where teachers have asked for help from the union?"

"Well, teachers don't receive enough disciplinary support here. That's an ongoing problem. And then just recently, they were told to fill in for other teachers who were absent—to serve as substitutes during what was supposed to be their prep time, so administrators wouldn't have to hire subs. The teachers came to me as union representative. We organized, and refused to fill in during the absences. Administrators ended up having to do the work of the subs they wouldn't hire. That lasted only one day! That was the end of it! Our psychologist only made it in the classroom until noon! The teachers' morale got a real boost. Administrators obviously couldn't handle the classroom. Our psychologist went to the school board the very next day and got the pay for substitutes raised so more subs would be available!"

"I'll bet that felt great!"

"You bet it did."

"Have you taken on any other new roles lately, David, besides union rep?"

"Well, I'm also representative for the school's employee assistance program, along with Thomas Monroe, our social worker. The school used to provide a paid EAP* person, but the funds got cut. Thomas and I volunteer our services now. Staff come to either one of us when they have problems. We assess their needs, and make referrals. It's all confidential, of course."

"What kinds of resources do you have around here for referrals, David?"

David listed for me the same ones that Norman Werner, Jim Gottwald, and Thomas Monroe had previously identified.

"Overall, David, how would you describe the situation in Orangetown today as compared with the time we both began our work here?"

"Let me put it this way," he replied. "Kids are harder to manage now. Their parents are angrier, and more likely to go to court. Administration has become more gun-shy around parents. As for teachers and administration, teachers seem to have earned more respect from administration, but they constantly have to fight for it."

"How do you personally like your work now?"

"Well, I'm a rare bird, I guess. I still enjoy working with the kids. But it's unusual to find anyone willing to work with children who have emotional disturbance any more. Most of my colleagues have switched over to learning disabilities or cognitive disabilities. The university program where I trained actually folded because it couldn't attract enough students."

"That sounds serious," I said. "What do you think is keeping students away from the field?"

"The work is very difficult," he replied, "and it doesn't get the respect or appreciation it deserves. Or the pay, for that matter."

"What do you see for the future, David?"

---

*Employee Assistance Programs.

"I don't know. But I'll be out there fighting for the rights of the teachers we have, and the rights of the kids. I'm an old war resister, remember, Carolyn!"

I grinned, thanked David sincerely, and went on my way.

Later, as I mulled over information I learned from Jim Gottwald, Norman Werner, Thomas Monroe, David Chase, and others during the many conversations I conducted during the revision of this book, I recognized some major themes. In particular, social workers and other school personnel believed they were being asked to do more with less, sometimes more than was humanly possible.

People I knew to be competent, experienced professionals described themselves as overwhelmed by the demands of their jobs. They perceived childrens' behavioral problems to be increasingly severe, including escalating physical and verbal aggression toward teachers, and increasing substance abuse. They described parents whom they tried to serve in good faith as increasingly angry and disrespectful. They reported a serious lack of vital resources to deal with the issues they encountered, and little support for their work from school administrators or the community at large. The picture people painted looked bleak on the surface, to say the least.

On the other hand, I was more than impressed by the creative responses that social workers, psychologists, and teachers as well were inventing day by day to deal with these difficulties. Almost all the social workers contacted, for example, were encouraging and undertaking new community-based work designed to deal with the shortage of resources by helping ameliorate or prevent social problems. People who described themselves as overwhelmed with work nevertheless took the time to learn grant-writing skills to secure funding to begin new community-based programs. What people said often sounded overwhelmed and despairing, but their actions told a different story. Their actions were future-oriented, aimed at preventing further problems, and carried out with a high degree of competence and commitment.

Myriad factors intertwine to produce the difficult conditions in Orangetown and Kingston today (and a neighboring urban area) that are described in this book. These conditions, I believe, are fairly representative of those in many parts of our nation today. I think we can do better. But if so, first and foremost we need to believe something better is possible. The work of the social workers and other professionals described in this book indicate that even a few dedicated individuals can make a difference—so something better *is* possible. But social workers and teachers cannot do it alone. Perhaps what we need is no less than a change in our national culture—something like the development of a world view that honors cooperation rather than competition. Then, we might be willing to invest in our people, especially our children. We have the financial resources to do so. What we lack is the vision and the will.

Clearly, we can't expect a single institution such as the public schools to solve today's growing social problems. Some children are so severely damaged by the time they get to school that it is almost too late to help them. It is all too easy then to escape responsibility by blaming their families. We in America today seem to like to blame, to point fingers, to punish, to incarcerate. It's the old "us" versus "them" mentality exerting its ugly force. But this approach doesn't work very well over the long haul. Too many "us's" become "thems" for too many reasons. Our prisons are already bursting.

Instead, we need to ask ourselves what our families need to succeed in their incredibly important task of raising competent, compassionate human beings. We need to ask what our communities need to help foster healthy families. We need to ask what our nation needs to engage it more fully in fostering healthy communities. We need to ask what the world needs to continue to provide the means for survival. We need to ask what each and every one of us can do as citizens. We need nothing less than an entirely different way of looking at our lives intertwined together on this little planet.

If a better "whole" is to be created, every part needs nurturance and care. Social workers understand this concept. Slowly, slowly, we can be instrumental in spreading the word.

DISCUSSION AND STUDY QUESTIONS

1. How would you justify the existence of social work in our society? How important is it compared with national defense? How important is it compared with police protection?
2. Should social workers be allowed to unionize? To go on strike? Is a strike justified if they feel underpaid? If they feel overworked? If they feel their working conditions are undermining their efforts to help others?
3. Why is it that private agencies cannot meet the needs of many people with problems such as those described in this book? Why was Emmett County Guidance Clinic also unsuccessful in meeting the needs of many potential clients?
*4. Under what conditions do you think society has a right to limit what people do? Should people pay taxes? Should they be allowed to reject help even if they are homeless? Should they be jailed if they have contagious diseases like AIDS? Justify your answers.
*5. Have you ever encountered people who do not respect your work as a social worker? How did their disrespect make you feel? Did you attempt to defend yourself? Why or why not?
*6. What kinds of programs or services do you think can best assist families to carry out their important job of raising future citizens? Why? How do you think such programs should be organized and funded?

---

*Questions notated with an asterisk are intended for advanced students who have had or are currently having some social work practice experience and who have made at least a tentative commitment to the profession.

Index